New Sinn Féin

Sinn Féin is a unique political party, not only within Irish politics, but also within the wider European context. It boasts a long revolutionary tradition, a historical affiliation with an armed group, a social radicalism and a vision of society that has inspired other parties and movements throughout the world.

As a consequence of Sinn Féin's connection with the IRA, the military side of the Republican Movement has tended to overshadow the political, both in terms of its internal operation and strategic choices and in terms of the attention that it has attracted from scholars, writers and journalists. However, since the 1998 Good Friday Agreement, Sinn Féin has experienced substantial growth, in terms of electoral results and party support, both in Northern Ireland and in the Republic of Ireland.

This book assesses the importance and relevance of Sinn Féin within the changing configurations of Irish politics, studying it as a political party on both sides of the Irish border. It investigates whether Sinn Féin can sustain the progress made over the last decade, retain its identity as the voice of radical republicanism, and ultimately, whether its vision of a united Ireland can prevail.

Containing interviews with key figures, such as Gerry Adams and Martin McGuinness, *New Sinn Féin* is essential reading for anyone with an interest in Irish politics, and the Republican Movement in particular.

Agnès Maillot is Lecturer in Intercultural Studies at Dublin City University, where she also teaches politics and history. Her main area of research is Northern Ireland, and particularly Sinn Féin and the IRA.

New Sinn Féin
Irish republicanism in the twenty-first century

Agnès Maillot

Routledge
Taylor & Francis Group

LONDON AND NEW YORK

First published 2005
by Routledge
2 Park Square, Milton Park, Abingdon, Oxon OX14 4RN

Simultaneously published in the USA and Canada
by Routledge
270 Madison Ave, New York, NY 10016

Routledge is an imprint of the Taylor & Francis Group

© 2005 Agnès Maillot

Typeset in Sabon by
Keystroke, Jacaranda Lodge, Wolverhampton
Printed and bound in Great Britain by
The Cromwell Press, Trowbridge, Wiltshire

British Library Cataloguing in Publication Data
A catalogue record for this book is available from the British Library

Library of Congress Cataloging in Publication Data
A catalog record for this book has been requested

ISBN 0–415–32196–4 (hbk)
ISBN 0–415–32197–2 (pbk)

In memory of Paul Brennan
1939–2003

Contents

Acknowledgements

This research is in great part based on interviews that I have carried out over most of 2003 with spokespersons for different organisations. I would like to express my gratitude to all of them for giving me their time, and in particular to the Sinn Féin Press Office in Dublin for making all the necessary arrangements and for enabling me to have access to many Sinn Féin representatives and leaders.

I also want to express my gratitude to my family, colleagues and friends for their incessant support throughout this project. More specifically, I want to thank Brian Duffy, Mick Heaney, Emmet Malone, Tommy McManus, Stuart Murray, Don Ryan, Stephen Schwartz and Douglas Smith for their advice, comments and help.

Finally, I am greatly indebted to Eoin Doogan and Bairbre Ní Chiosáin for their unswerving support, their enthusiasm and their generosity.

Introduction

Sinn Féin: the oldest political party in Ireland.[1] Ironically, this is the party from which most modern political organisations in the Republic are derived, as a result of splits within the ranks of the organisation. Yet for years it was shunned, despised, condemned, at times made illegal, hunted down by Special Branch forces. This was due partly to the controversial nature of its politics and strategies, illustrated by the wide range of adjectives attributed to the party. Fascists, left-wing radicals, terrorists, right-wing fanatics· this was quite an unusual and contradictory com bination to depict those who were, according to themselves, fighting in the name of Ireland to free their country from oppression, convinced that they had stayed true to the age-old dream of an island unified under the common name of Catholic, Protestant and Dissenter.[2] But if Sinn Féin garnered such animosity, such aversion, it was not so much due to its politics which few, for years, saw as a serious threat to the status quo between the main parties in the Republic; nor was Sinn Féin deemed capable of denting unionist power in Northern Ireland by politics alone. The main cause for this aversion could be spelt out in three letters: IRA, Irish Republican Army.

This situation altered dramatically in the new millennium. For two years, Sinn Féin ministers sat alongside their unionist counterparts, or at least those who accept to collaborate with them. Enemies of yesterday had successfully made compromises to work together in the institutions created by the Good Friday Agreement. Admittedly, unionists in the North of Ireland still deeply mistrust republicans for their failure, as they see it, to engage wholly with peaceful methods in a transparent manner. Southern politicians retain their long-standing suspicion and have said on occasion that they would not form coalitions with Sinn Féin. Nevertheless, by the end of the twentieth century, the republican[3] move-ment had become a force to be reckoned with, not solely because Sinn Féin substantially increased its share of the vote, particularly in Northern Ireland, but because it succeeded in presenting itself to its electorate as the voice of radicalism while fitting into the mainstream. Through years of debate, of internal soul-searching, of treading the uneasy path between dogmatism and innovation, republicans have found a voice within Irish politics and have pledged their organisation, North and South, rural and urban, to a policy that is both pragmatic and aspirational.

Sinn Féin's progress in Irish political life has been slow and at times difficult, but the outcome seems to vindicate those who had been advocating ground-breaking changes for some years. A survey of the party in the twenty-first century yields a totally different image to the picture that would have emerged in the early 1990s. In June 2002, Alex Maskey, Sinn Féin Belfast City councillor since 1983, was elected Lord Mayor of Belfast, the first republican ever to hold such a position. This was quite an achievement in a city that had only had one nationalist mayor in a century. Sinn Féin succeeded in having its candidate appointed thanks to the votes of the Nationalist SDLP (Social Democratic and Labour Party) and the Alliance Party, the non-aligned political force of Northern Irish politics. Maskey immediately set the tone, pledging to be the mayor of all the citizens of Belfast and therefore reaching out to all communities, including, of course, the unionists, but also ethnic minorities. He followed this up almost immediately when he attended in July 2002 a ceremony to commemorate the men who died in the Battle of the Somme in 1916. This was quite a controversial and unprecedented manner for a republican to reach out to unionists, since, for many years, involvement alongside the British troops in the First World War was seen as a betrayal of the nationalist aspiration. Yet it epitomised the image that republicans wanted to be associated with, that of a party willing to look at the past in an innovative manner, prepared to concede on some of its previously held positions and to contribute to the reconciliation process necessary to heal the traumas of the thirty-year-long conflict.

Alex Maskey's election was one of many successes that Sinn Féin can boast of in the last few years. A month previously, the party gained five seats in the Irish Parliament, Dáil Éireann, when it had only one outgoing deputy (TD). Sinn Féin increased its share of the first preference vote by 4 per cent, going from 2.5 per cent in 1997 to 6.51 per cent in 2002. The Sinn Féin vote rose to 8 per cent in the June 2004 local elections. Both the profile of these newly elected candidates and the areas that they represent reflect, on a more general level, the type of issues that Sinn Féin has taken upon itself to champion, combining socialist rhetoric with a discourse that links social justice with the reunification of the island. These electoral results were the high point of a promising electoral spate of successes for Sinn Féin. In June 2001 the party secured the election of four of the eighteen Westminster MPs for Northern Ireland, overtaking for the first time their nationalist rivals the SDLP, and confirming this advance in the 2003 Assembly with the election of twenty-four out of the 108 MLAs (Members of the Local Assembly).

Therefore, Sinn Féin in the twenty-first century is quite a different party to the traditional, old-style political movement that it was for most of the previous century. Yet the actors have remained unchanged in over twenty years, the structures do not seem to have been fundamentally altered, and the organisation still conjures up the past and claims the legacy of its forefathers. This then begs the question: What made this happen? What made it possible to go from a military strategy to decommissioning, with the in-between stage of the 'Armalite and ballot box'?[4] This process was slow, sometimes painful, and it is ongoing. It generated debates and divisions, as well as open criticism both within the ranks of the organisation itself and in the broader Irish political sphere. But the keys to the rise of republicans in Irish political life, on both sides of the border, are undoubtedly to be sought within the peace process that emerged in Northern Ireland in the early 1990s, and within the party's activist base and local community involvement.

The most striking achievement of the strategy outlined by the leadership of the movement is undoubtedly the fact that the momentous changes which the involvement of the party in a peace process entailed did not generate a major split. This was quite in contrast with past experience, as the party's history has been riddled with internal rifts and the threat of breakaway groups has been ever present. However, divisions were not about the ultimate goal of reunification, but about the strategies to achieve such an objective. Therefore, the party was unswervingly committed to a cause, but sufficiently vague in its programme and policies to attract a membership which was heterogeneous both politically and socially, one which was united over the issues of independence and reunification, but did not necessarily share identical ideological or strategic visions. Sinn Féin's main limitation as a party may also have been the strongest asset of the movement. It could summarise its message in brief formulae, such as Brits out, end partition. Over the years, it proved to be strong on principle, but weaker on policy. This does not mean that the leadership was incapable of producing policy documents, but what underlay the manifestos that were put together was their overall aspirational characteristic. Rather than dealing with bread-and-butter issues, Sinn Féin preferred a more flexible vision of a future when reunification would be achieved. The best example of this was the policy that dominated Provisional Sinn Féin's political agenda in the 1970s: *Éire Nua* (New Ireland). This was an extensive document that encompassed all sectors of public life and laid out a vision for a united Ireland. However, it was, essentially, aspirational. The party thus lacked the political credibility that would have been necessary when contesting elections and was not perceived as a serious contender by the electorate. Yet it was able to maintain a continuity in its commitment to the cause of which it had proclaimed itself to be the sole champion, that of Irish self-determination.

Sinn Féin viewed itself as a revolutionary party, and, to some extent, still maintains that perception. In line with most revolutionary movements, it was careful not to be too specific about its ideology in order to continue adhering to its objectives. As it clearly points out in its Members Training Programme, Sinn Féin views ideology as a flexible and constantly evolving concept, whereas principles are 'fundamental truths' and therefore 'don't change'. This document quotes two fundamental principles: the sovereignty of the Irish Republic as set out in the 1916 Proclamation, and the fact that sovereignty and unity are inalienable and non-judiciable. Around those two principles, strategies and policies are built, keeping in mind the four basic objectives of the party: the overthrow of British rule, the establishment of the Republic proclaimed in 1916, the upholding of socialist and republican principles and the restoration of Irish culture and identity (Members Programme, n.d.).

However, it is perhaps the looseness of the organisation's ideological vision that explains the longevity of the party and its survival in the face of great odds. Through the years, Sinn Féin has experienced major shifts that would have sealed the fate of any other political organisation. It has radically altered its position on a number of issues while still retaining its identity. The original Sinn Féin, founded by Arthur Griffith in 1905, was conservative and monarchist. Griffith was prepared to settle for a 'double monarchy' arrangement, whereby the British Crown maintained its jurisdiction over Ireland as long as the country obtained political and economic independence. This was altered in the aftermath of the 1916 Rising, when the idea of retaining a link – be it purely formal – with Britain was replaced with the republican ideal, which put a very strong emphasis on the concept of sovereignty. The party was divided over the issue of participation in the institutions of the newly formed Free State, and the dissidents broke away and formed Fianna Fáil in 1926. After this split, Sinn Féin seemed to be far more preoccupied with the oath of allegiance to be sworn to the British monarch in order to participate in the institutions of the Free State created by the 1921 Treaty with Britain, and with the purity of principles, than with social or political changes. Under the leadership of Tomás Mac Giolla and Cathal Goulding in the late 1950s and throughout the 1960s, there was a shift towards the left. This was acceptable to the movement as a whole so long as it did not clash with the basic tenets of what was perceived to be at the heart of republicanism. However, talk of class struggle started to supersede that of nationalist struggle. Marxist distinctions based on class replaced a more traditional vision based on geography and history. To aim to unite the working class was seen as a dangerous path by those who would eventually break away and regroup under the names Provisional IRA and Provisional Sinn Féin, since it was seen to undermine the fundamental dimension of the conflict: that of the colonial legacy which was maintained through partition and its institutions. Talk of class struggle was cut short with the emergence in 1970 of the Provisionals who became, in the early days of the conflict, the self-appointed defenders of one community, the nationalists. With the emergence of a new leadership in the north of the island in the late 1970s, however, socialism started to be reintroduced in a more coherent manner.

The ranks of the organisation were not cemented by ideology, but rather by a strategy that was inherently linked to the movement's identity, that of armed struggle. The stature acquired by the IRA throughout the years made it a powerful component of the overall struggle, and Sinn Féin became, in the words of Gerry Adams, the poor second cousin. To a large extent, Sinn Féin's association with an armed group not only hindered its progress within mainstream politics, but also meant that it seldom prioritised political means. For a sizeable fraction of republicans, the IRA had the right to take action if there was a perceived need to do so. Armed struggle was an integral part of the culture of the movement, the so-called 'armed tradition', one based on a reading of history that emphasised victimhood and resistance (see Arthur, in Coakley, 2002: 98). Nevertheless, not only did the IRA declare two ceasefires in the 1990s, it also accepted the reality of decommissioning. At the turn of the twenty-first century it seemed that the identity that the party had been built upon did not need to be justified by the revolutionary dimension of the armed struggle. The peace process enabled a new Sinn Féin to emerge, one that has gradually emancipated itself from its old partner and *alter ego*, although this was not yet translated fully into words, since the so-called 'war' was still not declared over.

Sinn Féin seems confident about the place it occupies and the role it will play in the new Irish order that has come about as a result of the Agreement. Its peace strategy clearly brings some dividends, especially in electoral terms. Whether the party can continue to grow, on both sides of the border, remains to be seen, as does its capacity to make inroads into the middle-class vote. Sinn Féin can count on several important assets. It is a young party which attracts enthusiastic recruits. Its leaders are unanimously accepted within its ranks, and their popularity is beyond doubt. Moreover, Sinn Féin is an ambitious party which calls itself 'the fastest-growing in Ireland' and it can show initiative. It aims to become the only authentic socialist party of the island and to impose itself as a radical force, as 'the party of the people of no property throughout this island'. However, Sinn Féin still has to iron out some contradictions. Although it claims to be socialist its tactics are also populist in nature, inspired by methods inherited from the actions of the IRA. Republican politicians are accused at times of resorting to vigilantism, as in the Dublin districts hit by the drugs problem. This is not without its setbacks, as was shown during the campaign for the June 2002 general election in the

Republic and the controversy surrounding North Kerry candidate Martin Ferris. Similarly, punishment beatings in Northern Ireland are still an obstacle on the road to respectability.

Having entered the mainstream of Irish politics, Sinn Féin still refuses to be seen as a mainstream party. It bases its future on difference while seeking a vote that is not merely a protest vote. It wants to be an all-Ireland party, yet there is a discrepancy between its strong share of the vote in Northern Ireland (with 23.5 per cent of the first preference vote), and its representation in the Republic of Ireland, where its strength is mainly to be found in border areas and urban, working-class constituencies (with the exception of North Kerry). For decades, it subjected the concept of liberation to the reunification of the island. It now seems that the focus has been reversed, and that it is social progress which will eventually lead to national liberation. The tensions that this is generating within its own ranks cannot be overlooked, and the manner in which this is played out on both sides of the border differs quite strongly. Sinn Féin has come a long way since the first IRA ceasefire in 1994. Whether it has the potential to travel further along that route in order to fulfil the vision it has of itself and of its country in general is what this book sets out to explore.

1 Historical overview

Sinn Féin today is but the latest incarnation of the party that was created in the early twentieth century and subsequently experienced many internal turmoils. From monarchist to republican, from abstentionist to fully electoralist, from the mainstream to the margins and back to the mainstream, Sinn Féin has undergone numerous transformations. It is credited with driving a substantial part of the island of Ireland to autonomy, but for the following decades it operated in the shadow of the IRA. Republican in outlook, socialist in policies, it was for years mainly associated with the issues of reunification and the Northern Ireland conflict. In the twenty-first century, the party calls itself the fastest growing political organisation in Ireland, a party on the move, and one of the main forces behind one of the most exciting developments on the island: the peace process. In order to assess how Sinn Féin became what it is today, how it has modelled itself on the struggle of its forefathers and yet has managed to emancipate itself to a considerable degree from its *alter ego* of many years, the IRA, as well as how the changes in tactics in the last decade of the twentieth century represent a watershed for republicanism, it is important to go back to the origins of the party and its principles.

Despite the many ups, downs and splits that Sinn Féin has gone through, the party has maintained its adherence to the cause of self-determination, which it views as the fight to obtain full independence from Britain, and ultimately, the reunification of Ireland. Republicans used two broad strategies to achieve these two objectives: abstentionism – the refusal of elected candidates to take their seats in parliament – and armed resistance. However, over time, these strategies mutated to become fundamental principles. As such, they were often confused with ideology, blurring the distinction between strategy and ideology. Neither abstentionism nor armed resistance, in themselves, had much to do with the social or economic vision of the party. Nevertheless, these strategies were what successive splits within the organisation were mainly about, and they were ultimately upheld as the fundamental philosophy of the party and of the movement as a whole. They were what distinguished Sinn Féin from the other political formations of the island, constituting the core identity of modern republicanism and guaranteeing its very survival in the face of what Sinn Féin perceived was an increasing denial of the nationalist agenda by the mainstream Irish political parties.

The abstentionist party

Although his name is rarely mentioned in recent republican literature, Arthur Griffith can be credited with developing the tactic of abstentionism and making it the signature of twentieth-century Sinn Féin. Griffith, a Dublin-based journalist, came to prominence within nationalist circles when he put forward a set of practical proposals under the name *The Resurrection of Hungary*, published in 1904. In this document, he described how the Hungarians 'refused to permit their representatives to appear in the [Austrian] imperial parliament. Six years of persistence in this attitude reduced the imperial parliament to impotence' (Griffith, 1904: 85). Griffith advocated a similar approach for his country, since in his view, as long as Ireland was governed from London, it was limited to the status of province, a situation that hindered it in its aspiration to become a nation.[1] Consequently, he proposed that all elected representatives form their own assembly in Ireland instead of taking their seats in Westminster. Griffith was not the first to suggest subverting the workings of Parliament to achieve concessions from London. The main nationalist party, the Parliamentary Party, also known as the Home Rule Party, had been using obstructionist tactics in Westminster, and at one stage even considered taking a more radical step by withdrawing all its deputies.[2] However, Griffith was the first to construct a policy around the idea of abstentionism that had practical and short-term implications.

At the heart of Griffith's vision of independence was also the concept of self-sufficiency, and this was to become the hallmark of his economic orientation. Griffith was convinced that political autonomy would have little weight if it was not supported by economic independence. In practical terms, he proposed to mount campaigns urging people to buy Irish products in order to promote indigenous industries. In upholding such protectionist and isolationist policies, Griffith was overestimating the resources of the island (Lyons, 1983: 254). Nevertheless, in his eyes, this formed part of a whole set of proposals, the 'Sinn Féin Programme', which he put forward at a nationalist convention in 1905. However, Griffith was not a republican. He did not seek to sever all links between Ireland and Britain, and favoured the establishment of a double monarchy under the British Crown, so long as his country obtained economic and political autonomy. Moreover, his conviction that armed resistance was counterproductive and that the way forward was passive resistance put him at odds with the Irish Republican Brotherhood.[3] Griffith's Sinn Féin thus offered a third way, one between the tradition of physical force and the Home Rule type of autonomy advocated by the Irish Parliamentary Party, one between insurrection and parliamentarianism. His main legacy to the later incarnations of the parties that were to retain the name Sinn Féin throughout the century was therefore abstentionism and self-reliance.

Griffith's Sinn Féin was rapidly overtaken by events. The Home Rule Bill, passed by the House of Commons in 1912,[4] greatly preoccupied the unionist politicians in the northeast of the island, who reacted by creating an armed defence force in 1913, the Ulster Volunteers. As a result, the Irish Volunteers were formed, which attracted members of the main nationalist organisations such as the Irish Republican Brotherhood, the Gaelic League[5] and Sinn Féin, which pledged to defend any future Irish government. When the First World War broke out, the Irish Volunteers split between those who urged support for the British war effort, and those who saw Britain's difficulties as an opportunity for advancing the cause of Irish independence. Among the latter were leaders of the IRB, who conspired to organise an armed insurrection which started on Easter Monday, 1916. The break with Griffith's ideals was clear, as this rising not only revived the tradition of armed resistance that Griffith had staunchly opposed, but it also implied the rejection of any continued link with the British Crown with the proclamation of a Republic read by Pádraic Pearse.

In total, sixty-four insurgents and 103 troops were killed before Pearse surrendered to the British authorities. Fifteen men seen as the leaders were executed in the following days, and hundreds were imprisoned. Yet far from being a setback for the cause of independence, the Easter Rising left a lasting impact on Irish nationalism. It gave the tradition of physical force a mythical dimension. Not only was such an action deemed inevitable by those who supported the ideal of a Republic insofar as it seemed the only effective means of putting forward the demand for national independence, but it was now equated with martyrdom, seen as intrinsic to the cause of Ireland. It also combined different political traditions: that of the republican nationalism of the Irish Republican Brotherhood with that of socialism expressed by James Connolly. After the rising, although the Labour Party maintained an independent position, a coalition emerged, bringing together those intent on fulfilling the goals set in the Proclamation. While it had little in common with Griffith's party, this coalition retained the name Sinn Féin. Led by Eamon de Valera, the organisation was heterogeneous and somewhat involved from a political point of view. It advocated independence but did not clearly spell out how an independent Ireland would be governed and managed. It fought the December 1918 Westminster general elections on an abstentionist ticket,[6] stipulating that its elected candidates would form their own assembly, although it did not specify clearly what such an assembly would do. The lack of political orientation was made clear by the surprisingly naïve comment of Sinn Féin's Vice-president Michael O'Flanagan in the aftermath of the election, when he stated: 'the people have voted for us. We must now explain what Sinn Féin is' (Kee, 1976: 627). Sinn Féin won seventy-three seats, the Nationalist Party six and the Ulster Unionist Party twenty-two (Lyons, 1983: 398). In keeping with the promise made during the electoral campaign, Sinn Féin's newly elected representatives, or at least those who were not in prison at the time or otherwise unable to attend, gathered in the Mansion House in central Dublin, forming the first Parliament since the 1800 Act of Union: Dáil Éireann. Along with a 'Declaration of Independence', the deputies voted a 'Message to the Free Nations of the World' and a 'Democratic Programme' outlining the objectives of the newly constituted provisional government. Thus, with abstentionism, Sinn Féin had succeeded in establishing what previous risings and insurrections had failed to do: a set of parallel institutions in Ireland that would rival the official British institutions still in place in the months to come. In effect, and without resorting to arms, Sinn Féin had taken over essential aspects of the management of the country, and could claim to have achieved a degree of self-government. Thus was created another powerful myth: abstentionism was more than a tactic, it was an essential key to independence. Curiously, what survived of this principle had far more to do with the strategy of abstentionism than with the potential that politics, as opposed to military action, could represent. Politics alone, at the time and for the following decades, was not considered sufficient to guarantee the ultimate goal of nationalists: full independence and sovereignty.

Dáil Éireann was exclusively composed of members of Sinn Féin, as the unionist and nationalist candidates had not responded to the call to assemble in Dublin. This implied a degree of confusion between the party itself and the newly created institutions. As the party admitted at the time, 'The work originally undertaken by Sinn Féin has become the province of Dáil Éireann. Sinn Féin having been released by An Dáil of the major portion of its various departments, is now practically confined in its sphere of activity to the work of organising elections and propaganda' (Sinn Féin, 1919). This would have been quite an accurate description of the organisation's work right up until the beginning of the 1990s. Yet it is possible that the merger between the institutions and the party reduced the vision of the role of a political machine and thus hindered development on the political front for the years to come.

In the aftermath of the 1916 Rising, the Irish Volunteers had been reorganised and trained under the leadership of Michael Collins, and they pledged allegiance to Dáil Éireann, thus becoming the Irish Republican Army (although as individual members they would still be referred to as

'Volunteers', or, in Irish, Óglaigh na hÉireann). On the day of the inauguration of Dáil Éireann, 19 January 1919, three Irish Volunteers killed two policemen in an ambush in Co. Tipperary, thus setting in motion a war of independence that was to last for two years. The IRA faced formidable opponents, not only the British army and Royal Irish Constabulary, but also the Auxiliary forces and former First World War soldiers who became known as the Black and Tans because of the uniform they wore, and whose ferocity soon acquired the status of legend in the country.[7] The war was based on guerrilla tactics, and the pattern that soon developed was one of attacks, counter-attacks and retaliation on both sides, until a truce was agreed in June 1921.

As a consequence of the War of Independence, the position of Dáil Éireann had rapidly become untenable. The British government declared it an illegal and dangerous association in September 1919, but it continued to operate underground, as did the republican courts which came to supplant the British judicial system in parts of the country. Westminster passed the Government of Ireland Act in November 1920, which provided for two parliaments, one in the six counties of the northeast of the country and another for the remaining twenty-six counties, both of which were granted a limited level of autonomy while London kept control over key areas such as defence, taxation and foreign policy. Ireland was thus, *de facto*, partitioned. Sinn Féin refused to have anything to do with these new institutions, since they so obviously fell short of the aspiration to independence. Elections were held to the new parliaments in May 1921. In the north, the Ulster Unionists won forty out of the fifty-two seats. In the south, Sinn Féin once again used the electoral campaign to field candidates for its own assembly, Dáil Éireann, the only one that it regarded as legitimate, and winning an overwhelming majority of 128 out of 132 seats. When the newly elected Parliament provided for under the Government of Ireland Act was due to meet, only the four Dublin University candidates who were not affiliated to Sinn Féin were present. The other deputies assembled in what became the Second Dáil. In republican thinking, the First and Second Dáils are the only legitimate and truly representative parliaments that Ireland has ever had, as the first was elected by the electorate of the whole of the island in 1918 and the second was not established by the British but by Sinn Féin itself (although it is ironic that the Second Dáil could be considered a partitionist assembly since it only had jurisdiction over the territory of the twenty-six counties). Thus the policy of abstentionism took on another dimension: it became enshrined as an inviolable principle. To sit at a parliament that was either 'foreign' (Westminster) or illegitimate (both Irish parliaments provided for by the Government of Ireland Act, neither of which was sovereign) was nothing short of a betrayal of the fallen patriots of the 1916 Rising and of the War of Independence, as well as of the previous generations.

Abstentionism came to acquire a hugely symbolic importance for republicans, epitomising the movement's refusal to accept any compromise solution as well as its strong belief in the precedents set by history.

Negotiations took place between Lloyd George's government in London and a delegation of Irish representatives, leading to the signing of the December 1921 Treaty which gave partial autonomy to the twenty-six counties, known as the Irish Free State, while firmly reasserting the bond between the Crown and the two local assemblies of the island. This deeply divided both Sinn Féin and Dáil Éireann, between those who followed Collins and Griffith's lead and saw the Treaty as a stepping stone towards full independence, and those, under De Valera, who castigated it as a betrayal of republican aspirations. The Treaty was put to a vote in the Dáil in January 1922 and was passed by sixty-four votes to fifty-seven; subsequently, during a national convention in March of that year, the IRA also split between those who remained faithful to the newly established Free State and those who opposed the Treaty and joined the force which became known as the 'Irregulars'. When a majority of the Irish people decided, in June 1922, to accept the Treaty, the split within the Sinn Féin and the IRA ranks, which had been more or less contained until that time, spread to the whole of the country. This resulted in a bloody and merciless civil war, setting former allies against each other, dividing the country and in some cases even splitting families. The Free State forces did not hesitate to execute their former brothers-in-arms turned enemies (seventy-seven men were executed between November 1922 and May 1923). The Irregulars, for their part, ambushed and killed Michael Collins on 22 August 1922, the very man to whom they had previously entrusted the destiny of their country and under whose leadership they had fought the War of Independence. A ceasefire was finally brokered in April 1923, when it was beyond doubt that the Free State forces had the upper hand from a military point of view. The Irregulars had been administered a further blow by the Catholic Church, which had threatened to excommunicate them. But the truce was by no means seen as a surrender on the part of the IRA, since it only involved a dumping of arms; armed struggle had merely been postponed.

After the Civil War, Sinn Féin's decline was rapid, as was shown with the elections of August 1923, when the party secured only 27 per cent of the vote. It considered the newly elected assembly illegitimate because, as it saw it, it derived its authority not from the Irish people but from the Treaty and, thus, from Britain. Sinn Féin's isolation was compounded by its refusal to sit in the new assembly. From then on, it progressively removed itself from the political process. Importantly, at that time, the main reason for doing so was not fundamentally due to the existence of a rival parliament in the northeast, Stormont (historians subsequently estimated that of the 338 pages dealing with the Dáil debate on the Treaty, only nine were dedicated to the issue of partition (Lyons, 1983. 445)). The main bone of contention rather seemed to be the fact that Ireland retained its attachment to the British Crown, epitomised by what Sinn Féin regarded as the odious oath of allegiance that the deputies had to swear to the British monarch. But this position soon became untenable, at least for those who were not content with a principled opposition to the new institutions. Sinn Féin's ranks were divided between those who sought a compromise solution on the oath of allegiance, and those who saw any softening of their stance as the abandonment of their loyalty to the Republic. The wording of the two motions put forward at the 1925 annual conference of the party (Ard Fheis) typified the orientations that the republican camp would take in the years to come. On the one hand, De Valera proposed that 'once the admission oaths of the 26-county and 6-county Assemblies are removed, it becomes a question not of principle but of policy whether or not republican representatives should attend these assemblies', whereas in the opposing camp, Art O'Connor, who was to become President of Sinn Féin, replied that 'it is incompatible with the fundamental principles of Sinn Féin as it is injurious to the honour of Ireland to send representatives to any usurping legislature set up by English law in Ireland' (*An Phoblacht* (*AP*), 19 February 1926). This was but one of the many debates that were to take place on the issue of abstentionism, debates that always opposed pragmatism and principle.

Although Sinn Féin continued to operate in the 1920s, it had become a marginal political force by the end of the decade. Its difficulties stemmed from the loss of the prestigious leaders who had followed De Valera in his newly founded party Fianna Fáil, and the consequent loss of substantial support. But perhaps equally significant was the fact that the bond that had united the party with the IRA had been severed in 1925, on the eve of the Sinn Féin Ard Fheis. In November of that year, the ruling body of the IRA, the Army Council, voted in favour of withdrawing its allegiance to the Second Dáil in order to avoid the split that was looming within Sinn Féin spreading to its own ranks. From then on the IRA was, *de facto*, independent. The organisation inflicted a further blow to Sinn Féin during the 1932 electoral campaign, when it openly called for a vote in favour of Fianna Fáil.

The decision to remain independent from any political party also caused problems for the IRA. The military organisation was riddled with internal divisions. Some leaders like Peadar O'Donnell advocated an alternative political process. The socialist route that he wanted to follow was unacceptable to most IRA members and he left to create his own organisation, Republican Congress. Others, like Seán McBride, chief-of-staff from 1936 to 1938, were of the view that once the Free State had enacted its own Constitution in 1937, there was little reason left for the IRA to pursue its campaign. When McBride proposed the creation of a political organisation, he was opposed by the Army Council and eventually severed his links with the organisation, forming, eight years later, a political organisation, Clann na Poblachta (Republican Family), that would actively take part in the parliamentary process. Yet there was always a third way, that of military action, which was still held in high esteem by a sizeable faction of the organisation. One of the main defenders of such action, Seán Russell, had been pushing for some time for a military campaign on British soil. This strategy was not unanimously agreed upon within the organisation, as some, like Civil War veteran Tom Barry, contended that any military action had to be limited to the north of Ireland (Bowyer Bell, 1983: 145). In order to contain the opposition within his own ranks and to lend legitimacy to the campaign, Russell turned to the surviving members of the Second Dáil to secure their support. Although in 1938 this body, which still existed in theory, only counted seven members whose function was primarily to act as the living memory of a more grandiose past, it was still considered, in republican circles, the embodiment of the government of the Republic. Russell's gesture itself was to have significant repercussions from the republican organisation's point of view. Not only did the Second Dáil condone the military plans, but it agreed to transfer its political authority to the IRA. The members of the Second Dáil vested the army with the political legitimacy of which they had previously been the guardians and thus reversed the situation that had existed until 1925, when it was the IRA that came under the authority of the Dáil. An unusual situation was thus created, where the IRA became the embodiment of the 'government of the Republic', the supreme political authority of republicanism, as the IRB had been before 1916. This entrenched a dynamic whereby the political party, whichever it was, would be answerable to the army, and not the other way around. For years afterwards, the balance of power between Sinn Féin and the IRA was to be strongly weighted in favour of the latter.

For the next two decades Sinn Féin was outflanked, on the one hand, by its former armed ally the IRA, and on the other, by Fianna Fáil which was seen by a large section of the Irish people as a legitimate representation of republicanism. Armed struggle came to supersede political action in the minds of those who wanted to overturn the institutions created by the 1921 Treaty. Sinn Féin, although still existent if only nominally, was resurrected when the IRA convention met for the first time since the Second World War in 1948.[8] Recognising the necessity for a political organisation, the convention decided to revive Sinn Féin, as it was deemed loyal and was still a household name in Ireland. The choice of Sinn Féin was also probably informed by the series of splits that had divided the IRA over the previous twenty years. Sinn Féin, if it accepted the supreme authority of the IRA, could serve a vital function without challenging the military organisation. It was at that time that the IRA also modified its strategy, deciding in 1949 to put an end to all military action in the newly declared Republic and to concentrate its activities on the north of Ireland.[9] The focus of the struggle became the reunification of the two parts of the island, a point that had not been particularly prominent in IRA discourse after the partition in 1920. In line with its new strategy, the IRA embarked on a 'border campaign'. The strategy underlying this campaign was to hit the Northern Irish state from the border areas, and ultimately, to make it ungovernable and thus make reunification inevitable. The Border Campaign, which ran from 1956 to 1962, claimed the lives of eighteen men in the six years that these sporadic actions lasted. Initially, the campaign benefited Sinn Féin, which succeeded in maximising popular support during the general election campaign of 1957 in the Republic of Ireland, when four of its candidates were elected to the Dáil, although they did not take their seats, having been elected on an abstentionist ticket.[10] But these manifestations of support were short-lived. By February 1962, the IRA admitted defeat and ended its military operations.

Socialism, reform and revolution

The 1960s represented a turning point in republican thinking within the ranks of both the IRA and Sinn Féin. On the one hand, the respective leaderships of the party and of the army clearly advocated a more visible political engagement while, on the other hand, some members were gradually becoming more suspicious of the emerging strategy that, in their view, implied the sidelining of the militaristic approach. This was to lead eventually to one of the most bitter splits in the recent history of republicanism. The new leadership that had come forward after the débâcle of the border campaign, embodied by Tómas Mac Giolla for Sinn Féin and Cathal Goulding for the IRA, started to reassess the movement's strategies and policies, concluding that the way forward lay in the formation of alliances on broad issues and in the ending of the isolationist nationalism that had prevailed until then. These leaders began to establish contacts outside of republican circles, with other political organisations such as the Communist Party of Ireland but also with trade unions. They embraced a more internationalist and socialist analysis not only of nationalism but of the existence of the two states and of partition. Instead of ascribing the cause of the situation solely to the British, Sinn Féin insisted on the necessity of breaking down all sectarian barriers. Therefore, unity was no longer just desirable from a geographic point of view; the prerequisite became the unification of the working class. Sinn Féin sought to replace what could have been perceived as a territorial analysis of the division of the island by one in which the key concepts became the 'proletariat', 'exploitation' and 'emancipation'. One of the most important changes, from this perspective, was that the first step envisaged in order to achieve this alliance of social classes was reform, a word which had been, up to that point, anathema in republican thinking. This new analysis consequently threw into disarray the entire vision of the state that had prevailed until then; reforms had never been an option because it was deemed impossible to reform a state that was, by its very nature – by its very existence – unworkable. To talk about reforms meant not only to accept that there might be some scope for progress within the state, but also to step over a forbidden line by lending legitimacy to the very institutions against which republicanism had been fighting for forty years. The split between the factions that came to be known as Officials and Provisionals had its origins in this antagonism: whether the way forward was collaboration with the institutions or continued rejection and, ultimately, whether the state should be reformed or overthrown.

Inevitably, the question which soon emerged was that of the role of armed struggle within the new objectives of the movement. Socialism was perceived by some as a credo imposed on republicans, and there was an ingrained suspicion of this ideology, which had already caused several splits in the 1930s and which was considered by some to be not only foreign, but contrary to Catholic teaching. Moreover, the new thinking entailed transformations in the structures of the movement. The IRA, which was still the so-called 'government of the Republic', would probably now have to take a more marginal role to accommodate the introduction of new policies. As the then leadership of both Sinn Féin and the IRA saw it, it would be impossible to break down the sectarian barriers that divided the working class, impossible to form alliances with trade unions and social organisations, if the IRA remained centre-stage in republican thinking and strategies. On a military level, thus, it seems that what the leadership had in mind was the creation of a National Liberation Front on the model of the Viet Cong that would involve the masses of the population, replacing the previous structures within which the IRA had operated and which were now seen as elitist.

These developments were taking place against the backdrop of the Civil Rights Movement in Northern Ireland, where a stronger voice than ever before was demanding basic civil rights such as 'one man, one vote'. For the leadership of Sinn Féin, the short-term objective was to support the introduction of these reforms, while their opponents within the movement viewed the situation as volatile in terms of its impact on security and advocated the strengthening of the military position. However, it is probable that this debate largely bypassed most of those involved in the Civil Rights Movement. Its activists were not looking for territorial unity, they were not questioning the partition of the island or the existence of the institutions; what they demanded was political and social changes and an end to what they perceived as their second-class citizenship.[11] Thus it is conceivable that republicans, both on the Official and on the Provisional sides, saw the Civil Rights Movement as a potential vehicle to move forward republican objectives. The leadership – the Officials – saw it as a possible platform, or stepping stone, towards the broader socialist agenda; on the other hand, the opposition – the Provisionals – sought to create sufficient unrest to prove the perennial point, namely that no reform would be meaningful as long as Ireland remained partitioned.

The outcome of this debate among republicans was a split that took years to heal. The leadership of both Sinn Féin and the IRA had come to the logical conclusion that the most effective manner to obtain reforms was to take the parliamentary route, and it consequently advocated an end to abstentionism. The old ghost of previous divisions resurfaced, once again with the same undertones of betrayal versus pragmatism, of short-term gains versus long-term objectives, of reform versus revolution. Those who sought to fight for reforms, and eventually for the end of partition from within the institutions, were opposed by those who found it utterly unacceptable to lend credibility to those institutions, since such an act would counter the very foundations of their struggle. But the lines that divided the two camps were not that clear-cut. To the leadership, embodied by Tómas Mac Giolla and Cathal Goulding, who would remain in what was called Official Sinn Féin, the language of reform was not necessarily incompatible with that of revolution. The type of revolution that they had in mind was probably one where the class struggle, and not the nation, would be placed centre-stage. Equally, their opponents, leaders such as Ruiarí Ó Brádaigh, Daithí Ó Conaill or Seán MacStiofáin, were not necessarily the single-minded militarists and reactionaries that the leadership portrayed. A substantial part of the analysis of these men, who were to found the Provisional Movement, was undoubtedly influenced not only by their reading of history but by the experience of those republicans living in the north. It is thus interesting to note that some leading republicans such as Gerry Adams joined the Provisionals not so much because they disagreed with the socialist orientation of the Officials but because they considered that their reading of the situation was mis-guided. 'For many of the dissidents the issue was not abstentionism itself but what it had come to represent: a leadership with a wrong set of priorities which had led the IRA into ignominy in August [1969]' (Adams, 1996: 129).

The future Provisional movement claimed that reforms, whatever form they might take, were impossible, as the state of Northern Ireland was based on the unionist veto, on injustices, and on an artificial legitimacy that was anything but democratic. The only effect of reforms would inevitably be to strengthen unionist power, as they would make the Northern Ireland state seem workable. They fought for the abolition of the Northern Ireland institutions, and claimed victory when the direct rule from Westminster was introduced in March 1972, although other observers attributed the fall of the Northern Assembly in Stormont to opposite causes; that is, the incapacity of unionists to reform their own state to make it more inclusive and thus more workable. The Officials on the other hand favoured a situation where Britain's involvement was kept minimal, since a direct intervention from Britain would postpone any resolution to the crisis. Thus their short-term objective was precisely the reform of the state.

The Provisional[12] republican movement that was born out of the 1969 to 1970 split was based on quite traditional principles: abstentionism (in other words, a refusal to sit on any institutional body and on the organisations affiliated to them), and a profound belief in the legitimacy and effectiveness of armed struggle. The men (and the few women) who constituted Provisional Sinn Féin and the Provisional IRA were fundamentally driven by the need to overthrow the state, to combat what they perceived as the corrupt nature of the Northern Ireland institutions, and to abolish partition. Their political discourse was not always sophisticated, and what the 1970s mainly achieved was an exaltation of armed struggle as a strategy, while the political role that Sinn Féin played was mainly one of mobilisation and protest. The leaders knew exactly what they were opposed to, and although they had a vision for a united Ireland, the political strategies to achieve reunification were not always clearly articulated. The policy document that was designed and presented as embodying the vision of republicans, *Éire Nua*, was never completely accepted within the ranks of the organisation, and had little, if any, impact outside republican circles. Politics took second place, and negotiations, when they did happen, were carried out by IRA commanders or by young northern leaders. Armed struggle commanded total respect among the republican rank and file. The rhetoric of martyrdom and that of the lessons of history was revived and the emotional appeal reached new heights. The armed struggle came to be the *raison d'être* of the republican movement, particularly from 1971 onwards when the Provisional IRA became a modern, well-trained and efficient paramilitary organisation.

This by no means implies that Sinn Féin was inactive during this period. On the contrary, it played an essential role in maintaining the momentum for the struggle. Its discourse was centred mainly on lending the armed strategy the legitimacy it needed in order to be supported by the local community in which the IRA recruited its volunteers. The role that Sinn Féin played was not solely that of the political wing of a paramilitary organisation, although there is no doubt that it did play an essential part, being the link between the clandestine IRA and the people in whose name the struggle was being waged. In that respect, it ensured a physical presence in those areas where it was necessary to retain a level of support. It also took part in elections, but more in order to subvert the system than to participate in it. For instance, Sinn Féin urged the electorate to actively boycott the Westminster general election of 1974 and the 1975 Convention elections.

The IRA remained centre-stage for most of the decade. The gradual intensification of its operations, along with an increased presence of the British army and the security forces, made it imperative for its organisation to be as sophisticated and professional as possible. By the end of the decade, it was becoming gradually more obvious that a military defeat of the IRA was unlikely and that the conflict would not be resolved by military means. According to a report written by a British army intelligence officer, James Glover, and intercepted by republicans in 1979, the future prospects for the IRA were quite bright.[13] The organisation was deemed capable of recruiting members, of attracting men and women with the necessary capability and know-how, and it would continue to benefit from sufficient support to remain operational (*AP*, 12 May 1979). Other ways to defeat the Provisional movement had been sought throughout the decade. Internment without trial had been introduced in 1971 in order to arrest and detain those deemed responsible for the continued unrest throughout Northern Ireland. Although a high number of people, mostly men, and practically exclusively from the nationalist community, were arrested and detained without trial, analysts agreed that this measure was, at best, counterproductive, since not only did it not succeed in its primary aim of arresting leaders of the IRA, it also antagonised the nationalist community into opposition to the Stormont regime, and subsequently to the British authorities. Progressively, the British army came to be seen as the enemy by a large section of the nationalist community, particularly after the events of Bloody Sunday, when British paratroopers fired on a peaceful Civil Rights march and killed fourteen civilians in Derry, on 30 January 1972.[14] Negotiations were attempted. The first of these took place in March 1972, when local leaders such as Gerry Adams, interned at the time, and Martin McGuinness, formed part of a team of negotiators that included some of the IRA and Sinn Féin's top men – Seán MacStiofáin, then chief of staff, and Dáithí Ó Conaill, Sinn Féin's Vice-president. The outcome of the discussions with British officials was a fragile three-day truce and a return to the impasse. The Provisionals did not seem entirely ready to grasp the complexity of the situation and simply demanded a British withdrawal and subsequent reunification of the island. According to some accounts at the time, the British were taken aback by the resolve and militaristic approach of their interlocutors. In his subsequent memoirs, the Labour Secretary of State for Northern Ireland, Merlyn Rees, gave a gloomy account of the exchange between the government's representatives and the Provisionals: 'These were hard men who talked and looked like soldiers. They thought solely in terms of military victory; there was no sign of compromise' (Rees, 1985: 27).

Three years later, following talks between clergymen and Sinn Féin representatives, the IRA declared an unlimited ceasefire in January 1975. This was to lead to one of the most controversial episodes in recent republican history, as the decision to declare a ceasefire was not unanimously accepted and was, in fact, opposed by the Northern element of the Army Council (Bishop and Mallie, 1987: 214). Republicans were expecting to obtain a British withdrawal, the end of internment and eventual reunification. What was thought to have been obtained, through eight months of fragile peace and repeated acts of mistrust, was, effectively, the end of internment and a gradual military withdrawal. What was in store, in the immediate future, was much worse. 'Ulsterisation' and 'criminalisation' became the new keywords of British strategists. Their objectives were twofold: the first aim was to normalise the security situation in Northern Ireland as much as possible by devolving greater powers to the police, notably the power to arrest and interrogate suspects, and by gradually diminishing the presence of the British army on the ground. The second aim was to put an end to the credibility that the IRA and other paramilitary organisations enjoyed in some quarters by portraying and treating them as criminals. This could be done through rhetoric, with a discourse that gradually started using terms such as 'mafia' and 'organised crime' to depict the paramilitary organisations. It could also be done through the courts, by expediting as much as possible those cases linked with terrorism. But more effectively, it was to be done in the prisons, the other heartland of republican resistance and politicisation.

Turning point: the 1980–1981 hunger strikes

Six years into a conflict that had caused over 1,500 deaths,[15] left thousands more injured, and sent scores of mostly young men and women to prison for political violence,[16] the Labour government in London decided, in late 1975, to withdraw the special category status that republican and loyalist prisoners had been granted in 1972. This was akin to POW status, in the eyes of the inmates at least, as they had the right to free association and were exempted from wearing a uniform or doing prison work. The Wilson government might not have foreseen the long and protracted crisis that this change in policy was to generate, displaying a lack of understanding of the Irish protest tradition, in which infringing prisoners' status has always been risky. By deciding to put an end to the special category status, the British authorities were determined to criminalise republican and loyalist prisoners, by assimilating them into the category of common criminals and placing them under the same prison regime.

Immediately after this decision was announced, republican prisoners declared their intention not to conform to the new prison regulations. By refusing to wear the uniform, protesting inmates were constrained to using a blanket as they were not allowed civilian clothing, and they soon became known as the 'blanket men'. By refusing to do prison work, they were confined to their cells for most of the day. The confrontation gradually escalated and the conditions deteriorated, leading to the 'dirty protest' where prisoners stopped washing and started spreading their own excrement on the walls of their cells. Each side predictably blamed the other, the prison authorities claiming that these conditions were self-inflicted, and the prisoners alleging that the authorities did not allow them access to even minimal facilities such as toilets and toothbrushes. After four years of living in this foul environment, and seeing no manner in which to further their demands, the prisoners decided to take their protest a step further and embark on a hunger strike.[17]

Hunger strikes have acquired, throughout history, a quasi-mythical dimension in republican circles. Over the years, prisoners have, at regular intervals, embarked on this type of protest to reject the prison system to which they were subjected.[18] Those who eventually died on hunger strike immediately joined the republican pantheon of martyrs. Their deaths were seen by their supporters as wholly unselfish and their protests as purely motivated by altruistic and idealistic reasons. Hunger strikes were always started within the prisons; it was the prisoners themselves who decided these tactics, and not the outside military or political command. In fact, the IRA rarely welcomed this type of protest, which was seen as a diversion from the 'real' struggle. Although the British and Irish authorities tended to accuse the republican leadership of manipulating their men inside the prison, this particular accusation seems unfounded. Obviously, it may be argued that some prisoners, especially the most vulnerable psychologically, might have joined the protest in a confused state of mind and not have been wholly prepared for what awaited them. Nevertheless, very few of the inmates who went on protest backed down, which was quite remarkable given the particularly difficult conditions that this generated.

The 1980 to 1981 hunger strike was somewhat different from the previous hunger strikes, in that all prisoners who volunteered for the strike did so after years spent on the 'blanket' and 'dirty' protests. At their height, the protests involved over 400 inmates in Long Kesh Prison, living in appalling hygienic conditions, which the then Primate of the Catholic Church, Cardinal Tomás Ó Fiaich, described as worse than those of the slums of Calcutta (in Coogan, 1980: 158). Most of the men who volunteered for the hunger strike shared a similar background. They had joined one of the republican organisations, either the Provisionals or the INLA,[19] at a relatively young age. A survey in *Fortnight* magazine at the start of the prison protest estimated that the vast majority of prisoners were between 17 and 21 years old, convicted on a first offence, and concluded that 'the war is essentially a working-class one' (*Fortnight*, May 1976). They had all been sentenced to lengthy detentions, and were, for the most part, poorly educated. Nevertheless, prison was a learning experience for most prisoners, who attended the 'republican university' as it was called and received, for most of them, their first real training in political history and theory. They also learned how to speak Irish, and in some cases pursued third-level education (Laurence McKeown and Ella O'Dwyer subsequently obtained a Ph.D. while in prison). But more importantly, all were united in their rejection of the new prison regime. They were convinced that their cause was just, that one day Ireland would be united and that their lives were a high but necessary price to pay for that reward. They were determined not to give up, and few of them did.

Ten men died before the issue was finally resolved between republican emissaries and the British government. These ten became associated, in republican thinking, with values such as martyrdom, sacrifice and altruism. They were seen as having enabled the Republican Movement to regain some of the moral ground that had been lost in a conflict mainly fought, up to then, on military terms. In the years to come, republicans would invoke those ten deaths as symbolising the ultimate republican sacrifice. One of the ten, Bobby Sands, became a household name for anyone remotely acquainted with Irish republicanism.

The lessons to be drawn from the ordeal of the hunger strikes were to pave the way for Sinn Féin's strategic choices from then on. Bobby Sands, the first prisoner to die, on 5 May 1981, after a fast that had lasted sixty-six days, epitomised the new image that Sinn Féin chose to put across, an image it wanted republicanism to be identified with. Sands was portrayed as an ordinary man, a typical volunteer of the IRA, the product of the conflict, and the victim, like so many others, of prevalent sectarianism. Sentenced in 1973, at the age of 19, to five years' imprisonment for possession of firearms, he benefited from special category status. When he was re-arrested in 1977 and charged with conspiracy, he immediately joined the protest. Sands' journey was thus common to a significant number of IRA volunteers, but he nevertheless became an emblematic figure within the Republican Movement. What made him stand out as the figure he represented in the following years, both in Ireland and abroad, was the way in which the circumstances surrounding his prison experience and death captured his contemporaries' imagination. His election to Westminster for the constituency of Fermanagh-South Tyrone in April 1981 was seen as legitimising his struggle and proved how much there was to be gained from such tactics. When he died, an estimated 100,000 people followed the funeral procession of this new martyr. And that is probably where the strength of the hunger strikes lay. With figures such as Sands, for the first time in over a generation, and maybe even since the Civil War, republicans were able to associate their movement with a mythical yet contemporary name. While forging their own myths, they could also point to the legitimacy of their struggle. Sands the inspirational figure was, first and foremost, a member of the IRA, who did not shy away from his military involvement and who made no apologies for it. For future generations, Sands would be presented as an ordinary young man caught in an extraordinary situation.

Republicans at the time correctly interpreted the hunger strikes as a turning point in their struggle. In his homily at Sands' funeral, Owen Carron, who had been his electoral agent and would later be elected for the same constituency, described Sands as 'a symbol for the unemployed, the poor, the oppressed and the homeless, for those who are divided by partition, for those who are trying to unify our country. He symbolises a new beginning' (*AP*, 9 May 1981). This is where one of the major changes that Sinn Féin would subsequently undergo could already be foreseen. Although the party had always claimed to represent the ordinary man, the victims of oppression, it had attributed the root cause of oppression mainly to British rule, or to British imperialism at best. Every ill that affected its constituents was ascribed to the British presence in Ireland, and this even permeated its analysis of the persistence of a strong loyalist tradition among sections of the Northern Ireland population. Unionism was thus seen as a by-product of British rule. The withdrawal of the British would, it was argued, consequently remove the causes and *raison d'être* of unionism. It was only from the 1990s onward that republicans would admit that unionism was more than a reactionary phenomenon, that it was an identity. Before 1981, the cure for all ills, on both sides of the border, was a British withdrawal. In the aftermath of the hunger strikes, this analysis of the northern conflict was gradually shelved and a more complex, pragmatic tone emerged.[20] The most notable introduction to this discourse was the working-class element, which had been cast aside since the early years of the conflict for fear that it would prove too divisive, after the split with the Officials at the end of the 1960s. Sinn Féin had, from 1981 on, a new, better-defined mandate, which did not centre only on national independence. It was going to embark on class politics, and this meant doing more political work than had been envisaged up until that time.

Gradually, the movement started liberating itself from some of the ideological rigidity that it had always viewed as essential to the unity of its ranks. Talking about what was potentially divisive had been considered a danger to the ultimate goal. Thus, freedom was a limited concept encompassing, mainly, territorial self-determination. With the hunger strikes and the opening up of the struggle to other sectors of public life, such as community groups or trade unions, leaders like Gerry Adams or Danny Morrison realised that this vision of liberation might have been too narrow and exclusive, and had to be broadened in order to be relevant to a wider section of the population. From the early 1980s, broader issues started emerging that Sinn Féin no longer avoided or ignored. This enabled more radical movements and individuals to contribute to the politicisation of

Sinn Féin. Symptomatic of this change was the discussion held at the 1985 Ard Fhéis and the subsequent vote on the right to choose on the issue of abortion. Although this decision was overturned the following year in light of the heated controversy it had stirred among the rank and file, the fact that this type of debate was taking place heralded important changes within the movement, and an implicit acceptance that freedom was not related solely to territoriality, that the oppressor could not be singled out as being the British alone. The tensions that this created within the movement have not, as yet, been totally overcome.[21] However, as with some more recent issues, Sinn Féin started to work with other groups not necessarily affiliated with its own organisation in order to broaden its political agenda and its appeal.

With the hunger strikes, for the first time since the Civil Rights Movement in the late 1960s, a mass movement surfaced in Northern Ireland, and then spread to the rest of the island.[22] The National H-Block/Armagh Committee was launched in 1977 to support the protesting prisoners. This organisation did not draw exclusively from the Republican Movement (although obviously there was a strong input from Sinn Féin). Furthermore, it reached to the other side of the border, thus achieving what no other group or movement had been able to do, mobilising a sizeable proportion of public opinion from the two parts of Ireland on the issue of prisoners' rights. This must have been enlightening for Sinn Féin, especially after the campaign around the theme of 'Brits Out' that had been mounted in 1977, but that had never succeeded in capturing the imagination of the Irish. The lessons of the H-Block campaign were clear. Sinn Féin could not do it alone, it needed broader support outside its usual constituency. Thus it reached out to other political parties, to pressure groups, to individual MPs and TDs, to trade unions. This was one of the fundamental lessons of the hunger strikes, one that informed the party's shift in position, one that could be said to have eventually led to its decision to embark on the peace process alongside the SDLP.

Armalite and ballot box

From 1981 onward, Sinn Féin enthusiastically embraced electoral strategies. The election of Sands to the Fermanagh-South Tyrone constituency in April 1981, and that of two representatives of the prisoners to the Dáil in July of that year, had shown republicans the potential benefits of getting involved in politics, although this particular tactic of 'borrowing' seats in the name of prisoners was not unprecedented.[23] Furthermore, at that time, Sinn Féin already had some experience of local politics, which had been tested in the mid-1970s, when it opened local clinics throughout the north. Indeed, during the 1975 ceasefire, in agreement with the British authorities, Sinn Féin opened and manned a number of 'incident centres' whose primary role was to monitor the ceasefire on the ground and to signal any incident that might have destabilised the situation. Sinn Féin was quick to capitalise on the potential that these centres represented. With the end of the ceasefire, these 'incident centres' were transformed into 'advice centres', which acted as political clinics where the local community could register its concerns and demands on issues such as housing and health. This gave Sinn Féin activists more grounding in their communities, and ensured that they maintained a presence and a role that had not been fully explored up until that time. This translated into the involvement of the party in local elections, the first ones being fought in 1979 in the Republic. Consequently, it was in those years that the debate over more active political involvement resurfaced, when a new leadership was already in control of the northern element of the movement and instigated a discussion on the way forward. The hunger strikes succeeded in making acceptable a political strategy that had been up until then the source of many divisions and splits. What this episode undeniably demonstrated was that getting actively involved in constituency politics had both short-term and long-term benefits.

Electoralism took on a new dimension for the Republican Movement. It was seen as a way in which to make republican sympathisers and activists more directly responsible for the struggle, by getting them to become actively involved within their communities. It introduced the idea of a 'republican veto', in other words ensuring that the SDLP was not the only voice for the nationalist community. The distinction between a 'republican vote' and a 'vote for violence' was thus made as clear as possible: the former was presented as an alternative to the status quo that the SDLP was seen to embody and not directly translated into support for the IRA. With the new electoral policies, republicans undoubtedly increased their share of the vote in the north, not so much by converting people whose allegiances might have been elsewhere, but by bringing on board those voters who had previously been left, or had chosen to remain, outside of the electoral system, those disenfranchised voters who could now identify with the alternative offered by Sinn Féin. Electoralism meant that Sinn Féin could consolidate the image that had been generated by the hunger strikes, that of the party of ordinary people. Indeed, Sinn Féin candidates at elections were local men and women, with a track record of involvement within their communities, who were, broadly speaking, young, dynamic and enthusiastic, most of whom had experienced imprisonment at some stage of the Troubles, and whose working-class credentials were not open to question. In other words, they were the mirror of the very people they sought to represent.

The hunger strikes led to the famous 'armalite and ballot box' strategy, a phrase coined by the then Sinn Féin director of publicity Danny Morrison, whereby politics and armed struggle would operate hand-in-hand.

Republicans enthusiastically embraced electoralism, and their choice seemed rapidly vindicated. When the British authorities announced in 1982 the establishment of a local Assembly for Northern Ireland on the basis of a 'rolling devolution',[24] Sinn Féin joined the electoral race, although it made it clear that such an institution was simply unacceptable and that its intention was to boycott it, just like the SDLP. Sinn Féin candidates obtained over 10 per cent of the vote, a result which augured well for the party's future electoral performance. Sinn Féin succeeded in strengthening its score in the June 1983 Westminster election, winning 13.4 per cent of the vote. Gerry Adams became the first Sinn Féin MP since the 1950s (Bobby Sands, technically, was not a Sinn Féin MP, since he ran under the banner of the H-Blocks candidates, as did Owen Carron). This result was maintained the following year by the score of Danny Morrison in the European election, when he obtained a total of 13.3 per cent of the vote. Sinn Féin had clearly demonstrated that its enthusiastic and mostly young workers could deliver a message which found an echo among the nationalist community, who saw abstentionism as a valid manner to register their opposition to the institutions.

These developments coincided with the emergence of a new leadership which had started articulating new ideas in the late 1970s. These were young men and women mostly from the north, and perhaps more importantly, who had been the natural intermediaries between the prisoners and the outside world, including the British authorities, during the prison protests and the hunger strikes. These new leaders were also in touch with their rank and file in a manner that the previous, mostly southern-based leadership, might not have been. The former generation of leaders, men like Ó Brádaigh, Mac Stiofáin or Ó Conaill, were from the southern part of the island, from middle-class backgrounds, and although their commitment to the struggle was beyond doubt, they were not as closely identified with the conflict and with those who were fighting on the ground as were the new northern leaders. The strategy consisting of fighting on the military and political fronts in parallel brought about immediate results, but it also meant a rethinking of the priorities of the movement as a whole. Obviously, even if republican leaders were adamant that a vote for Sinn Féin was not a vote for the IRA or a vote for violence, there was an inescapable correlation between the two. But as Danny Morrison recognised early on, the strategy had its own inherent limits. He therefore admitted that 'perhaps it is not entirely possible to harmonize the relationship between armed struggle and electoral politics' (*Magill*, September 1984).

The situation in the Republic was quite different, and in spite of its efforts, Sinn Féin did not seem capable of making any significant electoral breakthrough. This was made obvious during the 1982 general election, when Sinn Féin decided to test its level of support. The fact that it only put forward candidates in five constituencies, in an attempt to build on the support won by those who 'borrowed' the seats in the name of the prisoners, was in itself an indication of the weakness of the party. Its dismal share of the vote, 1.2 per cent of the first preference vote on a national scale, proved that the discourse of oppression used in the north had little currency on the other side of the border. More immediately, it pointed to the obvious fact that abstentionism was not relevant in the south, where the electorate had long accepted the legitimacy of the institutions. This principle had already been slightly eroded the previous year, at the 1981 Ard Fheis, when it had been abandoned as a strategy in local councils in the north and in the European Parliament. This did not, according to the party, represent a major shift in policy: the local councils were not directly associated with the partition institutions and the Brussels Assembly was totally outside of that equation. But in light of the 1982 results, the inescapable conclusion was that abstentionism for the Dáil was hindering the progress of the party, and it was probably only a matter of time before a decision would be taken on the issue. This debate had been started earlier, triggered by some prisoners who, being removed from the everyday obligations and commitments that the movement outside had to conform to, could be far more open and pragmatic in their approach to the way forward. Some of them were even quite visionary, suggesting as early as October 1981 that abstentionism, that benchmark of republican ethical purism, be dropped for the sake of the future development of the movement. As one prisoner put it,

> A lot of people feel they must have some sort of representation at parliament and therefore the abstentionist policy may not appeal to them. I don't think that Owen Carron going to Westminster may be damaging to our struggle. I think we should fight the war on as many fronts as possible, and if the support is there, we may as well use it.
> (Beresford, 1987: 111)

This was not going to happen immediately. The following years were dedicated to preparing the rank and file of the movement for this possibility. When an amendment urging the dropping of abstentionism for the Dáil was put to the vote at the Sinn Féin Ard Fheis for the first time, in 1985, it was easily defeated, but the following year it obtained the two-thirds majority necessary for the amendment of the party's constitution. In the meantime, the IRA Convention met, for the first time since the creation of the Provisionals, and condoned the change in policy. The Sinn Féin leadership, by obtaining the backing of the IRA, had ensured that it would not be seen, as had its predecessors in 1969 to 1970, to be questioning the role of the armed struggle. It also made certain that the almost inevitable split that would ensue was not going to harm the movement.

'There is going to be no bloodshed over this issue. We should part as friends, in sadness not in anger. We have been down the road of feuding before and we are not going down that road again' was the message from the Sinn Féin President to his party's delegates (Adams, Presidential Address, 1986). The movement did have to part with lifelong republicans such as Ó Brádaigh and Ó Conaill, who had dedicated their whole careers to their cause. Feeling betrayed, let down and passed by, these men left the movement they had contributed to founding in 1970 in order to form their own organisation, Republican Sinn Féin. The leadership of the move-ment had successfully demonstrated not only its considerable influence and prestige, but also that it was possible to adapt the party to a given situation instead of waiting for the situation to conform to the republican analysis, which had been the case previously.

Yet in spite of their electoral successes in the north, their drastic reappraisal of their own strategies, and the apparent willingness of the IRA to support these changes, politics were not, in the eyes of Sinn Féin, a sufficient response to the situation. As if to reassure his supporters, Gerry Adams stated quite simply that 'if the British government listened to the ballot box, no one would be reaching for the armalite' (*AP*, 16 June 1983). These were difficult times, when republicans were facing resolute enemies. Few, if any, could have foreseen that the IRA would, before the end of the century, declare a ceasefire, much less that this would be followed, after much soul-searching and controversy, by acts of decommissioning of weapons. Neither was the climate in Northern Ireland at the time likely to lead to any settlement that would involve reaching an agreement by a majority of political forces as well as by the British and Irish governments. At a time when no immediate end to the conflict was in sight, it would have been quite optimistic, even unrealistic, to envisage a situation where Sinn Féin representatives would hold ministerial seats alongside unionists. Those were bleak days, when unemployment was soaring on both sides of the border and economic depression was a fact of life, when republicans seemed to see no way of making any political progress under the Thatcher-led government and were still relying on a more militaristic approach to bring about her downfall, as had almost happened in Brighton in October 1984 when a bomb exploded in the hotel where the Conservative Party was holding its annual conference. The explanation given by the IRA for this action was quite simple: 'the language of force is the only reasoning the British government understands' (*Iris*, 1984).

As the Brighton bombing displayed, the lessons drawn from the hunger strike and the electoral involvement of Sinn Féin by no means implied a side-tracking of the IRA. Republicans no longer viewed politics as secondary in the ultimate task of achieving a British withdrawal, and saw correctly that the analysis that had prevailed until then, which had permeated their movement in the previous decade, potentially thwarted the prospects of a settlement. But they were still in no doubt, at least in their public discourse, that armed struggle was the fundamental vehicle for reaching their objective. They succeeded in justifying their strategy to their immediate supporters by quoting history and pointing to the heroic nature of the fight. It was a dirty war, where all sides concerned committed unjustifiable acts of violence. However, republicans were convinced that they held the higher moral ground, because in their eyes their cause was intrinsically just, because they were clear as to what their objectives were, and because the enemy, the British, was considered to be fighting a dirtier war. Pointing to the corruption of the state, to the collusion of the security forces with loyalist paramilitary forces, they justified their continued battle against both the state and the establishment.

For the Thatcher government, the primary objective seemed to be to crush the IRA and Sinn Féin, and few means were spared to achieve this. The authorities used the political route to try to stabilise the situation while isolating Sinn Féin. The main proposal of the decade was the Anglo-Irish Agreement signed between Dublin and London in November 1985, which unleashed a series of protests from the unionists, who were united in their rejection of the document mainly because of the role that the Irish government was given in the affairs of Northern Ireland. Republicans were equally opposed to the document, which they saw as an attempt to isolate them and thwart their political progress by pushing the SDLP towards centre-stage and by stepping up military and security cooperation between the two sides of the island. But politics was not the only means used by the authorities to deal with republicans. The judiciary was also used to try to put as many suspected IRA volunteers as possible behind bars. In the Diplock, non-jury courts, the testimony of former IRA Volunteers turned informants was considered admissible as evidence for the first time in 1981, leading to the conviction of numerous suspected IRA members. Christopher Black, arrested that year, named thirty-eight people. Between 1981 and 1983 alone, this 'supergrass' system, as it came to be known, led to the arrest of at least 600 suspects on the basis of the testimony of some thirty-five informants (Cunningham, 2001: 58). On appeal, most convictions were overturned, for lack of evidence, leading lawyers and civil rights defenders to condemn the system. It was abandoned in 1986.

The British authorities also responded to IRA activities by resorting to undercover operations and summary executions of suspected IRA members, which for republicans amounted to a 'shoot to kill' policy. One of the most contentious incidents took place in Gibraltar in March 1988, when three unarmed volunteers, who had come to prepare a military operation in this small British possession in the Mediterranean, were shot and killed by an SAS commando team. But the controversy that surrounded this type of action did not seem to deter the British government from its objective. It did not hesitate to resort to censorship, imposing in

October 1986 a ban on the broadcast of interviews of members of pro-scribed organisations or individuals who supported or invited support for those organisations. A few years earlier, in 1982, the government had enforced a provision of the Prevention of Terrorism Act (1975) on exclusion orders, barring politicians such as Adams and McGuinness from entering Britain. Finally, in 1986, the Irish Republic signed the European Convention on the Suppression of Terrorism, which paved the way for the extradition of suspected offenders to Northern Ireland. This policy was controversial within Irish political circles, and a number of extradition cases were rejected on appeal. In one such instance, the defendants, two former prisoners who had escaped from the Maze Prison in Northern Ireland in 1982, won their case, the court ruling that if extradited they would risk being 'attacked or injured by the illegal action of the prison staff' (*Irish Times* (*IT*), 14 March 1990).

The 1980s were also a time of internal turmoil for republicans, a time when their organisation suffered many setbacks, which seemed to reach their peak in 1987. In May of that year, an IRA unit about to attack an RUC station in Loughall was ambushed by the SAS, who had apparently been tipped off by an informer, killing all eight members of the IRA unit. At the end of October, a large arms shipment from Libya was seized on board the *Eskund* by French police off the coast of Brittany. But another major problem for the IRA was the number of operations which went badly wrong, costing the lives of civilians. This severely hindered Sinn Féin's progress. In November 1987, the IRA planted a bomb on Remembrance Day in Enniskillen which killed eleven people and injured sixty-three. According to the explanation provided subsequently by the IRA, the bomb had been intended for soldiers and military personnel, but went off at the wrong time. In the summer of 1988, seventeen people were 'mistakenly' killed in IRA operations, in spite of the Sinn Féin leader's appeal for more professionalism: 'You have a huge responsibility. Sometimes, the destiny of this struggle is in your hands. You must show incessant attention' (*IT*, 12 November 1987). Nevertheless, IRA oper-ations continued to claim civilian lives, and, beyond the human tragedy that this entailed, they had devastating effects on the organisation as a whole. In March 1993, in the city centre of Warrington, England, two bombs were detonated, killing two young boys and injuring fifty-one people. This prompted widespread condemnation, and a march in Dublin was attended by 20,000 people demanding peace. The fortunes of the IRA seemed to be at a low ebb, and this was compounded by an increasing number of attacks from loyalist organisations, who in 1992, and for the first time since the start of the Troubles, claimed more victims than the IRA. At the beginning of the 1990s, the prospects for peace were, at best, dim.

The long road to peace

Nevertheless, talks behind the scenes had been initiated in 1988 between Gerry Adams and John Hume. The SDLP leader insisted on the principle of consent, while Sinn Féin pushed for the ultimate goal of self-determination, both agreeing that an internal solution was not acceptable. Although John Hume was sharply criticised for taking part in talks with a leader whose party was closely associated, in the eyes of the politicians and the media alike, with the IRA, the talks continued for a number of months in 1988, and resumed in 1993, when the two leaders published, in September, a joint communiqué summarising the principles agreed during their talks. This led to the Downing Street Declaration by the British Prime Minister John Major and the Irish Taoiseach (Prime Minister) Albert Reynolds in December 1993. While the British recognised the right to self-determination and insisted on the importance of the principle of consent, the Irish conceded on the eventual amendment of the constitutional articles which claimed jurisdiction over the north of the island. The two governments announced the establishment of a Forum for Peace and Reconciliation. Significantly, this document opened a door for Sinn Féin, which up until then had been left outside of any official negotiating process, declaring that any party which renounced violence would be included in future talks. After much soul-searching, consultation with the grassroots and a special Sinn Féin conference in Letterkenny, Co. Donegal, to examine the document, the IRA declared a ceasefire on 31 August 1994. The peace process had begun in earnest.

This was only the beginning, and the next few years were to prove difficult for all sides. The long-standing lack of trust between republicans and the British, on the one hand, and republicans and unionists, on the other, meant that for months, Sinn Féin was not allowed to sit at the negotiating table. This in turn led to increasing frustration in republican ranks, many feeling that their leadership might have been duped by the author ities. Different attempts were made at finding a way forward. After a one-day summit in London, the British and Irish Prime Ministers published a joint proposal, the Framework Document, in February 1995. It advocated three strands, or dimensions: an internal one, an all-Ireland one and a British-Irish one. But this was followed almost immediately by controversy over the issue of decommissioning, when the Secretary for Northern Ireland, Patrick Mayhew, announced in March of that year, while in Washington for the St Patrick Day's celebrations, that disarmament was a prerequisite for any party to attend negotiations. This issue was increasingly to become a bone of contention in the multi-party talks both at the time and subsequently. The American Senator George Mitchell was asked to draw up a report on the conditions to the talks, and his recommendations, which became known as the Mitchell Principles, were published in January 1996,[25] requiring that all parties adhere to basic principles of non-violence.

Nevertheless, the IRA was becoming increasingly frustrated at what it saw as the lack of progress and continued British prevarication. This led the organisation to put an end to its seventeen-month ceasefire, by detonating a bomb in Canary Wharf, London, in February 1996, which killed two people and caused extensive damage. The peace process seemed to be at a standstill, and the proposal by the Irish and British governments to hold elections on 30 May to a forum of representatives that would have a mandate to participate in all-party talks was greeted with scepticism by Sinn Féin. It nevertheless nominated candidates to these elections and obtained 15.47 per cent of the vote, its best result since it had embarked on the electoral strategy some fourteen years previously. The marching season[26] in the summer, however, served as a reminder of how wide the gap was between the two communities in the north, particularly in the Drumcree area of Portadown, where the refusal from the Garvaghy Road residents to let an Orange Order parade go through provoked a stand-off for several days. Sinn Féin seemed to be resigned to the fact that it would have to wait for a change of government in London for the impasse to be broken, Martin McGuinness admitting in July 1996 that 'I doubt that the peace process can be resuscitated by a British government led by John Major' (*IT*, 25 July 1996). Until such time, the party remained outside the mainstream political process, and was excluded from the talks that started in Stormont in September 1996 because of continued IRA activity.

The British general election of May 1997 paved the way for change. Tony Blair's landslide Labour victory and the new team he appointed to the Northern Ireland Office led by Mo Mowlam heralded a new beginning. Sinn Féin had fared well in the 1997 elections, securing two seats and 16 per cent of the vote, and becoming the third largest political party in the north, ahead of Ian Paisley's Democratic Ulster Unionist Party. This success was mirrored in the south, where, for the first time in over forty years, a Sinn Féin candidate was elected to Dáil Éireann in May of that year.[27] When London and Dublin announced in June that decommissioning would no longer be a prerequisite to entering talks, the IRA responded by announcing, a month later, its second ceasefire. In September 1997, Sinn Féin entered the multi-party talks and subscribed to the Mitchell Principles.

The road that led to the signing of the Good Friday Agreement in April 1998 was fraught with obstacles. However, on that day, as all commentators noted, history was made when most of the political parties agreed neither to lose nor to win, but to make and win concessions.[28] The Agreement was a carefully balanced document where principles were enshrined, institutional mechanisms put in place and safeguards given to both communities. A 108-member assembly would represent the people of Northern Ireland, which would elect a ten-member executive to be appointed on a proportional basis, so as to reflect all political shades. The North–South Council, where ministers from both sides of the island would sit, would enhance cooperation in a number of areas, and the British government would be represented at the Council of the islands which would also include representatives of the Scottish and Welsh assemblies. Both Irish and British governments were prepared to put an end to their territorial claims over Northern Ireland, by the repeal of the 1920 Government of Ireland Act[29] by Westminster and the redrafting of Sections Two and Three of the Constitution[30] by the Republic of Ireland, thereby conforming to the fundamental principle of consent. Among the other provisions of the Agreement were the reform of the police service, the establishment of a Commission on Human Rights, and procedures to deal with the issue of reconciliation and victims.

The Agreement was to be approved by the electorate of both parts of the island by referendum. The difficulties that lay ahead were evident during the campaign to promote a Yes vote by all the participants. Gerry Adams and the leader of the Ulster Unionist Party (UUP), David Trimble, explained in similar terms to their constituencies that this was not a perfect agreement, but that it was the best that could have been achieved in the circumstances. Sinn Féin held a special Ard Fheis to secure the approval of its members, and was greatly helped by the provision of the Agreement that stipulated the early release of prisoners by May 2000. On the unionist side, there was a level of unease at this very same provision, to which was added the fact that decommissioning, although recognised as a necessity within the Agreement, was not a prerequisite for parties to sit on an executive. On 22 May 1998, the Irish voters resoundingly approved the Agreement, with an overall 85.46 per cent Yes vote for the whole of the island. The Republic had agreed by 94.49 per cent to amend its constitution, while in the north, 71.12 per cent chose to give the Agreement a chance. However, exit polls estimated that 99 per cent of the nationalists had voted Yes, which put the unionists' share of the Yes vote at slightly over 50 per cent. Unionism thus seemed far more hesitant to endorse the Agreement, and this was to have important political consequences in the years to come.

If the Good Friday Agreement was the climactic point of the multi-party talks initiated some months before, it was only the first step on the road towards a political and institutional normalisation of the situation in Northern Ireland. Some of the major differences that had emerged during the negotiations that led to the Agreement remained. There was a deep level of discontent among some within the republican camp who saw the document as a betrayal of the ideals of their forefathers and who were ready to pursue a military strategy. Those who disagreed with the direction taken by the leadership of Sinn Féin had left to form their own organisations, such as the thirty-two-County Sovereignty Movement and the Real IRA. They crudely demonstrated their opposition to the Good Friday Agreement by detonating a bomb in Omagh in August 1998 which killed thirty people. Drumcree was still the scene of violent stand-offs, of manifestations of territorial claims, of contradictory readings on the meaning of history.

The establishment of the Northern Ireland institution was stalled for some time due to the controversy surrounding decommissioning. Several attempts were made by the British and Irish governments to break the deadlock. One such initiative was taken on 1 April 1999, when the two governments proposed the nomination of ministers who would, however, have no power until devolution was implemented, once the IRA actually started decommissioning. This 'collective act of conciliation', as it was termed, was rejected by both Sinn Féin and the UUP, the latter maintaining that Sinn Féin would not be allowed in government without prior decommissioning. In July of the same year, the Secretary of State Mo Mowlam announced that Sinn Féin would be allowed in government without prior decommissioning, but to allay unionist fears, she signalled a halt to the early release of prisoners if there was no move on weapons after the establishment of the executive. However, following the unionist rejection of the deal, the British and Irish governments announced a review procedure. George Mitchell returned to Belfast in September to chair the review that was to last eleven weeks, at the end of which a succession of events was announced. On the same day the executive would meet, the IRA would appoint an interlocutor to the International Independent Commission on Decommissioning (IICD) chaired by retired Canadian General John De Chastelain. On 27 November 1999, David Trimble narrowly won the support of his party on this proposal, which paved the way for the first power-sharing executive to be nominated two days later. Sinn Féin ministers entered into the Northern Ireland government for the first time in history, with Martin McGuinness taking the Education Department and Bairbre de Brún the Health portfolio.

However, when the IICD reported in February 2000 that it had received no indication as to when decommissioning would actually start, David Trimble resigned as First Minister and Peter Mandelson, who had replaced Mo Mowlam in October 1999, suspended the institutions. A new initiative by the British and Irish Premiers, Tony Blair and Bertie Ahern, led the IRA to open up its dumps for inspection, while the British government agreed to cut down the number of troops. Trimble once again narrowly won the backing of his party's council to re-enter the executive, but his position was critical, as he obtained 459 votes against 403. On 26 June, the first inspection of an IRA arms dump was carried out by the IICD.

However, there were indications that anti-Agreement unionists were gaining ground. In the South Antrim by-election of September 2000, the UUP lost its seat to the DUP's William McCrea, a staunch opponent of the Agreement. David Trimble's leadership was under increased difficulty in the absence of actual progress on decommissioning, and stepped up the pressure on Sinn Féin by barring its ministers from attending the North–South Ministerial Council. A renewed British–Irish initiative in June 2001 in Weston Park, England, failed to end the impasse. However, in August 2001, the IRA made an offer to the IICD to put its weapons beyond use in a verifiable manner. This was not sufficient for the UUP leader, who remarked that there was a difference between initiating a process and actually starting it. The institutions were once again suspended for a period of twenty-four hours. The following day, on 11 August, three men were arrested in Colombia, accused of being on an IRA mission to train the FARC.[31] The IRA announced a few days later that it was withdrawing its offer to the IICD. The summer ended with the escalation of tensions in North Belfast, where several hundred small Catholic schoolgirls had to be escorted by the police and the army to walk to their nearby school, as they had to walk down a loyalist road where hostile demonstrations were organised daily. The stand-off between Sinn Féin and the Ulster Unionist Party escalated in the autumn of 2001. On 18 October the UUP announced the withdrawal of its three ministers from the executive when its motion to have Sinn Féin excluded failed. However, five days later, the IRA revealed that it had effectively put part of its weapons beyond use, for the first time in its history. This was followed by a second act of decommissioning in April 2002, which stabilised the process for a time.

However, a series of events cast a shadow over the IRA's commitment to the process, or at least fed the existing suspicion that it had not entirely ceased its operations. One was the raid in the Castlereagh police station in East Belfast on 17 March 2002, when three masked men stole what were described as highly sensitive files. This led to the arrest, some three weeks later, of a number of republicans, some of whom were quite high-profile figures such as Raymond McCrea, a former hunger striker. Although Sinn Féin categorically denied that those arrested had anything to do with the break-in, this was used by republicans' political opponents to cast doubt upon their democratic credentials. A further blow to the institutions came in October 2002, when the Sinn Féin Stormont offices were raided by the police on the suspicion that they were being used by the IRA as the basis of an intelligence-gathering network. The institutions were suspended, and Tony Blair issued a warning to republicans, saying that 'we cannot carry on with the IRA half-in, half out. Remove the threat of violence and the process is unstoppable' (*Guardian*, 18 October 2002).

In spite of all these difficulties, Sinn Féin still saw the Good Friday Agreement as a step forward, one that was made cautiously but which nevertheless involved taking risks and implementing sea changes within the organisation. In order to play its part within the new situation created by the signing of the Agreement, it had to accept an internal solution, albeit under another name, even though it maintained its final objective of reunification. It had to convince its grassroots that the IRA might one day be redundant. These were huge steps, landmark changes for a party that was always at its weakest when its principles were questioned. These steps were taken with the confidence that they could deliver results to republican constituents and rank and file, but also that they did not undermine in any way the ultimate republican ideal of reunification. The years following the signing of the Good Friday Agreement were momentous for all sides of the divide in Northern Ireland. These new developments allowed Sinn Féin to present itself as a party capable of responding to immense challenges, but also of reaping huge rewards: its direct contribution to the first power-sharing government in the history of Northern Ireland, the possibility of making a significant electoral breakthrough in the Republic, and the prospect of going down in history as one of the parties that helped resolve the oldest conflict in Europe.

2   The peace process

The story of the peace process is a success story for Sinn Féin, if measured in terms of the party's electoral expansion on both sides of the border. However, for critics of Republicans, it is also the story of a party that has been, by and large, at the heart of the major disagreements that have riddled the Ulster Unionist Party and that have stalled the implementation of the Good Friday Agreement (GFA). At the core of these controversies are opposed readings of the clause on decommissioning contained in the Agreement, which called on all participants:

> to continue to work constructively and in good faith with the Independent Commission, and to use any influence they may have, to achieve the decommissioning of all paramilitary arms within two years following endorsement in referendums North and South on the Agreement and in the context of the implementation of the overall settlement.
>
> (GFA, 1998: 24)

Decommissioning: the fault line

For the Ulster Unionist Party and the SDLP, as well as for the British and Irish governments, this placed a responsibility on Sinn Féin to put pressure on the IRA to decommission. Therefore, lack of progress on this issue has led to the major crises in the peace process: the delays in establishing the Northern Ireland Executive in November 1999; the suspension of the institutions in February 2000 and again in July 2001; the failure to restore these very institutions on several occasions and, in particular, in October 2003. Sinn Féin's answer to these accusations is straightforward: as a political party it has no weapons to decommission. It further contends that it has effectively used its influence to ensure that the IRA embarked on the process of putting its weapons beyond use.

In late 2003, another attempt to restore the institutions failed on the issue of decommissioning, prolonging the political crisis and making the situation appear, once again, intractable. However, it is undeniable that progress on this issue has been made by all sides since the Good Friday Agreement. Both Sinn Féin and the Ulster Unionist Party have considerably shifted their positions on the question of IRA weapons. Unionism went from a position of 'no guns, no government' to one where David Trimble led his party into coalition with two Sinn Féin ministers without prior decommissioning. On the republican side, decommissioning, which was initially bluntly ruled out, has become, in the words of Martin McGuinness, a 'collective responsibility' (McGuinness, interview, 2003). The IRA has agreed on three occasions to put arms beyond use, thus doing what Adams termed in 2003 'the unthinkable'.

Decommissioning was, from the very start, an issue which had to do with security or military considerations but equally important was its political value. The assessment given early on by the then RUC Chief Constable was quite bleak:

> it was perfectly clear from all of the intelligence assessments that the Provisionals were not going to hand in their arms. Indeed, some individual reports made it clear that some prominent players said they wouldn't hand in as much as a single rifle. In pragmatic terms, the issue of decommissioning was less important for the security forces – because of the build up of home-made equipment than it was on the political front.
>
> (Taylor, 1997: 349)

In other words, if the IRA really wanted to go back to war, no matter how many weapons were decommissioned, it was deemed to have the capacity to do so.

Decommissioning was not raised at the inception of the peace process. Indeed, it was not on the agenda when the IRA declared its first ceasefire in August 1994. One member of the movement told a journalist a month after the IRA's announcement:

> if there was any question that we should surrender our weapons, we would all be opposed [to the ceasefire]. But this is not on the agenda. The army will not cease to operate during that time. It will not fall into oblivion. The collecting of information and of finance, like all other activities, will continue as usual.
>
> (*Fortnight*, September 1994)

This assessment illustrated the difficulties that were associated with the issue of disarmament within the Republican Movement, and indicated how difficult it would be to find ways to assuage both internal and external fears regarding IRA weapons.

In the aftermath of the IRA ceasefire, the major disagreement involving republicans was not about weapons, but about the absence of the term 'permanent' in the IRA's statement, since the British government expressed doubts regarding the organisation's future intentions. Sinn Féin emphasised repeatedly that the only precondition that had been set to their inclusion in talks was the IRA cessation of activities, and it tended to see any new issue arising as a sign that the British – and unionist – politicians were moving the goal post. When the British Prime Minister John Major announced that his government was prepared to accept the IRA ceasefire as a working possibility, another precondition emerged in February 1995: the IRA had to hand in part of its arsenal before Sinn Féin could be included in the multi-party talks. This last condition, known as the 'Washington three',[1] was to set the terms of the debate on decommissioning, which became a keyword, a permanent fixture within the peace process.

The British government's position shifted, with the announcement, jointly with the Irish government, of a 'twin-track' approach in November 1995. Exploratory talks would be held regarding the timing and content of talks, and an independent commission, led by US Senator George Mitchell, would be set to look at ways to deliver on the disarmament of paramilitary weapons. Its report, published in February 1996, recommended that decommissioning should no longer precede talks but happen in parallel.[2] It advocated the establishment of an independent commission that would oversee the proceedings. Finally, acknowledging the difficulties that the prerequisite of decommissioning entailed for the Republican Movement, the Mitchell report recommended that all parties adhere to six principles which would guarantee their commitment to peaceful and democratic means in order to be included in the talks.

Republicans initially refuted the validity of decommissioning. In his keynote address to his party's Ard Fheis in 1995, Adams applied the term 'decommissioning' not to the IRA or to any other paramilitary organisation, but to 'the British Crown Forces', and called for 'the disbandment of the RUC' (Ard Fheis, 1995). This sentence was repeated, word for word, the following year. Although this could have been construed as an effort to deny the issue, it was partly a response to the fear among the ranks of the organisation that decommissioning would be used as a bargaining tool by the unionists and the British who would condition the early release of prisoners on IRA disarmament. Republicans, however, did not see any justification to the prerequisite for decommissioning, seeing it, in the words of Gerry Adams, as a 'means to undermine the rights of voters of this party' (Ard Fheis, 1998).

The negotiations which led to the signing of the GFA were held without any organisation having handed in a single weapon, when the Labour government (elected in June 1997) declared that Sinn Féin would be included in the talks if it signed up to the Mitchell Principles. The Ulster Unionist Party was deeply uncomfortable with this situation and pressed, along with other participants, for the issue of decommissioning to be included in the final text of any agreement. But this was still deemed insufficient by a section of the UUP, among them Jeffrey Donaldson,[3] who walked out of the negotiations one hour before the Agreement was signed in great part because of his opposition to the approach taken on this matter.

For many republicans, the issue of decommissioning was a highly important point of principle. Never in its history had the IRA surrendered its weapons. The different ceasefires that had taken place, be they in 1923 after the Civil War or in 1962 after the Border Campaign, had not resulted in the surrendering of arms. Nevertheless, on both occasions, the IRA had admitted defeat. This was not the case with the 1994 ceasefire, since neither the IRA nor the British authorities considered that the republicans had been defeated. What probably worried both governments and unionists alike was that as they saw it, the IRA had a track record of going back to violence if it saw fit. But for many republicans, and not necessarily the most extreme, the fact of giving up the IRA weapons would have been equated with an acknowledgement not solely that the war was over but that it had been lost. It would take some time for the leadership to convince its supporters that decommissioning did not mean surrender. This level of confidence seemed to have been achieved by 2003, when veteran republican Joe Cahill was given a standing ovation at his party's Ard Fheis for his speech on the peace process, which he concluded by saying: 'We have won the war. Let us win the peace.'

In the immediate aftermath of the signing of the Belfast Agreement, the IRA's attitude to decommissioning was clearly spelt out in an interview in April 1998, when a spokesperson for the organisation stated: 'let us make it clear that there will be no decommissioning by the IRA' (*AP*, April 1998). Nevertheless, in September of that year, republican leaders established contact with the International Independent Commission on Decommissioning (IICD) established in August 1997 and chaired by retired Canadian General John de Chastelain, although they were careful to stress that they were only exposing the views of the party and were not acting as intermediaries for the IRA. Gerry Adams stated repeatedly that he would work within the Agreement and would use his influence on the IRA to resolve the issue, while maintaining that this was a matter for the IRA, since Sinn Féin did not possess any weapons. Furthermore, the IRA ceasefire was portrayed as genuine and therefore as sufficient guarantee that it no longer represented a danger to peace. But for the unionist politicians, this was far from convincing. As they hardly made a distinction between the IRA and Sinn Féin, which they regarded as one and the same organisation, they saw it as Sinn Féin's responsibility to deliver on decommissioning.[4]

Nevertheless, David Trimble agreed to lead his party into government alongside Sinn Féin in November 1999, but this decision was predicated on actual IRA decommissioning. By February 2000, as no progress had been made, he resigned as First Minister, which effectively meant that the institutions were suspended. The IRA announcement, in May 2000, that it was initiating a process 'that will completely and verifiably put IRA arms beyond use' (*IT*, 16 May 2000) paved the way for the institutions to be restored. Two inspectors were appointed by the British government – Marti Ahtisaari, a former Finnish President, and Cyril Ramaphosa, former Secretary General of the ANC – who observed that the weapons and explosives were securely stocked and that they could not be used without their detecting it. However, in an attempt to put further pressure on Sinn Féin, the Ulster Unionist Party barred the two Sinn Féin ministers from attending the North–South Ministerial Council in October 2000.

The IRA made its first concrete gesture in the following year, in October 2001, putting, for the first time in its history, part of its arsenal beyond use. The proceedings, supervised by the IICD, were to be kept confidential and the exact amount of weapons destroyed was not to be revealed. A second act of decommissioning took place in April 2002. However, the institutions were suspended in October 2002 when the IRA was accused of operating an intelligence network from the Sinn Féin offices in Stormont Castle.[5]

Throughout the following year, the efforts of the participants to restore the institutions were heavily focused on decommissioning. Nevertheless, Sinn Féin insisted that this could not be the sole focus of negotiations. In its view, there are still matters outstanding that need to be resolved. Central to the republican objective of 'taking the guns out of Irish politics' is what Sinn Féin calls demilitarisation; in other words, the withdrawal of the British military presence. This process has been underway for some time, according to the British authorities. A report updating the progress made in this area, published in 2003, outlined the measures taken since the start of the peace process. The total number of troops in Northern Ireland was 13,000, the lowest since the British army was sent to Northern Ireland in 1970, and down by over 5,000 since 1992 when they totalled 18,500. Moreover, the report stressed that almost half of the surveillance sites had been demolished since 1994, as well as more than fifty of the 105 military bases and installations (*Responding to a Changing Security Situation*, 2003: 1).

'Taking the gun out of Irish politics', for Sinn Féin, also means that other paramilitary organisations have to decommission. The party contends that while the IRA has been in the spotlight on that particular issue, very little pressure has been brought to bear on the loyalist organisations. The other parties, however, counter the validity of this argument by pointing to the fact that Sinn Féin is the only party with links to a paramilitary organisation which sat on the executive, and as such, its situation cannot be simply paralleled with that of other parties, even if they still call on those paramilitary organisations to decommission their weapons.

Several attempts were made to break the logjam. While Sinn Féin insisted that the elections for the assembly had to be held as scheduled, in May 2003, the two governments outlined the conditions for the restoration of the institutions in a Joint Declaration. One of these concerned the continuation of 'paramilitary activity'. This was mainly a reference to the so-called 'punishment beatings', which designate attacks on civilians by paramilitary organisations for what they term 'antisocial behaviour'. According to the statistics of the RUC/PSNI, which started keeping track of such attacks in 1973, the number of casualties resulting from paramilitary-style attacks rose in the aftermath of the Good Friday Agreement, from 207 in 1999 to 305 in 2003. The figures for 2004 included only the first four months of the year, but, compared with the same period for the previous year, showed only a relative decrease, with ninety-six and eighty-seven respectively (PSNI statistics, 2004). However, according to some organisations, these statistics could be underestimated by about 30 per cent or more, since victims are reluctant to go to the police for fear of reprisals. The fact that punishment beatings continue attests to the importance that some organisations grant to that type of retaliatory measure, according to a Superintendent of the PSNI in 2002: 'paramilitaries still firmly believe they have the right to police their own areas and it is their way of continuing to exert control' (*Guardian*, 19 March 2002).

The Joint Declaration of the British and Irish governments also asked for 'transition from violence to exclusively peaceful and democratic means [to be] brought to an unambiguous and definitive conclusion' (*Joint Declaration*, 2003: 4). In response, the IRA sent a message to the two governments, in which it stated that 'we are resolved to see the complete and final closure of this conflict. The IRA leadership is determined to ensure that our activities, disciplines and strategies will be consistent with this' (IRA statement, 13 April 2003). However, Tony Blair wanted more clarification on the IRA statement, and asked three specific questions: was the IRA prepared to declare an end to all paramilitary activity, a total decommissioning of its weapons, and the end of the war? The clarifications given by the Sinn Féin President were deemed insufficient and the elections were, effectively, postponed.[6] This episode showed a continued lack of trust between the different parties, one claiming that the IRA's intentions were not fully clear, the other accusing its adversaries of breaching protocols, of playing word games and ultimately of going back over the scenario that had been agreed.

The fact that the Ulster Unionist Party accepted to sit in government with two Sinn Féin ministers in late 1999, despite the absence of decommissioning by the IRA, was seen as a leap of faith. Yet republicans have castigated the UUP leader for holding back the process, and have voiced concerns on occasion at the decision to suspend the institutions which, in their view, has more to do with saving David Trimble's leadership. They saw the resignation of the First Minister on two occasions, in February 2000 and again in July 2001, as unilateral decisions taken by the UUP leader, and supported by the British government, in view of the mounting pressure that Trimble was experiencing within his own party. Similarly, when the institutions were suspended for the third time in October 2002 over the allegation that the IRA was operating a spy ring in Stormont, Sinn Féin considered this episode an attempt to save David Trimble's leadership by making republicans appear responsible for this new crisis, so that, according to an *Irish Times* headline, 'Sinn Féin [would take] the rap and Trimble the reprieve' (*IT*, 8 October 2002).

However, after weeks of intense negotiations in Downing Street, a sequence of events aimed at breaking the impasse was announced in October 2003. British Prime Minister Tony Blair declared that the assembly elections, which were initially due in May 2003, would be held on 26 November 2003. In the meantime, the IRA was to carry out a further act of decommissioning, which was to be preceded by a comprehensive statement by Gerry Adams and a declaration of the UUP leader that he accepted the terms of the republican leader's statement. On 21 October 2003, everything seemed to go according to plan: Adams delivered a lengthy statement in which he spelt out, more clearly than he had ever done before, the fact that the days of the armed struggle were beyond them. 'As president of Sinn Féin, I have set out a peaceful direction which I trust everyone will follow. Sinn Féin's position is one of total and absolute commitment to exclusively democratic and peaceful means of resolving differences' (*IT*, 23 October 2003). David Trimble then welcomed Adams' speech. Both statements, according to Sinn Féin publicity officer Dawn Doyle, had been approved by both leaders, David Trimble having sought and obtained some minor changes in the statements from Adams and the IRA (Doyle, interview, 2004). Consequently, a third act of decommissioning was presided over by General De Chastelain and the IICD. However, the carefully crafted succession of events fell into disarray when the UUP leader estimated that the information conveyed by De Chastelain in his press conference did not disclose enough information on the act itself. The debate that followed centred around whether the IRA should provide details on the amount of arms that had effectively been put beyond use. However, a spokesperson for the Commission specified that De Chastelain would resign if forced to divulge such details, as it had been agreed that both the location of the event and the precise amount of weapons involved would be kept confidential. Sinn Féin seemed dismayed at this turn of events, stating its belief that the proceedings had gone according to what had been agreed, and concluded that David Trimble had 'lost his nerve' (McGuinness, interview, 2003). Adams summarised the republican bafflement when he stated: 'One man's decommissioning is another man's humiliation.' The palpable resentment on the republican side was matched by that of the unionists, who felt that Trimble had taken enormous risks over the five years since the signing of the GFA. A more 'malign scenario', in the words of UUP member Roy Garland, was suggested, one where the IRA, by refusing to act in a transparent manner, had deliberately attempted to undermine pro-Agreement unionists, effectively putting David Trimble in an untenable position (Garland, interview, 2003). Sinn Féin strongly denied this scenario, arguing that it would much rather work alongside the pro-Agreement parties within the assembly and that the situation where the strongly anti-Agreement DUP is in a majority presents serious problems.

Republican leaders contend that they cannot afford to move too fast on the issue of decommissioning, and that they must keep pace with their own constituents, given the difficulties that such a choice involves for a sizeable section of their rank and file. Party chairman Mitchell McLaughlin talks about the republican project in the following terms:

> what is the project about? Developing an alternative to armed Republicanism. In other words, we're going to leave it behind us. It's very hard to argue that, when the British government decide they don't like the possibility of an election result, and they stop the election. But we have to stay true to our strategy, which means we have to find a solution to these new problems. There is a very clear strategic direction, which is moving Republicanism away from armed insurrection as the response to political problems, or to the denial of political aspirations. We believe we have a strategy and it's working for us.
>
> (McLaughlin, interview, 2003)

Undoubtedly, some in the unionist camp acknowledge the difficulties that decommissioning present for the republican leadership. David Adams of the former UDP (Ulster Democratic Party, linked to the UDA) wrote in the *Irish Times* that 'selling decommissioning in largely abstract form to the volunteers has probably been difficult enough without the added problems that an itemised listing by Gen. De Chastelain would bring' (*IT*, 24 October 2003). But the difficulties in the unionist camp are equally severe. In the same article, David Adams explained that 'irrational as it may seem – and despite the 'war is over' statements from Sinn Féin and the IRA, the unionist electorate would feel conned' [by the lack of transparency].

The unionist position on decommissioning deals with raw emotions, those of a community which, in great part, sees itself as the victim of thirty years of conflict, and who emphatically puts the blame for the violence on the IRA (see Chapter 6). This perception has been challenged on many occasions by republicans, but it nevertheless means that it is extremely difficult for unionists to share power with those who are perceived to have inflicted the hurt, all the more so if they are seen to retain the capacity to inflict more hurt. No matter how many times republican leaders and IRA spokespersons insist on the fact that their weapons are silent and that a sizeable faction of them has been put beyond use, the IRA is still seen as a potential danger. This is compounded by the fact that unionists do not accept that the conflict was a 'war' and therefore cannot find any legitimacy in the reasons that drove men and women to take up arms. Their failure to renounce those very same weapons once and for all is incomprehensible to them.

In the view of UUP's Ken Maginnis, a close ally of David Trimble who retired from Westminster in 2001, the 'Agreement places a clear obligation on David Trimble and Ulster unionists to ensure that society in Northern Ireland can never again be held hostage to the bombs and bullets of political terrorists' (Maginnis, 1999: 8). He therefore refutes the argument that unionists have 'conjured up a spectre in order to exclude anyone from the democratic process' (Maginnis, 1999: 10). On the contrary, the only possible way forward is seen to be necessarily linked to progress on decommissioning, for 'where there has been a culture of violence for almost 30 years a mere cessation of military operations on a temporary basis does not allow things to radically change' (Maginnis, 1999: 21).

Not all in the unionist camp, however, see the merit of the demand for decommissioning. David Ervine, leader of the Progressive Unionist Party (PUP), a political party close to the loyalist paramilitary organisation UVF, sees this issue as a means used by mainstream unionism to stop Sinn Féin fully entering the democratic process. In his view, 'decommissioning was a disastrous issue. It is not conducive to creating democratic conditions. It's all about morality. The unionist position relies on morality, which is problematic as each sub-culture creates its own morality' (Ervine, interview, 2004). It is all the more disastrous that it has been used cleverly by the Sinn Féin leadership which 'has sold weapons in exchange for political gains' (Ervine, interview). The removal of the causes of conflict, to use a republican phrase, is not, according to him, about physically handing in weapons, although he admits that all organisations have a duty to go down that road. It is about the IRA clearly stating that the war is over.

The SDLP is also critical of the manner in which Sinn Féin has used decommissioning as a 'bargaining tool'. Seán Farren, former SDLP Minister for Further Education, stresses that, according to the terms of the Agreement, decommissioning should have been completed within two years. In hindsight, this deadline could now appear somewhat unrealistic, but for Farren, republicans have been 'dragging their feet on this issue' and have not complied with the GFA (Farren, interview, 2004). Although the SDLP, unlike the Ulster Unionist Party, does not want to see clarity over the amount of weapons decommissioned, Farren is convinced that a time scale would have enabled the process to move forward and the institutions to be restored.

In contrast, the DUP is adamant that total decommissioning must take place as a prerequisite for any political process. Its starting point is that the IRA should never have had any weapons in its possession in the first place. DUP MP Gregory Campbell argues that 'apart from the morality of violence, there is a certain tactical advantage in having a private army, having an ace up their sleeve, which the other parties do not have' (Campbell, interview, 2003). The DUP will therefore only alter its position of not engaging with Sinn Féin when the latter is considered similar to the other political parties; that is, when it is no longer associated with a paramilitary organisation. In the meantime, as party leader Ian Paisley put it in the aftermath of the 2003 assembly elections, 'anyone in my party who talks to Sinn Féin will be expelled' (*IT*, 29 November 2003). This position will be reviewed only when the IRA has ceased to exist. A declaration to this effect, however, will not be sufficient. 'It is not what we need to see, but what we need not to see any longer: guns, Colombia, Castlereagh,[7] punishment beatings. When all of this has stopped, then the DUP will review its position' (Campbell, interview).

The all-Ireland agenda

The Democratic Ulster Unionist Party is deeply suspicious of the peace process because it sees it as a strategic choice made by republicans to achieve reunification, once they realised that what could not be obtained by force of arms could be achieved by politics. Campbell explains that 'down through the decades the Irish Republican has twisted and turned, changed and amended its short term strategic goals but always kept firmly in sight the long term objective of achieving a united Ireland' (Campbell, 2000: 3). To twist the well-known axiom of Prussian military thinker Carl Von Clausevitz,[8] the manner in which republicans use politics is thus seen as the mere continuation of war by other means. Nevertheless, the Sinn Féin objective, for the DUP, remains as ominous as ever, since reunification is seen as the denial of Protestant culture and identity. In this regard, the DUP views the peace process as strongly biased and ultimately dangerous. This party does not fundamentally believe that republicans are genuine in their commitment to peace, which it sees as a path chosen because of the potential results it could yield, and not because of an ideological or moral belief. This makes it all the more difficult for Ian Paisley's party to accept the bona fide of any gesture coming from the IRA or from Sinn Féin, and it feeds into a logic whereby opposition to the peace process and to the Agreement is presented as the only way to save the Union. Indeed, moving alongside republicans, making deals with them, even talking to them, goes against the interests of unionists as it promotes the reunification agenda.

The DUP's analysis, in spite of its strong partisan views on the conflict and on republicans, has one merit, because it rests on an obvious truth: the unification of the two parts of the island is indeed the ultimate goal of republicans. This has always been the case, as reunification is central to their vision of the Irish nation. As the IRA indicated in its April 2003 statement, 'we are Irish republicans. Our objective is a united Ireland. We are not unionists or British and no one should expect us to set aside our political objectives or our republicanism' (IRA statement, 13 April 2003).

Embarking on the peace process was indeed a strategic choice, but this does not necessarily imply that Sinn Féin's commitment to peace was not genuine. There are many reasons why Sinn Féin made this choice. There was, undoubtedly, a belief by some members and leaders of the organisation that armed struggle was at times not morally or ideologically justified, and could even prove counterproductive. But there was also a realisation that the Irish situation could no longer be seen in isolation to what was happening in the international context. Indeed, the world order that had prevailed until the late 1980s was rapidly evolving with the fall of the Berlin Wall, allowing some external players such as the USA to become more directly involved in the resolution of the conflict. As one academic put it, the Irish peace process was 'one piece in a mosaic of [American] selective interventions designed to prevent any resurgence in isolationism following the end of the Cold War' (Briand, 2002: 172). Furthermore, according to Sinn Féin's Chairperson Mitchell McLaughlin, the peace process was 'the logic of the EU. While it took account of domestic considerations, it also took account of the Cold War or the peaceful reunification of Germany. All these issues can be brought together into historic convergence' (McLaughlin, interview).

Finally, the peace process brought to light the fact that, in Adams' own words, the conflict was not 'intractable'. While the pragmatic and strategic necessities that a peace process would entail might not have been fully worked out initially, its ultimate objective was, from its very inception, clearly spelt out by republicans: reunification. According to them, this strategic and ideological choice has been vindicated in the light of the developments that have occurred since the early 1990s. Sinn Féin is prone to contend that it is the party which started the peace process. The speeches of its leaders all converge on this theme; in essence, without republicans, there would be no peace process. Adams claimed that '10 years ago, it fell to republicans to seize the initiative and take the courageous steps necessary to bring peace to Ireland' (*PR*, 23 March 2002). These 'courageous steps' do not merely relate to the IRA ceasefire, since republicans regularly remind their audiences that peace is not simply the end of armed conflict. The process was presented as a demanding task, both for republicans and for their opponents, in the sense that compromises, or 'sacrifices' as they are sometimes called in the republican repertoire, would be necessary from all players.

Sinn Féin insists that it was the first party to have put forward a peace strategy, '*Peace in Ireland*', approved by the Ard Fheis in 1992. Adams recognises that the process was the result of the 'collective work of a number of people, of the informal movement of organisations and forces' (Adams, interview, 2004). Evidently, it may also be argued that there would be no peace process if it had not been for the initiative of John Hume, who established contact with Adams in 1988 in spite of his party's opposition to holding talks with republicans and in spite of the vilification that the SDLP leader had to endure at the time, on both sides of the border. Gerry Adams acknowledges that 'John Hume's role in the peace process was fundamental for its success' (Adams, interview). However, the fact that republicans claim to be at the root of the process could also signify that they see their party as the only political formation which is indispensable for the process to move forward. Adams rejects this view, since seeing Sinn Féin as the engine behind the process 'does not suggest that we have played a greater role' (Adams, interview). Sinn Féin has been consistent in stressing that the only prerequisite for a peace process to work was that it had to be inclusive. Martin McGuinness insists that 'there can be no precondition to progress, we do not want preconditions' (McGuinness, interview). Whenever preconditions have been imposed on entering talks, this has inevitably led to the exclusion of republicans, along with the smaller loyalist parties associated with paramilitary organisations.

Nevertheless, the peace process can and has survived when some of the parties have decided to absent themselves from the proceedings. Therefore, the fact that the DUP did not take part in the all-party negotiations that led to the GFA was deemed regrettable by Sinn Féin, but its absence did not stop what had already been set in motion; that is, the drive towards an agreement between the majority of the parties of Northern Ireland. In the republican analysis, all parties, including the DUP, have their role to play. However, when new rounds of negotiations were started in October 2003 with the British and Irish governments to find a manner in which to restore the institutions, only two parties took part in those talks, namely Sinn Féin and the UUP. Martin McGuinness insists that his party ensured that 'the SDLP was not sidelined', and that its exclusion from the talks was a decision taken by the two governments (McGuinness, interview). Adams adds that he raised the issue of the absence of the other parties with the two governments, but concludes that 'we don't have the guest-list for Downing Street' (Adams, interview). SDLP leader Mark Durkan took the view that the fact that the negotiations were carried out by what he termed a 'gang of Four' was prejudicial to the outcome of the talks: 'This still remains a fairly exclusive process as far as the two parties and the two governments are concerned. The rest of us are meant to be treated as though we're the consumers of whatever hype or spin they come up with' (*IT*, 23 October 2003). However, neither government considered that they had excluded anyone. Martin Mansergh, Fianna Fáil senator and special adviser to the Taoiseach, considered that:

> in my experience, involving some or all of the other parties in this type of negotiation makes little difference to the outcome. One wonders why the SDLP could not confidently make more of a virtue of the fact that they are not part of the problem and have already fully signed up to the solution.
>
> (*IT*, 25 October 2003)

The peace process has afforded republicans a newly invigorated discourse on reunification which is presented as inevitable, as the only progressive choice, but also as a reality within their grasp. There is a sense that reunification is no longer an aspiration. Republicans talk of their vision for the future, of their sense of direction:

> We are translating that vision into an achievable objective. Republicans in previous generations had this idea of passing on the torch which is a defeatist perspective, we're not going to succeed but keep this vision alive, and maybe somebody else will succeed at some time. But now Republicans have a sense of being on the threshold of a whole new beginning, a national democracy, a social revolution. We are now starting to put together the policy portfolio of a party that's involved in the mainstream, as leading a particular strand of the overall political agenda. And that's on the basis of not only being an all-Ireland political party but a party which has a strategy for all-Ireland policies which is attracting support.
>
> (McLaughlin, interview)

Republicans seem convinced that history is on their side. In their eyes partition has always been synonymous with a repressive situation, insofar as it allowed the worst manifestations of imperialism and colonialism to come to the fore, subjecting the nationalist minority to the status of 'second-class citizens' in a system that governed by coercion and not by consensus. Therefore, progress and the future are necessarily equated with doing away with partition, as this is the only way in which true liberation can come about. What makes reunification inevitable, according to McLaughlin, is to be found partly in the demographic reality of the Northern Ireland situation. 'It's not because Sinn Féin exists that it's inevitable. Before we became involved electorally I think that you could analyse the demography of the Six Counties and there you could find the clue to the insecurity of unionism' (McLaughlin, interview). He refers to the possibility of unionists losing their majority status, since demography was showing, until recently, a much higher increase in the Catholic population than in the Protestant. Indeed, the balance between the two communities has shifted quite dramatically in the course of forty years. The 1961 census showed a 63 per cent Protestant majority to 35 per cent Catholic, while the 2001 census figures put the ratio at 53 per cent Protestants to 42 per cent Catholics, although analysts noted that the increase in the Catholic population had not been as noticeable as previously forecast.

However, these figures do not necessarily translate into a stronger body of opinion in favour of reunification. As a survey has shown, it is not accurate to equate Catholics with reunification. When asked to state their preference for the future status of Northern Ireland, 58 per cent of Catholics gave unification with the Republic as their first preference, to 20 per cent who wanted to remain within the UK (the ratio for Protestants was, unsurprisingly, 3 per cent to 83 per cent). Furthermore, the same study showed a fluctuation in opinion among Catholics, with an increasing number favouring a 'third way' which was neither remaining in the UK nor unification (McGinty, April 2000: 2). The vision put forward by McLaughlin has been criticised as inaccurate and sectarian, in that not only does it present religious affiliation as a manner in which to categorise people into homogeneous political groupings, but it also undermines the principle of consent that underpins the GFA. As Dermot Nesbitt (UUP) remarked, 'This type of sectarian head count must end. We need mature debate, not knee-jerk number crunching with a sectarian calculator' (*IT*, 20 December 2002). However, another survey indicated that while a majority of 57 per cent still preferred the option of Northern Ireland remaining in the UK, 79 per cent would accept reunification if this was the wish of the majority, which would tend to prove that the concept of consent has been, by and large, accepted. Interestingly, when asked: 'At any time, do you think it is likely or unlikely that there will be a united Ireland?', 15 per cent of the respondents (and 42 per cent of Protestant respondents) believed that this was likely (McGinty and Darby, 1999: 3).

Demography is not the only reason why republicans stress the inevitability of reunification. Other well-rehearsed arguments abound in their analysis. The existence of two separate entities leads to two social systems, two education systems, different infrastructures, which in their view make the running of the overall system inefficient and costly.[9] Sinn Féin Secretary General Robbie Smyth concludes therefore that 'the argument for reunification has been won' (Smyth, interview, 2003). Sinn Féin contends that most parties in the south are now putting reunification on their agenda, after having neglected this issue for years. Adams points to the fact that Fianna Fáil has recently made its subtitle, 'The Republican Party', more prominent, in an attempt to reinforce its identity as a party committed to reunification. Martina Anderson, who is in charge of supervising the party's all-Ireland implementation of the Agreement, talks of 'intensive meetings at the highest level between the SDLP and Fianna Fáil about merging and becoming an all-Ireland party' (Anderson, interview, 2003). Sources in the SDLP have indeed indicated that a merger had been considered, although no concrete steps seem to have been taken. Nevertheless, for the time being, Sinn Féin can boast of being the only party organised throughout the whole of the island, which gives it an advantage over its adversaries if the inevitability of reunification is indeed a consensual reading of the present situation. Adams has stated on several occasions that his party does not wish to force the unionist community into a united Ireland. In his view, 'the challenge around Irish unity is making it a practical imperative for the majority of people of this island including a majority of unionists', and this challenge includes 'getting the British government to enter into a strategy to go in that direction' (Adams, interview).

Sinn Féin proposes a number of strategies to advance the case of reunification, all, according to the party, provided for within the framework of the Good Friday Agreement. The first, and most immediate, is to widen the areas of cooperation of the north–south bodies that were established in order to promote links between the two sides of the island in limited areas. Sinn Féin wants further implementation bodies that would look at areas such as policing, justice, agriculture, rural development, social economy and pollution. In January 2004, the party published a discussion paper, *Rights for All*, which it presented as a 'framework of principles which [we] believe should be enshrined as rights in a progressive society' (*Rights for All*: 3). Calling upon local communities, trade unions and volunteer groups to engage in a debate, this document outlined Sinn Féin's vision of rights, ranging from the rights of children to the protection of the environment and the fight against discrimination. One of the stated objectives was 'to build an inclusive society which addresses the political allegiances of Unionists and guarantees their rights and entitlements so that they have a sense of security and a stake in the new Ireland' (3). One of Sinn Féin's more pressing demands in the reunification agenda, however, is to ensure that the citizens of Northern Ireland have a voice in the Irish Parliament.

So far, the calls for representation for the citizens of Northern Ireland have not been heeded, and the expansion of the North–South Council has not taken place, as the institutions were suspended in October 2002. However, these proposals constitute, in the eyes of republicans, practical steps towards achieving their ultimate goal. Nevertheless, Sinn Féin is not the only party committed to reunification. The SDLP also sees its dedication to that objective as unswerving, and it claims on its website that it is '100 per cent for a united Ireland'. According to Seán Farren, 'The GFA provides the most practical and viable template' for achieving this goal (Farren, interview). The Agreement provides for the holding of a referendum on unification, which the SDLP wants to see held within the lifetime of the next assembly. It insists that the protection and inclusion that nationalists sought in Northern Ireland within the UK must be guaranteed to unionists in a united Ireland. To ensure that this is the case and that unionists can overcome their fears of such a prospect, Farren proposes an unlimited period of devolution within Northern Ireland, so that they 'would continue to work within institutions they are familiar with and would have the satisfaction of knowing what they are buying into' (Farren, interview). Sinn Féin, however, is seeking a poll on both sides of the border, and not only in Northern Ireland. In Farren's view, Sinn Féin's vision of reunification would place unionists in a position whereby constitutional changes would happen and only then would they be in a position to negotiate, which is not seen as an attractive model. In that respect, the SDLP presents itself as the 'only party that can deliver a united Ireland', because of its track record of persuasion and its 'unblemished record of peace and partnership' (Constitutional Issues, n.d.).

Sinn Féin in government

The institutions that emerged from the GFA were seen by republicans as an opportunity to advance further the case of reunification. Nevertheless, the idea of Sinn Féin representatives sitting on the Northern Ireland Assembly could have been, potentially, highly contentious among the republican rank-and-file, because it could have been read as a recognition of the partition between the two sides of the island and therefore of the possibility of reforming the system from within. But Adams presented this to republican supporters as a stepping stone, as an 'historic' decision, but also as an opportunity, both for the party's development and for the cause of reunification: 'our party is the only national one in Ireland and we have to build our political strength everywhere on this island if we are to secure the national advances we require' (1998 Ard Fheis). However, espousing a rhetoric that strongly supports the executive and the assembly could potentially imply that an internal solution was workable, which would in turn undermine the argument for reunification. This is countered by

Conor Murphy, Sinn Féin group leader in the assembly until 2002, in whose view 'the institutions are all-Ireland, and they're all interlinked' (Murphy, interview, 2003).

In embracing the GFA, Sinn Féin was conscious that one of its strongest selling points, the one that would convince its supporters, was the North–South Ministerial Council, seen as the formalisation of the cooperation between the two parts of the island. This body was crucial in that its capacity to yield results would be seen as a vindication of Sinn Féin's vision of reunification. Martina Anderson therefore regards the North–South Ministerial Council as a potential on which to build, although she argues that the areas of collaboration designated within the Agreement are not contentious and that they will not, per se, 'bring about unification'.[10] She explains that her party, at the time of the negotiation, did not 'have the political strength that it has now. Ireland and Britain agreed to what the unionists would tolerate, that is, two states operating as equal partners' (Anderson, interview, 2003). Sinn Féin has other visions for its operation. Not only is the objective of republicans to increase the areas of cooperation, but also to enable some cross-cutting in terms of social inclusion and poverty, to ensure that this did not 'become another institution that is not going to impact on people on the ground, to ensure that you're not creating another layer of bureaucracy' (Anderson, interview). Whether the north–south bodies really made any difference or were even perceived as an area of interest by the electorate or by the public at large remains to be seen. But unionists also correctly identified this area as being central to Sinn Féin's overall strategy, and it was probably no coincidence that David Trimble chose to ban the two Sinn Féin ministers from attending the North–South Council of Ministers in September 2000 as a means of putting pressure on the party to deliver on IRA decommissioning. The UUP leader admitted that 'by excluding Sinn Féin from the North–South meetings, we are hurting them significantly because we are proving to them that there is a unionist veto' (*IT*, 11 January 2001). For Sinn Féin, David Trimble was clearly in breach of the Agreement, as nothing in that document allowed for this type of sanction. Meetings between the two Sinn Féin ministers and their Republic of Ireland counterparts did take place during that period, in spite of the UUP leader's strong criticism of Irish politicians: 'they must know that they are being used as an electoral stunt by Sinn Féin, so why are they doing it?' (*IT*, 24 May 2001). Sinn Féin challenged this decision in the courts, and won its case when a Belfast court ruled that the barring of ministers was unlawful. The UUP leader appealed the court's ruling, but lost his case again, the Court of Appeal ruling that decommissioning could not hinder other crucial strands of the GFA.

The challenge that entering the institutions represented for Sinn Féin was significant, not only in view of the question of principle involved, but also for practical reasons. Sinn Féin representatives had limited experience of political work outside of their own constituencies, more often than not confined to the working of local councils. The party as a whole was not very familiar with parliamentary practices, because it had not taken part actively in parliamentary life since 1923 (with the exception of one TD who took his seat in the Dáil in 1997). Furthermore, Sinn Féin was keen to retain its radical edge, to continue to be seen as a militant, activist-led party. Entering into not just an assembly but a coalition government presented a further challenge. The spectre of past experiences when Sinn Féin entered mainstream politics is ever present, and conjures up images of betrayal, of institutionalisation and, eventually, of the loss of the radical identity that distinguishes Sinn Féin from other political formations. 'I think there were quite a few that thought it was too much of a contradiction for us, that it would force us to implode, the contradiction of being part of a conservative coalition' (Murphy, interview).

Finally, because of the connection of the party with the IRA, there was considerable pressure on the Sinn Féin representatives and ministers to deliver not only on policies but on their democratic credentials. This challenge was going to be all the more significant given that the two Sinn Féin ministers,[11] Bairbre de Brún and Martin McGuinness, were in charge of two departments which combined more than half of the budget of the whole executive, health and education (£2.3 billion and £1.3 billion respectively, out of a total of £5.8 billion in 2000). Moreover, these two areas were ones that affected the entire community, be it in terms of social class, of ethnic or religious background or of geographical location.

The appointment of Martin McGuinness as Minister for Education came as a shock for many unionists. His credentials for this particular post were immediately questioned, considering his alleged past involvement with the IRA (he admitted subsequently that he had, effectively, been second-in-command of the IRA unit in Derry in 1972) but also because he had left school at the age of 15 and had been educated, in his own words, 'in the university of the Bogside' (*IT*, 7 November 2000).[12] Initially, his nomination was greeted with hostility in some quarters, some schools organising protests such as pickets and walkouts. Although Sinn Féin considered these manifestations to be politically orchestrated, they were nevertheless an indication of the unease created by this situation.

The choice of this ministry was a logical one for Sinn Féin. Indeed, as was suggested by one academic, 'Sinn Féin's choice made strategic sense for a radical nationalist party; the ministry gives it access to a high-profile, big-spending, potentially redistributive and socialising ministry' (O'Leary, 2002: 355). However, the new minister set about enthusiastically fulfilling his duties, not only because education was an area regarded as essential to the republican 'equality agenda', but also because he was aware that he would be closely scrutinised by allies and adversaries alike. 'I have put myself heart and soul into this job because I am only too aware that there are people who would love to see me fall flat on my face, and I have no interest in giving them that satisfaction.'

McGuinness set ambitious objectives for his department, such as reforming the education system and making equality the central axis of all policies. In order to achieve these goals, his department proposed some far-reaching, and even controversial, reforms, in particular, one regarding the abolition of the 11-plus exam, an examination that 11-year-old pupils take in order to determine what type of secondary school they will attend. This exam, which had been in operation in Northern Ireland since 1947, was defended by those who saw it as a guarantee of the quality of the education system, but was also sharply criticised by others who considered it too premature, too elitist and who condemned if for perpetuating a two-tier secondary school system. McGuinness did not conceal his outright opposition to the 11-plus, but announced the establishment of an independent commission to examine the issue. Its report, published in October 2001, *Education for the 21st Century*, recommended the replacement of the two-tier system with one that would promote schools of equal rank, as well as the replacement of the 11-plus with a system of continuous assessment.

McGuinness took initiatives aimed at fighting inequalities in the system, by putting forward policies promoting human rights, combating racism and improving special needs education. His department also did away with the League Tables, an annual publication which ranked schools according to the performances of their pupils. However, his policies were not unanimously welcomed. McGuinness was accused of favouring his own constituency and, more generally, the Catholic schools, although he denied this vigorously. Admitting that he was invited more often to Catholic schools, he nevertheless stressed that discrimination 'would be stupid, would be wrong, it would be politically disastrous and I would have no part in it' (*IT*, 7 November 2000). Many unionists saw the abolition of the 11 plus as a decision that would undermine the grammar schools, and UUP MLA Derek Hussey concluded that this was done 'without any regard to the establishment of a replacement process', leaving 'education in limbo' (*Derry Journal*, 21 November 2003). However, one of Martin McGuinness' last announcements, before the institutions were suspended, was precisely that the 11-plus exam would be held in 2004. The direct rule minister who followed McGuinness in education announced, in January 2004, that this exam would be abolished in 2008.

McGuinness' record as Minister of Education was seen as positive by some of the main teachers' unions. The Ulster Teachers Union considered his nomination 'preferable to the part-time tenure of a direct rule minister from London', a view that was echoed by the Irish National Teachers' Organisation, whose Northern Secretary explained: 'I feel

Mr McGuinness has made it his business to be as visible and user-friendly as possible. . . . Overall marks out of 10? I'd give him seven' (17 April 2001). The Churches also commented positively on McGuinness' record, the Education Secretary of the Church of Ireland Board of Education stressing that they had been given fair treatment, as well as a courteous and considerate hearing (18 May 2001).

The other Sinn Féin minister, Bairbre de Brún, who was in charge of the health portfolio, was sharply criticised from the beginning of her tenure. Although her personal political background was less controversial than that of her colleague in education (she was born and educated in Dublin, then became a secondary school teacher and moved to the north in the early 1980s), she attracted severe and sometimes quite personalised criticism from her political opponents. As she explained to an *Irish Times* journalist in an interview on 2 May 2002, 'for some, it's the fact that I am a woman in a position of power, for some it's a question of political beliefs, for some it is the fact that I am an Irish speaker. For some people the question of cultural practice seems to impact on their view of another person's ability or integrity.' Some of her opponents, however, seemed to question her ability to run the department. The difficulties that she had to face were also due to her portfolio being, according to her party colleague, MP Michelle Guildernew, a 'poisoned chalice' (*IT*, 9 November 2001), in the sense that her job would involve taking decisions that would inevitably be unpopular. Her first two months in government were quite controversial. One of her first tasks, for example, was to decide on the location of a Belfast maternity hospital, between the Royal Maternity in West Belfast and the Jubilee in South Belfast. Her choice of the former was motivated, according to her, by its proximity to the children's hospital and A&E department. But this was seen by her adversaries as a political decision which benefited her own West Belfast constituency.

Bairbre de Brún inherited a situation in which the waiting lists for hospital beds were the longest in the UK, the result, according to her, of 'years of neglect' (*IT*, 2 May 2002). She also had to oversee the rationalisation of the health system, for which she established a review to study acute hospital services and the public health strategy. This news was greeted by some of her assembly colleagues with dismay, such reviews being considered the last thing that the health services needed as they were seen as a substitute for action. The Hayes report, published in June 2001, recommended the concentration of accident and emergency units, and the closing down of some of those units, particularly in the hospital in Omagh in favour of the unit in Enniskillen. This choice was a particularly difficult one for de Brún, given that both hospitals were in the constituencies of Sinn Féin MPs Pat Doherty and Michelle Guildernew. Ironically, when a similar debate developed in the Republic the following year, Sinn Féin TD and health spokesperson Caoimhghin Ó Caoláin was among the most vociferous critics of the government's plans for rationalisation. Speaking of the plans to close down Monaghan's A&E and maternity units, he pledged to 'keep the pressure on until we get what we want, a proper hospital with adequate services' (*IE*, 1 October 2002). Although it could be argued that the two situations were different, it was clear that the imperatives of government made Sinn Féin ministers take decisions that were sharply criticised by their own party colleagues when coming from other government ministers on the other side of the border.

De Brún's ambition was, ultimately, to take a holistic approach to the area of health by looking at the issue within the broader context of 'environment, poverty, social and economic determinants', a vision that was contained in the document produced by her department, *Investing for Health*. This view is shared by NGOs such as Combat Poverty and substantiated by reports such as the one published by the Institute of Public Health in 2001 which stated that up to 6,000 deaths could be avoided in Ireland if poverty was eradicated. However, she was condemned by her critics for having failed to improve the overall services, such as the shortening of waiting lists. De Brún, while pointing to the achievements of her department (100 more nurses in training, more ambulances), admits that 'people were expecting change. While some did happen, a lot more didn't' (de Brún, interview, 2003). She argues that the suspension of the institutions prevented her department from carrying out the work needed, but also that 'equality and human rights are controversial. They are seen as a package for nationalists, instead of being viewed as an improvement to society as a whole' (de Brún, interview). As noted in an academic paper on the review of the Good Friday Agreement, 'devolution could have been used to commission more policy research, make more use of experts and ask new questions. But on health, for example, the emphasis remained primarily on how many hospitals had acute functions rather than on ill health and its relationships to social exclusion' (Wilford and Wilson, 2003: 17).

Sitting on the executive was paramount for Sinn Féin, for a number of reasons. According to Bairbre de Brún, this gave her and her colleagues the opportunity to 'bring decision-making closer to people who up until that time not only felt alienated from the institutions of the state for political, ideological and constitutional reasons, but also to people who felt detached from governmental institutions' (de Brún, interview). Indeed, the views held by the public at large indicate that there is a preference for devolved government over direct rule. In a study on the performance of the executive and the assembly, the picture which emerged was one where public opinion perceived Westminster as still having the most influence over how Northern Ireland is governed (51 per cent), as opposed to 28 per cent who believed the assembly had the most influence. However, when asked which institution ought to have more influence, 65 per cent quoted the assembly against 17 per cent who favoured Westminster, a finding which, according to the authors of the survey, indicated 'strong levels of public faith in the Assembly' (McGinty, May 2002: 1). The same study surveyed the public's perception of the improvements achieved in two areas, namely health and education, which also happened to be those under the responsibility of Sinn Féin ministers.[13] The findings indicated widespread dissatisfaction with the progress that had been made within the health sector, with 39 per cent of respondents stating that it was getting worse in 2001 as opposed to 28 per cent who had held that opinion the previous year. Fewer respondents believed that the services were improving: 11 per cent in 2001 and 9 per cent in 2000. Education fared somewhat better in the survey, with 24 per cent of people estimating that the situation had improved in 2001 to 12 per cent who believed it had not, the remaining 64 per cent seeing no change or stating that it was too early to give such an assessment.

The Northern Ireland executive, which lasted from December 1999 to October 2002, with two interruptions, was unprecedented, in the sense that it brought together four political parties who compete against each other in the electoral field, who have different social and economic visions, and who do not necessarily see eye to eye on the priorities of government. Sinn Féin ministers were indeed criticised by their colleagues; they took decisions which have proved unpopular among the unionist community, such as the 11-plus exam discussed above. More particularly, they were strongly condemned by unionists for their refusal to fly the Union Jack above their departments so long as they were not allowed to fly the Tricolour alongside, a gesture which was seen as being in 'flagrant breach' of the Agreement and representing a lack of respect for the unionist community.

Republicans and unionism

Sinn Féin's enthusiasm for government, which explains its strong criticism of the suspension of the institutions and its repeated calls for their restoration, was due to the republicans' belief that sharing power would improve the perceptions that both communities had of each other. According to de Brún,

> in the new situation following the GFA, it was important that people within the nationalist community should be seeing unionists in power without excluding the others. Thus it was important to change the view of unionism. It was equally important that unionists who might have been fearful of Martin McGuinness and myself becoming ministers would see us being able to have a positive impact.
>
> (de Brún, interview)

Sinn Féin's analysis of unionism has considerably altered in the course of the peace process. Republicans still seem to struggle to come to terms fully with what exactly unionism means and how it is defined. As the IRA said in its April 2003 statement, 'we do not claim to fully understand unionist perceptions. But we are prepared to listen and to learn'. Unionism is certainly no longer seen in the dichotomous terms which were used to portray that section of the community for years. In the 1970s, Sinn Féin's understanding of unionism was limited, partly because there was virtually no contact between the two communities; therefore there were few possibilities for republicans to gain an insight into unionism. But while unionist leaders were seen as the arch-enemy of republicanism and of a united Ireland, the unionist people were seen in a somewhat less negative light. The policy document drafted by Provisional Sinn Féin in the 1970s exposing its vision for a united Ireland, *Éire Nua*, contained an important section that was supposed to assuage unionists' fears and to make the idea of their inclusion within a united Ireland attractive, or at least less daunting. To that end, the document advocated a federal system in which each of the four historical provinces of Ireland (Leinster, Munster, Connaught and Ulster comprising nine counties) would have an autonomous parliament. This, in theory, would have enabled unionists to retain their majority, albeit a less marked one. The appeals to unionists were multiplied, such as the one pronounced by the then Sinn Féin President Ruiarí Ó Brádaigh in 1976: 'We need you, we want you, there is a place for you in the New Ireland. We say to you: come and join us, and together we will dismantle British rule and the Northern State and the Southern State' (*IT*, 26 April 1976). Whether this message was heard by those to whom it was addressed is doubtful. Whether it had any impact on their vision of reunification is even more unlikely. Nevertheless, the Provisionals repeated this type of message throughout the 1970s and early 1980s, omitting from their analysis the fundamental fact that unionists did not wish to dismantle British rule in the northern state, and only wished for the so-called southern state to stay out of their daily lives. The federalist aspect of the document was dropped at the 1981 Ard Fheis, Danny Morrison stating bluntly that 'you will have as much trouble getting the Loyalists to accept a nine-county parliament as you will in getting them to accept a united Ireland, so why stop short?' (*AP*, 5 November 1981).

In the 1980s a new discourse started to emerge within republicanism, one which tried to come to terms with unionism as an identity that could be seen as valid within any configuration of reunification. Nevertheless, loyalism was still regarded as a construct, which served partitionist and sectarian interests. As such, it could claim no historical heritage or roots: 'this notion of having different roots is part of the present-day mythology of loyalism, which was invented to serve the purpose of justifying partition as well as the sectarian divisions within the six counties' (*Loyalism*, n.d., 3).[14] This blunt analysis was toned down in the *Scenario for Peace* document published in 1988, where loyalists were described as a 'national minority in Ireland', but still seen as 'deriving an artificial psychological strength from the British presence, from the Union'. A measure of pragmatism was added, when the document conceded that 'we do not wish to turn back the pages of history or to dispossess the Loyalists and foolishly attempt to reverse the Plantation' (*Scenario*, 1988: 5). But unionism, or at least its leadership, was still equated, for the years to come, with injustice and inequalities. Gerry Adams stated in his 1996 presidential address to the Ard Fheis that 'the UUP leadership, supported by this British government, do not want change. They are conservative in their instincts and in their politics. They want to maintain a status quo which perpetuates supremacy, inequality and repression' (Adams, 1996).

However, some contact between Sinn Féin and unionist representatives had been taking place since the late 1980s. According to Roy Garland, member of the UUP, initial meetings were held at that time between leaders such as the then Sinn Féin Secretary General Tom Hartley, Mitchell McLaughlin and himself, although these were not approved of by his own party (Garland, interview, 2003). He even faced, at one stage, expulsion from his party for having taken an initiative which contravened UUP policy until the negotiations for the GFA started in earnest. This 'outreach work', as Sinn Féin's Jim Gibney calls it, aimed at building bridges between the two communities and fostering a better understanding of each other. These contacts are still ongoing, being viewed as 'one of the most crucial areas for republicans to be involved in' (Gibney, interview, 2003). Contacts between Sinn Féin and the unionist community are not limited to the highest echelons of the political leaderships. They also involve leaders of Protestant churches, middle leadership within unionism, and loyalist representatives.

In spite of these contacts, unionists are presented as a fearful community, still very much confined within a siege mentality. Republicans talk of a sense of isolation, of a fear of the future which stems, according to Gibney, from the fact that 'their tenure is insecure, that they don't have a rooted mentality, having one foot on the island and the other on the other island' (Gibney, interview, 2003). Therefore, following the contact hypothesis according to which social contact between majority and minority groups will reduce prejudice (Allport, 1966), republicans view dialogue with unionism as fundamental to challenge the stereotyped notions that each community has of each other. This is all the more essential since republicans do see this phase as the 'end phase of the struggle for reunification', in which 'a negotiated conclusion is central, and the unionist people are an indispensable element to this' (Gibney, interview). This is not an easy process; republicans recognise that the conflict has affected both sides and that emotions are still raw. 'At times, these contacts lapsed into recrimination, when the embers of the past got the most of the participants. However, the objective is to manage the anger, in order not to undermine the project' (Gibney, interview). Some shared experiences are possible, as is the case with the loyalists, who share a working-class background, a prison experience, but this does not always yield positive results. Indeed, David Ervine (UUP) argues that meetings between his party representatives and Sinn Féin were used by the latter to gather intelligence on his own party members, and had to be cut short (Ervine, interview).

The contacts at local level are seen as fundamental. For a number of years, Sinn Féin councillors have been sitting on local councils with their unionist counterparts, be they from the UUP or the DUP. Eoin Ó Broin, Sinn Féin local representative for North Belfast, believes that the work in the Belfast City Council created a 'good environment conducive to the development of other forms of collaboration. It's in the interest of politicians not to be competing against each other. It doesn't work all the time, but 90 per cent of the decisions reached are cross-party and consensual' (Ó Broin, interview, 2003). Although the DUP maintains its official line that it refuses to engage with Sinn Féin on any level whatsoever, the reality seems to be more pragmatic. Relations are icy, but there is a level of cooperation between the parties. Ó Broin concedes that there is 'a huge issue of trust'. But he quotes an informal conversation with a member of the DUP who claimed that 'at least with Sinn Féin you know where you stand. What they say is what you get' (Ó Broin, interview).

Republicans see their electoral mandate as fundamental in great part because it gives them the opportunity to work alongside the unionists. In this respect, Alex Maskey's tenure as Mayor of Belfast was seen as an opportunity to open up City Hall to all traditions, which he did in a number of ways. One was to fly the Tricolour in his office, alongside the Union Jack, which he made a solemn promise not to remove (*IT*, 5 September 2002). This move angered unionists who argued that a 'foreign flag' had no place in Belfast City Hall. Indeed, the early days of the executive had been marked by a similar controversy, when Sinn Féin ministers announced that they would not fly the Union Jack above their respective departments unless they could also fly the Tricolour alongside it. Republicans referred to the clause of the Agreement which called for all participants to 'acknowledge the sensitivity of the use of symbols and emblems for public purposes, and the need in particular in creating the new institutions to ensure that such symbols and emblems are used in a manner which promotes mutual respect rather than division' (GFA, 1998; 23). However, the unionists' reading of the Sinn Féin ministers' decision was quite different. In the eyes of Steven King, adviser to David Trimble, the importance of this point for the unionist community could not be underestimated, as it struck a sensitive chord in their sense of identity:

the Tricolour flies over Leinster House all the time. In the British tradition the national flag flies over government buildings on certain prescribed days. Is it any wonder, therefore, that when Sinn Féin ministers refused to observe the established practice, unionists suffered a crisis of confidence in the devolution settlement?

(*IT*, 19 May 2000)

Maskey dedicated his term of office to being, in his own words, 'the mayor of all citizens'. One of his objectives was to show that cooperation was possible on a number of levels, and was essential in dealing with fundamental issues such as interface violence in North Belfast.

North Belfast has a large number of interfaces; that is, common boundaries between Protestant/unionist areas and Catholic/nationalist areas, in a relatively small, predominantly working-class area. It has experienced some of the worst manifestations of sectarian violence since the start of the peace process, finding its most obvious expression in the events surrounding the Holy Cross episode, when schoolgirls attending a Catholic school were prevented from walking down a predominantly Protestant street in North Belfast. The pictures of young children being escorted by the police to go to school, and being jeered at by the bystanders who had gathered to insult and intimidate their parents, shocked world opinion. These scenes were seen as the worst manifestations of tribal and territorial reflexes, and were interpreted as epitomising the refusal of one community, the loyalists, to fully embrace the peace process. They exemplified the fears that the peace process had generated for that community, fears of being left behind, of being bypassed by the nationalist agenda. 'In North Belfast, the Protestant/unionist community feels they have been losing more than anyone else: that they are losing local territory, their rights to cultural expression and potentially their political influence. Aggression has thus become one prominent aspect of their defensive strategy' (Jarman, 2002: 18). But Holy Cross also made the nationalist community question the peace process. 'If this could happen in the context of the Agreement, what tangible effect or meaning could it have?' (Ó Broin, interview). Local Sinn Féin councillor Gerry Kelly spoke of the Agreement being 'in great danger' after the Holy Cross episode.

Interface violence in North Belfast claimed five lives between 2001 and 2003, according to Ó Broin. The interpretations of Sinn Féin and the DUP on the reasons for this violence differ substantially. Sinn Féin puts the onus of the blame on loyalist paramilitaries, and on the DUP's strategy which is, as the party sees it, one of territorial segregation, where they want to limit the 'expansion of the nationalist community' (Ó Broin, interview). On the other hand, Peter Robinson produced a document for the DUP in which he claimed that interface violence was orchestrated by republicans in order to undermine the police service, to 'keep the

Volunteers' busy and to create new victims. Interestingly, the DUP also sees the republican strategy as one of 'territorial expansion', in order to 'increase the chance of republican elected representation' (DUP, *Insight*, November 2002). The party launched a discussion document in June 2004, *Template for Interface Violence,* which contained 'practical mechanisms to deal with the various types of violence' (1), such as the monitoring of incidents and liaising with governmental bodies and NGOs. It recommended the setting-up of local groups to work on prevention, response and maintenance. But its application on the ground might be more problematic, as sectarian violence is still a regular occurrence throughout Northern Ireland. According to the findings of several pieces of research, the Agreement has done little to improve relations between the two communities. Segregation is still predominant in working-class areas, being the rule in 98 per cent of the NIHE estates in Belfast and 71 per cent throughout Northern Ireland. There are still approximately twenty-seven walls or fences dividing unionist and nationalist districts in Belfast alone. This has led some researchers to conclude that an already dichotomous situation has been compounded by the 'two tribes thesis copper-fastened within the terms of the Agreement and within the systems and structures of the Assembly' (Jarman, 2002: 13).

However, the institutions arising out of the GFA gave politicians the opportunity to work side by side. Francie Molloy, Sinn Féin Chairman of the Finance Committee in the assembly,[15] described his overall experience as positive. According to him, there was 'agreement on a day-to-day basis, and disagreement over constitutional issues' (Molloy, interview, 2003). He acknowledged the DUP's refusal to engage with Sinn Féin, manifested in the fact that its representatives refused to address him directly when he chaired meetings, but he sees this tactic as bluff, as a defensive strategy. 'There is common ground with the DUP', which was translated into very few decisions, two according to Molloy, ever having to be put to a vote.

The public perception of how successful politicians had been in cooperating with each other was not so positive. Forty-three per cent saw them as having collaborated 'a great deal or a fair amount', while 50 per cent believed they had cooperated 'not very much' or 'not at all' (McGinty, May 2002: 3). But whatever level of cooperation between the two sides, there are major obstacles still to be overcome in order to bridge the gaps that exist between the two communities. Unionists still distrust their republican counterparts, and have been quite sharp in the vocabulary employed towards them. In one instance, David Trimble talked of republicans needing to be 'house trained', referring to their lack of experience in governmental matters (*Observer*, 28 May 2000).

The peace process and the Agreement undoubtedly presented unionism with a dilemma. The momentum that the process generated was positively received by British political parties, by international opinion, by the EU, as representing the way forward. To decide not to engage with it was not an option if unionism did not want to find itself isolated. The alternative was seen as being equally difficult: to take part in a process which implied negotiating with Sinn Féin while there was still no decommissioning, and later, to form a government with its representatives. The agreement also posed a significant challenge to unionists, as they had closely identified with the institutions of Northern Ireland created in 1920. According to the DUP, the widely held belief that the manner in which Northern Ireland was governed prior to the abolition of Stormont in 1972 was discriminatory against Catholics is nonsense: 'The belief that the constitution of Northern Ireland's place within the UK consigns them to second-class citizenship is absurd' (Campbell, 2000: 7). This, according to Martin McGuinness, is one of the major flaws of the DUP analysis, in that 'they are not prepared to say that there were inequalities' (McGuinness, interview). Academic Duncan Morrow points out that this is in great part what makes the Agreement so challenging for some unionists. 'To favour the Agreement is to begin, and as yet only implicitly, to acknowledge that the traditional unionist state has failed and the Britishness in Ireland must be negotiated, not imposed' (Morrow, 2000: 14). The fact that unionism is seen as being on the defensive is also due to other factors, such as the fact that it is not a united camp. Politically, there are many different formations. Religiously, Protestantism is, as Archbishop Robin Eames reminds us, 'for historical reasons, a fragmented body' (Eames, 2000: 4). Therefore, it has not been able to present a coherent and united front during the peace process.

Fighting harder? Polls and policing

The results of the November 2003 assembly elections were seen as a symptom that public opinion in Northern Ireland was increasingly polarised, with the two 'extreme' parties, the DUP on the one hand and Sinn Féin on the other, winning a majority of votes within their respective communities. The victory of the DUP was analysed by Gregory Campbell as the unionists regaining their voice and no longer accepting the second-class status that the conflict and the peace process had reduced them to. Ironically, the DUP's terminology is identical to that used by nationalists in the late 1960s to condemn the discrimination that they suffered from. However, the view that unionists are now discriminated against, and therefore that the 'tables have turned', according to Campbell, is not corroborated by any empirical evidence or data, which does not mean that the feeling of unease in the unionist community is not deep.

The outcome of the elections gave the majority in each camp to two parties that seem to have little understanding of each other. The DUP confesses that it is 'difficult for unionists to comprehend that nationalists can vote for and support murder', while the unionists shunned the loyalist parties linked to paramilitaries, the Progressive Ulster Unionist Party and the Ulster Democratic Party (Campbell, interview). When this position is challenged by the fact that Sinn Féin also has social and economic policies, the DUP's answer is that 'so did the Nazis, and yet they killed 6 million people' (Campbell, interview). Equally, Sinn Féin has little time for the politicians of the DUP which it views as sectarian and regressive. But republicans are more pragmatic when it comes to their relationship with DUP representatives, with whom, they say, they can and have done business. They see the refusal of the DUP to engage with them as bluff, while according to them the reality shows a more moderate position where republicans and DUP councillors and MLAs have indeed collaborated on some issues.

The assembly election was one that Sinn Féin had been pressing the British government to hold, since it saw the postponement of the May 2003 election as a disenfranchisement of the electorate. Intensive lobbying was carried out in the weeks preceding the initial date set for these elections. However, following the IRA declaration in April and the perceived lack of clarity surrounding its future intentions, the British government announced the postponement of the elections. On the day that the elections were due to be held, republicans organised protests throughout Northern Ireland to highlight what they saw as the anti-democratic stance taken on this issue. For critics of republicans, elections were not a priority as there was nothing that the candidates would be elected to. However, Sinn Féin was not the only party which opposed the postponement of the election. Taoiseach Bertie Ahern openly disapproved of the decision taken by the British authorities, stating that 'I disagree with them and I think it creates more problems than it solves, but that's where it's at' (*IT*, 2 May 2003).

In spite of the fact that Sinn Féin and the UUP failed to reach an agreement in October 2003 on the issue of decommissioning which would have allowed for the institutions to be restored, the elections to the assembly went ahead as they had already been announced by the British government. Sinn Féin's main electoral battle takes place within the nationalist constituency, as cross-community voting remains the exception rather than the rule. Indeed, the analysis of vote transfers showed that, in spite of the calls from Sinn Féin for its electors to transfer their vote to any of the pro-Agreement parties, including the UUP, 83.3 per cent of its transfers benefited the SDLP, while only 1 per cent went to the UUP (*IT*, 1 December 2003).

As electoral competition is played out almost exclusively within each community, Sinn Féin's main competitor is, quite obviously, the SDLP. The relationship between these two parties has been stormy at times.

Down the years, the SDLP was relentless in its condemnation of IRA actions, and there have been many occasions when Sinn Féin castigated its nationalist rival for being too willing to compromise on the national question. Both parties worked side by side within the peace process, but never forgot that when it came to elections, they were campaigning within the same constituency, the nationalist community. Ever since Sinn Féin decided to enter electoral politics, its objective, whether overtly stated or not, was to outperform the SDLP, since this particular area of politics had been, until the early 1980s, the uncontested territory of constitutional nationalism. As early as 1982, the vote for Sinn Féin was measured not only in terms of the percentage that its candidates obtained, but also in comparison with the SDLP. Sinn Féin was initially in a weaker position, given its abstentionist position, its connection with the IRA and its lack of experience in electoral practice. However, it was also capable of maximising its strength, in terms of its strong and energetic canvassing and campaigning tactics.

Although the vote for the SDLP remained, until the beginning of the twenty-first century, relatively stable, there is no doubt that as Sinn Féin left behind its more controversial image, it started to make serious dents in the traditional SDLP support. Apart from the Westminster general election of 1992, when Gerry Adams lost his West Belfast seat to the SDLP's candidate Joe Hendron, its vote has increased consistently at all elections.[16] It overtook the SDLP for the first time in the 2001 Westminster elections, when it obtained 21.7 per cent of the vote and secured four seats (West Belfast, Fermanagh/South Tyrone, Mid Ulster, West Tyrone). However, the SDLP was not far behind, with a total share of the vote of 21.0 per cent and three seats (South Down, Foyle, Newry and Armagh). In the space of two years, therefore, Sinn Féin was able to make serious headway into the nationalist electorate, obtaining 23.5 per cent of the vote to the SDLP's 17 per cent. In terms of seats, Sinn Féin and the SDLP's strength in the assembly was exactly reversed, with 24 and 18 seats respectively.

Several factors can explain the fact that Sinn Féin was able to take such a lead over the SDLP. In the two years between the Westminster general election and the assembly election, there were three acts of decommissioning on the part of the IRA, two Sinn Féin ministers sat on the power-sharing executive, and Sinn Féin waged successful campaigns, notably on the holding of elections. To these may be added the results of the 2002 general election in the Republic, where Sinn Féin obtained more than 6 per cent of the overall vote, and the performance of Alex Maskey as Mayor of Belfast. These enabled Sinn Féin to retain a high profile, not only during negotiations, but in between, in spite of the setbacks suffered by the party, such as the arrests in Colombia (see Chapter 5) or the disclosure of an alleged spy ring in Stormont. According to the SDLP's Seán Farren, Sinn Féin's good performance was greatly helped by the fact that the two governments have tended to focus on what he calls the 'problem parties', that is, the UUP and Sinn Féin, at the expense of the other parties such as the SDLP. 'The periodic breakdowns and the periodic arrivals of the Prime Ministers in their helicopters have put the problem parties centre stage' (Farren, interview, 2004), giving other parties a peripheral role. As a consequence, this has created a perception where 'the focus of power was on Sinn Féin and the electorate saw republicans as key players'. David Ervine of the PUP partly ascribes the responsibility for Sinn Féin's successes to the Ulster Unionist Party, which nationalists perceive as being 'reticent, implacable, not reasonable'. He further points to what he terms the 'unfair game' that Sinn Féin plays: 'in-your-face, street politics and agitation' (Ervine, interview).

What explains Sinn Féin's electoral successes is undoubtedly the fact that it has a strong campaigning machine which relies on a large number of activists canvassing potential constituencies in a systematic and visible manner. As was the case for the 2002 general election in the Republic of Ireland, Sinn Féin calls on all its representatives, on both sides of the border, to lend their support to the campaign. Therefore, TDs were canvassing side-by-side with their northern counterparts throughout the north, giving the campaigners a higher profile. But for Seán Farren, it is the spotlight in which Sinn Féin has been kept that has allowed for some of its candidates to obtain electoral gains. He quotes the example of his own North Antrim constituency, where the Sinn Féin candidate, who was 'virtually unknown' to the electorate, was swept in by his party and won a seat (Farren, interview).

Sinn Féin's explanation is obviously quite different. The party suggested an electoral pact with the SDLP that was turned down by the latter, which enabled Sinn Féin to come across as an accommodating party and depicting its nationalist rival as being defensive and unaccommodating. McGuinness therefore talks of his party having been 'rebuffed' by the SDLP, when republicans had been 'proactive. We are quite deliberate, quite focused in our approach. It is about developing nationalist consensus politics to the maximum' (*IT*, 18 November 2003). Ultimately, Sinn Féin's message was one where it presented itself as the party that could deliver on key issues such as demilitarisation, the Irish language, equality and human rights, and policing. In short, in the words of Gerry Kelly, the party's spokesperson on policing, 'many disaffected SDLP voters have come to us. The key to this is policing' (Kelly, interview, 2004).

Policing is indeed a key issue, or to use Kelly's expression, a 'touchstone issue'. The former police force, the RUC, established in 1922, was overwhelmingly composed of members from the Protestant community, as in 1992 only 7.78 per cent of its full-time members were Catholic. Considering the long history of mistrust and resentment on the part of the nationalist minority towards those Sinn Féin considers 'the agents of repression', it was deemed necessary to introduce reforms. This was necessarily going to be a fraught exercise, given that the unionist community identified with the RUC and saw it as a force which had paid a heavy toll throughout the past thirty years. Indeed, this was recognised, in the midst of a controversial debate, by the granting of the George Cross to the RUC on the visit of Queen Elizabeth to Northern Ireland on 12 April 2000. Two hundred and ninety-eight members of the RUC have lost their lives in the Troubles, which represents 9 per cent of the total deaths, which is in sharp contrast with the number of people whose death the organisation is responsible for (1.5 per cent) (Fay *et al.*, 1999: 168–169). Nevertheless, republicans saw the RUC as the 'paramilitary' force of the Northern Ireland state, at the service of the unionist community, one that did not hesitate to cooperate with the loyalist paramilitary groups, as the Stevens report brought to light (see Chapter 6). Therefore, the reform of the police force was a fundamental element of the GFA, which provided for an independent commission to be established in order to 'make recommendations for future policing arrangements in Northern Ireland including means of encouraging widespread community support for these arrangements' (GFA, 1998: 26). This commission was chaired by former Hong Kong Governor Chris Patten, who after lengthy consultations with community groups, individuals and political parties, published its report at the end of September 1999.

In total, the Patten report contained 175 recommendations, some of them far-reaching. It advocated, *inter alia*, the establishment of a Policing Board, which would comprise nineteen members: ten assembly members selected on the d'Hondt basis and nine independent members drawn from business, trade unions, voluntary organisations, community groups and the legal profession. The Board's primary function was 'to hold the Chief Constable and the police service publicly to account' (107). Furthermore, a District Policing Partnerships Board was to be established in each district council to reflect 'community concerns and priorities'. Some measures were advocated to improve the transparency of the police service as well as the representative character of the service to reflect the overall composition of the population of Northern Ireland, in order to achieve 'an equal number of Catholics and Protestants'. Finally, the Patten report recommended that the RUC, while not being disbanded, change its name to Police Service of Northern Ireland, and adopt a new badge and symbols.

These latter recommendations were particularly controversial within the unionist community, as the name RUC is an integral part of their past, one they strongly identify with. Changing it thus meant erasing a vision of their own identity. But it also implied that on a more basic level, there was a perception that the sacrifices and losses among the force were not recognised, and that the so-called unacceptability of the force was being legitimised. Indeed, the RUC, unacceptable as it might have been for one community, was the police force that the other community not only manned (it was, almost exclusively, a Protestant force) but initially set up. Therefore, to change its name was tantamount, in the eyes of unionists, to conceding that the force had been, somehow, illegitimate. But it is for this same reason that nationalists campaigned to have the old name dropped. A survey carried out in 2000 among young people illustrated how perceptions on the police force differed, with 60.5 per cent of Protestants surveyed disagreeing with the change of name, compared to 4.1 per cent of Catholics (McGinty, May 2002: 3).

Although Sinn Féin was initially suspicious of what Patten could actually deliver, being seen as a Conservative appointed by the British government, the report was deemed 'more radical than what we expected' (Kelly, interview), although it did not go far enough in the sense that it was not the complete overhaul that republicans had been seeking. It was nevertheless considered a 'basis upon which we could work' (Kelly, interview). The Policing Bill introduced in the House of Commons in May 2000 (which Sinn Féin calls the 'Mandelson Bill') was seen by both Sinn Féin and the SDLP as a dilution of the Patten report, notably on the issues of the name, symbols and emblems of the police force, but also on the role of the Police Board and the appointment of its members.

However, following a series of intensive negotiations which culminated in Weston Park (England) in July 2001, a Revised Implementation Plan on Policing was announced by the British government in early August 2001. The SDLP identified ninety-four changes to the Policing Bill, which enabled the party not only to participate in the Police Board and District Policing Partnerships, but also to 'encourage nationalists, particularly the young, to join the new police service in order to help make and shape a new service acceptable to all' (SDLP, 2001: 7). Among the gains considered significant were the implementation of the Patten recommendations on name, flag and badge, the strengthening and enhancement of the powers of the Policing Board with powers formerly resting with the Chief Constable and the Secretary of State, and the new powers granted to the Police Ombudsman to investigate policies and practices. However, Sinn Féin announced that the revised plan did not go far enough and, consequently, that it would not endorse the proposals nor would it nominate members to the Policing Board. Sinn Féin is still seeking the creation of an unarmed policing service, the banning of plastic bullets, the end of repressive legislation, enquiries into allegations of collusion between British security forces and loyalist paramilitary groups, and the transfer of powers of policing and justice to the assembly (Manifesto, 2003: 26).

The latter point is a key demand for republicans, as it is seen as the only way to ensure the accountability of the police force. This was one of the recommendations of the Patten report, one which was agreed upon in the British and Irish Joint Declaration of April 2003. According to the SDLP, Sinn Féin's refusal to sit on the Policing Board is no more than 'bombastic rhetoric', as 'if Sinn Féin forgo their place, then they can't complain if they don't know what's going on' (Farren, interview). In fact, Seán Farren sees Sinn Féin's position on policing as counterproductive, since it is implicitly handing over its seats to other parties, including the DUP. The party is also considered inconsistent in the light of its criticisms of the DUP's refusal to fully participate in the institutions (Farren, interview). Kelly, however, still views the system as 'based on secrecy', and the only way to ensure a new departure is, according to him, to introduce a system of checks and balances. For the PUP, however, the issue of policing has little to do with what the nationalist population wants, and the reasons behind the republican position are internal to the party. Indeed, this is an issue that is strongly debated within Sinn Féin, as the number of motions put to the Ard Fheis testifies. There is staunch opposition among the rank and file to the acceptance of a Northern Ireland police force, and one motion stated specifically that 'this Ard Fheis reflects the feeling of the broad republican constituency by stating that any Six-county police force is totally unacceptable' (Clár, 2003). This motion was not passed, nor was the one asking that 'no Sinn Féin representative can sit on any Policing Board or similar body while Britain has juris-diction over the Six Counties' (Clár, 2003). However, the leadership is cautious on this issue, professing to understand the uneasiness of its rank and file, and has pledged not to enter into any policing arrangement without the prior agreement of the whole party, through a special Ard Fheis.

Sinn Féin's electoral success is due in great part to the image it has succeeded in putting across, that of a party which is, on the one hand, pragmatic, prepared to make compromises and to listen, and on the other, unswerving about its fundamental commitments, such as demilitarisation, human rights and policing. The SDLP's approach, one that consistently advocated conciliation, has been seen to have been successfully espoused by Sinn Féin, leaving the SDLP with a weaker and at times uncertain identity. Some researchers believe that Sinn Féin has an important debt towards the SDLP. In the words of Jennifer Todd, 'Sinn Féin has refash-ioned its own republicanism, borrowing large parts of SDLP discourse, including its flexibility and pragmatism, although offering a more radical egalitarianism, and a sharper nationalist focus' (in Coakley, 2002: 83). In the words of Seán Farren, Sinn Féin is successful because it 'shouts louder'. In the words of Martin McGuinness, it is successful because it 'fights harder'. The battles left to fight are significant for the republican movement, as not only do they involve their relationship with the other parties and the two governments but also with their own supporters and rank and file, on issues such as policing or the future of the IRA. The next assembly, when the institutions are restored, could prove all the more challenging for Sinn Féin.

3 From political wing to political party

The peace process and the IRA ceasefires propelled Sinn Féin into the limelight, affording its leaders coverage on the airwaves and a degree of credibility that they had been denied for years. From its inception and especially since the Downing Street Declaration of December 1993, the peace process has been, arguably, one of the most important news stories coming out of Ireland, and considering the role that Sinn Féin played in it, it has greatly contributed to casting the party in a different light. Progressively, Sinn Féin started to replace the IRA in headline stories covering the Republican Movement, a new status which the party seemed keen to retain. With a blend of activism and conciliation, Sinn Féin leaders opted for respectability, while at the same time cultivating their working-class roots and claiming a historical legacy, one which pulled together revolutionary politics and armed struggle. In the process, they fashioned an image that captured this new-found confidence, and were keen to come across as serious, trustworthy and professional politicians.

The politics of imaging

Republicans have had quite a lot of first-hand experience in cultivating a self-image, having always been aware of the importance of the media, and having had to make sure, through the years, that their message was heard, in spite of the censorship on the broadcast media that prevented them from appearing on the airwaves both in Britain and Ireland. Hence they have acquired, according to media consultant Pat Montague, 'a clear sense of their own political strategy. They have a sense of self-belief, they know exactly where they're going, they're clear on who their audiences are, which gives them an edge over other political parties. Sinn Féin are confident about their mission, and this is a key skill in terms of communications' (Montague, interview, 1998). Sinn Féin leaders are indeed capable of articulating a message that has found an echo among an increasing number of Irish voters. Some of their critics still sneer at what they see as the dogmatic rhetoric that republican spokespersons use. *Irish*

Times columnist Vincent Browne commented that this was due in great measure to the fact that 'they all say the same thing, using the same words, evading the same questions in the same way' (*IT*, 15 June 2002). Indeed, at times, it seems that there are parts of the republican discourse that are immutable, passing from one leader to another, from one press release to another. Nevertheless, this rhetoric is partly what gives Sinn Féin a sense of identity, of cohesion, which in turn helps to lend credibility to its policies. This is a deliberate strategy. Parts of the message conveyed by the spokespersons are identical, reduced to sound bites such as 'seize the opportunity', 'take the guns out of Irish politics'. According to Sinn Féin's Director of Publicity Dawn Doyle, 'these messages are hammered home everywhere: in the media, among activists. When themes run, the language used is the same' (Doyle, interview, 2004). There is, according to Doyle, a very pragmatic necessity for this: 'several people could be doing an interview at the same time. The message has to be easily articulated. Any nuances can be used in a detrimental way' (Doyle, interview).

Republicans have acquired the reputation of being quite savvy in their public relations. A survey carried out by Liz Fawcett for the University of Ulster found that political journalists gave Sinn Féin and the DUP top marks for their media relations. 'While there's some sophisticated spin-ning of the type associated with Alistair Campbell from these parties, the main factor is simply that they deliver what journalists want – and fast. Sinn Féin is clearly the most highly rated in this regard – but the DUP isn't far behind' (Fawcett, 2001: 1). For Sinn Féin, this is due to the way in which the party approaches publicity. It has eight full-time press officers, who cover both sides of the island. What makes their operation unique, according to Doyle, is the fact that they are, primarily, activists, involved in their local cumainn (sections) and in local campaigns. The political message is not decided upon by the press officers but collectively by the party, which has overall control over how this message will be worded and delivered.

Sinn Féin's relationship with the media was not always easy. For years, the party tended to blame censorship and the media for the manner in which it was perceived by public opinion. In Jim Gibney's words, 'republican views are smothered beneath a wet blanket of censorship, and when they are not, they are distorted beyond recognition' (Gibney, Bodenstown, 1992). For almost two decades, Sinn Féin was banned from the state-owned media in the Republic. Section 31 of the 1960 Broadcasting Act gave the Minister for Post and Telegraphs the discre-tionary power to issue directives to the media, a power that was used in October 1971 when an order was signed by the then Minister Gerry Collins instructing the broadcast media 'to refrain from broadcasting any matter that could be calculated to promote the aims or activities of

any organisation which engages in, promotes, encourages or advocates
the attaining of any particular objective by violent means' (Curtis, 1984:
191). Initially this ban was vague enough to allow the broadcast media
to interview Seán Mac Stiofáin, the then chief-of-staff of the Provisional
IRA. All interviews with IRA spokespersons were subsequently banned.
A new directive in 1976 extended the application of the ban to a number
of political organisations, including Sinn Féin. This led to a contradictory
situation, whereby a party which was legal and allowed to operate within
the jurisdiction of the Republic, and even present candidates at elections,
was nevertheless virtually barred from access to the mass media. From
then on, as journalist Tom McGurk remarked,

> under the long shadow cast by Section 31, ministers from Conor
> Cruise O'Brien on ran the place like their personal fiefdom. Apart
> from the censorship aspect of Section 31, it also created a political
> dependence culture whereby RTE was regarded from the Dáil as
> something akin to a dog on a lead.
>
> (*SBP*, 8 April 2001)

Section 31 could be said to have greatly curtailed both the work of
journalists and the information that was put across to the Irish public, and
it led indeed to a level of disinformation. When Owen Carron, Bobby
Sands' electoral agent, was elected to Westminster in August 1981, the
only camera crew present at the polling station was from RTE. Being pro-
hibited from interviewing the new MP, as he was a member of Sinn Féin,
they had to settle for the defeated Unionist candidate (ICCL, 1993: 6). But
the ban also meant that no member of Sinn Féin could be interviewed
in a private capacity, no matter what the topic being discussed. This at
times led to ludicrous situations, such as the interruption of a radio call-
in programme on gardening when the caller happened to be a member
of Sinn Féin. It also meant that coverage of issues beyond the conflict and
beyond the IRA was greatly impaired, as was the case with the 1990 strike
in the Gateaux factory, where RTE could not interview the union leader
Larry O'Toole, because of his affiliation with Sinn Féin. O'Toole took his
case to the High Court, which effectively ruled that RTE's interpretation
was incorrect. RTE appealed this decision to the Supreme Court, which
again ruled against the broadcasting company. Although this judgement
was considered by republicans at the time as a victory, Section 31 was
'one of the most damaging things for Sinn Féin. We couldn't put our side
of the argument. It was an insult to viewers, as they weren't allowed
to make up their minds' (O'Toole, interview, 2003). This permeates
the analysis of republicans to this day, and Section 31 is blamed for the
party's poor electoral performances and for the negative image that its
leaders suffered from during this period. O'Toole quotes the remark

of one of his constituents as evidence of this: 'I'd vote for you, Larry, but I don't like that guy Adams' (O'Toole, interview).

Britain was much slower in introducing such a measure, as it only came into effect there sixteen years later, in 1988, when the then Secretary of State Douglas Hurd announced 'restrictions' on the electronic media. At first sight this legislation was far less rigid than its Irish counterpart, since the ban did not apply during elections, nor to Sinn Féin spokespersons interviewed in a personal capacity. Furthermore, the media were able to slightly subvert this ban by using voice-overs or subtitles when interviewing Sinn Féin representatives. The irony of this was that the accents of the dubbing artists were surely more comprehensible to a British audience than the strong northern twang of the republican leaders. Whether this legislation significantly changed the manner in which Sinn Féin's message was relayed by the media is, ultimately, open to question. Journalist Ed Moloney has argued that the media in Northern Ireland had already been applying a level of self-censorship when it came to reporting on republicans, and that they had gone along with the process of ostracising Sinn Féin in the 1980s. For instance, the media did not question the unionist refusal to be interviewed in the same programme as Sinn Féin representatives. By and large, they contributed to cornering Sinn Féin into an image where it was, solely, the political wing of the IRA by only covering stories that related to the IRA and by ignoring the party's involvement in social or economic issues. At the end of the 1980s,

> Sinn Féin interviews and press conferences became almost exclusively contests between defensive Sinn Féiners and reporters trying to get a revealing and damaging response to the latest IRA disaster. Coverage also concentrated on alleged internal IRA–Sinn Féin divisions even though a split, at least a serious one, never developed.
>
> (Moloney, 1991: 15)

Given this climate of censorship, Sinn Féin became quite familiar with the techniques of propaganda, and gained experience in the setting up of its own alternative communication strategies. Apart from the Socialist Workers' Party, which publishes a fortnightly paper, Sinn Féin is the only party in the Republic of Ireland to have its own publication, *An Phoblacht*. The history of *An Phoblacht* goes back a long way, as it was already the title of the paper published in Belfast in 1915 under its English name, *The Republic*, but was also the publication of the IRA from 1926 until July 1937. *An Phoblacht* disappeared on the eve of the Second World War, when republicans were facing momentous difficulties, and was revived in 1948 under the name *United Irishman*. The leaders who formed the Provisional Movement in the aftermath of the 1969 to 1970 split in the Sinn Féin and IRA ranks were keen to ensure that they had an outlet for their message and policies. One of Provisional Sinn Féin's first actions was to set up its own newspaper, and *An Phoblacht* was published as a monthly publication, with the first issue coming out on 31 January 1970. In Belfast, another monthly paper was created in March of that year, *Republican News*. Both newspapers became weeklies within two years, and were published separately until 1979 when they merged to become *An-Phoblacht Republican News*, edited from Dublin.

In an environment that was seen as hostile to republicanism in general, it was important for the party to ensure that it could use its own outlet which would, furthermore, be entirely dedicated to the cause. Republicans were well aware of the importance of propaganda, as was British intelligence officer Maurice Tugwell, who commented that 'without its aid, the leadership would be powerless to mobilise the masses, inspire confidence and dedication, and focus hatred. Strategy leading towards a military decision can be strengthened by propaganda that lowers enemy morale and makes rebel victory seem inevitable' (in Wilkinson, 1981: 17). In the context of the 'propaganda war', as the conflict was called, especially in the 1970s, *An Phoblacht* was indeed full of such stories and reports. It proclaimed the victory of the movement on various occasions, and used techniques such as opinion polls to demonstrate its support and invalidate the point of view of the enemy. Although journalist Liz Curtis remarked in the early 1980s that republican sources compared well with other sources, such as the British military personnel, when it came to the measurement of veracity and accuracy (Curtis, 1984: 268), *An Phoblacht* was none the less a tool at the service of the so-called war, and it used information in pursuit of the movement's ends. One of its headlines, 'British morale cracking', was the conclusion of a so-called survey carried out by the newspaper, the outcome of which 'proved' that, under IRA pressure, British army morale was declining. The report also stated that there was an 'increasing intake of drugs and alcohol as a result'. However, this was based on quite an unorthodox sample, consisting of 'conversations with the military and police, as well as with nurses and doctors' (*AP*, 7 November 1973). Counter-propaganda on the British side was fierce, and extended to quality newspapers such as the London *Times*. On the day of Bobby Sands' funeral, its reporter wrote that 'the Catholics buried Robert Sands yesterday as Protestants lamented their 2,000 dead from 12 years of terrorism' thus implicitly laying the blame for all those deaths solely on the IRA (Curtis, 1984: 108).

An Phoblacht was at the height of its influence during the hunger strikes, when it sold some 45,000 copies (compared with the 20,000 copies a week sold in the early 1970s, according to a special issue of *An Phoblacht* in 1988). Ironically, with the advent of the peace process, the sales of *An Phoblacht* started to decline, and its circulation is now approximately 15,000 copies a week, according to its editor Martin Spain. An article on Ireland's alternative press ascribes this partly to the lifting of Section 31 and the British broadcasting ban because, with the removal of these restrictions, *An Phoblacht* lost a 'world exclusive' (Pettit, 1997: 14), that of being the only source of information quoting directly, and not second-hand, IRA and Sinn Féin spokespersons (although this assertion would need to be qualified, since the print media had not been included in either of the bans). But equally, the paper could no longer afford to be, nor be seen to be, merely a propaganda tool reporting from the 'war zone', and needed to be rethought and reshaped. This presented a double challenge: that of retaining its militant edge while opening up its contents to a wider readership. As the conflict was the main story that filled the pages of the paper for years, a critical reappraisal of its editorial line had to be made, while keeping in mind that *An Phoblacht* must not lose its identity as the paper of militant republicanism. Editor Martin Spain recognises the difficulties involved, as the readerships' expectations vary according to the geographical location: 'audiences in the North expect more coverage on sectarian violence and the peace process, whereas in the South, they'll be more keen to see us tackle socio-economic issues' (Spain, interview, 2003).

Although *An Phoblacht* is a self-sustained and relatively small operation with only one editor and one staff journalist, the rest of the writers working on a freelance basis, it is experiencing difficulties, as its sales are dropping and its traditional network of readers is waning. But now that Sinn Féin has access to the mainstream media, and has its own website, is the newspaper still as useful, and necessary, a tool as it was ten years before? Doyle acknowledges that there is an ongoing debate within the movement regarding the role of the paper. 'The irony is that as the party has grown, the audience has gone up, but the sales are down' (Doyle, interview). Whether the paper becomes a monthly or fortnightly, republicans still see the importance of conveying their own message to their audience, claiming that some stories would never be uncovered or given the attention that they deserve if it were not for *An Phoblacht*, such as that of sectarian violence in North Belfast which has been kept at the top of the newspaper's agenda. As Spain puts it, 'it is a tremendous vehicle at the disposal of the party, as it reaches and cements a "community of republicans"' (Spain, interview). It would also seem that republicans still believe in the power of their own propaganda machine, and that they are prepared to ensure that their voices penetrate every household where this might make a difference to their fate. Thus, the Dublin southwest constituency publishes its own magazine, *Dublin News*. Its summer 2003 issue focused heavily on the work of local TD Aengus Ó Snodaigh. In this twelve-page newsletter, Ó Snodaigh appeared in a total of ten pictures, being photographed alongside senior citizens, party colleagues, with other activists on the Bin Charges campaign, or simply at his desk. For assiduous readers, the sense of this politician's ubiquity is reinforced by a series of articles tackling a variety of issues and his name is quoted in twenty-four out of the forty or so articles. The local TD's omnipresence thus becomes an essential dimension of the image that the party wishes to convey to its local constituents, namely that its representatives are hard-working, committed and serious politicians.

An Phoblacht was never overtly targeted by censorship legislation. This may be due to the fact that it is not unanimously seen as a fully fledged newspaper. It did not appear in the list of publications of the 1996 Report of the Commission of the Newspaper Industry in Ireland (Pettit). It is not listed either on a website that purports to study the media on both sides of the island and that claims to include 'a comprehensive range of information' (medialive.ie). Its journalists do not have Dáil accreditation, and have to rely on second-hand reports of Dáil proceedings. The reason for this is that, as a political party paper, it is not eligible for accreditation. Its application was thus rejected in 2000, and the paper was awaiting the outcome of its renewed application in the autumn of 2003. As it is still embargoed by Easons, one of Ireland's largest newspaper retail outlets and distributors, and cannot afford to pay the main newsagents to stock issues of the paper, its distribution is still erratic. The paper's rudimentary distribution system is composed of a network of members whose task it is to sell the publication every week. From the party's point of view, this has the advantage of keeping a visible presence on the streets, in bars, colleges and in other public places where the newspaper is sold. It also gave the members something concrete to do, at a time when there were 'restrictive tasks that they could be involved in. But now, there is lots of work, and members have less time' (Doyle, interview). Furthermore, to some extent, by the very nature of its distribution, the paper is in great part preaching to the converted. However, *An Phoblacht* is now online (it was, according to its editor, the first Irish newspaper to appear on the internet, before the *Irish Times*), and according to the paper's editor, it receives an average of 10,000 hits a week (Spain, interview).

Shifts in public perception

Undoubtedly, Sinn Féin's increasing credibility was the fruit not only of a process of modernisation of the party's image, but also of the new political landscape that was emerging in Northern Ireland. While its political presence in the north in terms of electoral support was stable from the mid-1980s onward, and increased substantially at the end of the century, this was far from the case in the Republic, where, at the end of the 1990s, Sinn Féin still had some way to go before it became a relevant force in political life. Although the decision to play a part in national politics came about with the dropping of the abstentionist rule for Dáil Éireann in 1986, the strategies put in place by the party only came to fruition in the general election of 2002, with the first tangible electoral success for more than four decades.

This breakthrough was made possible partly due to changes in public perceptions. Until the mid-1990s, Sinn Féin had quite a negative image among public opinion in the Republic of Ireland. This was due in great part to its long association with the IRA, which made the party unacceptable to a sizeable proportion of the electorate. It also meant that Sinn Féin was, almost exclusively, associated with the Northern Ireland conflict, and was thus seen as a single-issue party not necessarily capable of having a programme of government for the Republic. With the peace process, and following the party's political gains, the attention of republican policy-makers, media advisers and strategists gradually turned to the Republic of Ireland, which was seen as an essential battlefield in its drive for expansion.

However, if an audit of the situation of the party in the Republic had been carried out in the mid-1990s, it would have made grim reading for Sinn Féin strategists. Opinion polls carried out before the signing of the Good Friday Agreement in April 1998 showed a level of support throughout the years that was consistent, but abysmally low.[1] Indeed, it ranged between 1 and 2 per cent of the total potential electoral support, a figure which was regularly confirmed by the party's share of the actual vote. Whether or not the IRA was on ceasefire did not seem to alter considerably the electorate's voting intentions. Two polls carried out in 1994, one in March and one in November, both showed support at 2 per cent (IMS, 24 March 1994 and Lansdowne, 24 November 1994). The same pattern emerged in 1997, before and after the resumption of the IRA ceasefire: while Sinn Féin got 2 per cent of the actual vote in the May general election of that year (therefore, before the second IRA ceasefire), only 1 per cent of the electorate declared their intention to vote Sinn Féin the following December if an election were to be held (MBRI, 1 December 1997). In the run-up to the signing of the Agreement, Sinn Féin was credited with 2 per cent of support (March 1998), with that figure rising only very slightly to 3 per cent in October (IMS, 15 October 1998), the highest percentage that the party recorded in twenty years, but still a fragile basis from which to build.

Quite obviously, the greatest hindrance to Sinn Féin's development was its public image as the political wing of the IRA. This association was, and still is, regularly used by politicians and commentators alike to identify the party, although, according to TD Caoimhghín Ó Caoláin's emphatic statement, Sinn Féin 'is not the wing of any other organisation' (*IT*, 24 October 1997). Notwithstanding this deeply ingrained public perception, there were some indications that the public's view was gradually shifting, in the sense that it did not see the relationship between the two components of the Republican Movement as being necessarily negative. Indeed, in 1993, before the first IRA ceasefire, only 18 per cent of the people surveyed believed that Sinn Féin should be allowed to participate in all-party talks with no preconditions (IMS survey, 7 October 1993). This proportion rose to 26 per cent in February 1996, immediately after the attack by the IRA on Canary Wharf in London, which in effect announced the end of the first IRA ceasefire (Coopers & Lybrand, 22–23 February 1996). Furthermore, a few months later, 75 per cent claimed that the two governments should maintain links with Sinn Féin, in spite of the direct reference to 'escalating IRA violence' contained in the question put to the survey respondents, as opposed to 18 per cent who stated that links should be severed (IMS Survey, 4 April 1996).

Nevertheless, no matter how often the leaders of the party repeated that the two organisations were separate entities and that Sinn Féin did not speak for the IRA, most of the electorate in the Republic of Ireland remained unconvinced. When public opinion was surveyed in September 1997, two months after the second IRA ceasefire, about the relationship that Sinn Féin maintained with the IRA, 23 per cent considered the two organisations to be distinct and separate, against 66 per cent who saw them as one and the same (IMS, 18 September 1997). But the manner in which the electorate looked at this particular relationship was far from cut and dried. Although a majority felt quite certain that there was an organic link between the two organisations, 42 per cent considered, in the run-up to the 1997 Westminster general election in Northern Ireland, that a vote for Sinn Féin was a vote for peace, as opposed to 37 per cent who saw it a vote for violence (IMS, 29 June 1997). In other words, it would seem that Irish public opinion, while not entirely trusting that Sinn Féin as a party was truly independent from the IRA, accorded its leaders an important role, seeing them as the leaders of a political force who could contribute to delivering peace and who could keep the IRA in check.

Sinn Féin's long association with the Northern Ireland conflict and, as a consequence, the perception that it was, essentially, a party of the north, were further handicaps to be overcome in the Republic. As a general rule, Northern Ireland does not rank very high in the electorate's preoccupations at election time. A study on the ranking of issues considered relevant by the electorate before elections has shown that Northern Ireland tends to figure low on the list of important issues. With the exception of the May 1981 election, when 14 per cent of the electorate saw it as the most important issue (at the height of the hunger strike, with five candidates representing the H-Block prisoners), the issue has remained consistently low: 1 per cent quoted it as the most important issue in February 1982, none in November 1982, 3 per cent in January 1987 and 1 per cent in December 1996 (Trumbore, 2001: 126). In this regard, the 1997 general election was an exception to the rule as, according to the findings of an exit poll, 14 per cent of those questioned cited Northern Ireland as one of the issues that had influenced their decision as to which party to vote for. Nevertheless, if this issue is not a priority, it is seen as an important criterion for distinguishing between the parties. Fianna Fáil used Northern Ireland in its 1997 and 2002 campaigns, calculating that its role in the peace process would be viewed positively (Doyle and Connolly, 2002: 161). But the fact that the north was perceived by only 4 per cent of the electorate as being the most important issue in 2002 meant that the electoral debates were going to be focused on other issues. Sinn Féin had to fine tune its policies regarding those particular areas in order to establish its credentials as a fully fledged political party.

Undoubtedly, the peace process produced important political benefits for the party in terms of the image that it was able to project. The fact that its leaders were given a high media profile for the political role that they were carrying out, rather than simply for their alleged association with the IRA, was an important development. Furthermore, at both national and international levels, the Sinn Féin leadership was being presented as capable of carrying out high-profile negotiations both with local politicians and with foreign diplomats and statesmen. Interestingly, although Irish public opinion generally associated Sinn Féin with a violent past, it was nevertheless beginning to exonerate the party for this because of the role it played in the peace process. Obviously, this did not immediately or automatically translate into a higher share of the vote. There was still a perception that what took place in the north of Ireland did not necessarily apply to the rest of the island. One such case in point is the debate over whether Sinn Féin should be allowed to enter a coalition government if it was in a position to do so. There is a discrepancy between what applies in Belfast and in Dublin. The electorate was more open to the idea of Sinn Féin playing a role in government in the north than in the Republic. In May 1997, 32 per cent thought that Fianna Fáil and the Progressive Democrats should accept Sinn Féin's support were they to depend on it to form a government, as opposed to 54 per cent who were against that proposition (MRBI, 28 May 1997). Nevertheless, public opinion was more flexible on the place of Sinn Féin within the executive in the north, since 40 per cent thought that Sinn Féin should enter the executive without prior decommissioning as opposed to 44 per cent who felt that this pre-condition must be fulfilled (IMS, 18 May 1998).

Public opinion on this issue was in line with that held by the main political parties, whose stated public position was that Sinn Féin was still considered an unacceptable partner. In February 2002, Fianna Fáil leader and Taoiseach Bertie Ahern outlined the reasons for his refusal to consider a coalition with Sinn Féin: the continued existence of the IRA and the unfinished decommissioning process, its refusal to cooperate with the Policing Board in the north, and the vigilante-type methods that republicans were accused of using in some areas. Ahern added that even if Sinn Féin's position on the above issues was reversed, 'there would be insufficient time to establish confidence for government participation to be realistic' (*IT*, 21 February 2002). Fianna Fáil maintained this line throughout the whole 2002 electoral campaign, claiming that the participation of Sinn Féin in any government would clash with Article 15 of the Constitution which states that 'No military or armed force, other than a military or armed force raised and maintained by the Oireachtas, shall be raised or maintained for any purpose whatsoever' (Constitution of Ireland, available online).

Sinn Féin leaders and some commentators pointed to what they saw as the inherent contradiction in such a position. As the then North Kerry councillor Martin Ferris noted, Sinn Féin already sat alongside Fianna Fáil ministers in the North–South Ministerial Council. For republicans, this type of rhetoric amounted to a diversionary tactic used by the main parties to marginalise them, but they did not believe that this position stood up to scrutiny. There were, obviously, other reasons why Fianna Fáil was reluctant to enter into negotiations with Sinn Féin in the Republic, such as those outlined by Foreign Affairs Minister Brian Cowen regarding the incompatibility of their political programmes, particularly on economic issues (*IT*, 25 January 2002). Gerry Adams castigated the Fianna Fáil leadership for their hypocrisy. In his view, the argument that the existence of the IRA meant that Sinn Féin did not accept the armed forces of the state was not compatible with the calls for republicans to get involved in the north's policing service, and he also pointed to his party's record in the peace process where its representatives had been privy to highly sensitive and confidential information and had proved themselves to be trustworthy partners. But the bottom line was, quite simply, that Sinn Féin was not, and would not be, acceptable as long as the IRA remained in existence. No matter how Sinn Féin leaders were to argue the invalidity of these points, the particular Rubicon of forming a coalition with Sinn Féin would not be crossed as long as the IRA had not disbanded, a position that was approved by unionist leader David Trimble (*IT*, 28 May 2002). In some ways this question was academic, as the party claimed not to be interested in entering into any coalition arrangements with anyone, and might not even have been in a position to do so. Interestingly, however, the voters' point of view on that question evolved somewhat between the general elections of 1997 and 2002. In a poll carried out in May 2001, 47 per cent stated that they would accept Sinn Féin as part of their next government while 45 per cent were opposed to the idea, which represented a significant evolution from the respective figures of 32 per cent and 54 per cent of the May 1997 survey (5 May 2001). Ultimately, however, this was more of a theoretical issue, since a situation where Sinn Féin would be in a position to hold the balance of power was, in 2002, quite unlikely.

For years, Sinn Féin was faced with the inescapable reality that the party's name remained closely associated with the IRA. Denying the links between the two organisations was clearly not enough to convince public opinion, and though such denials could be politically expedient, they could also prove to be internally damaging. But there were other ways to overcome the apparently negative impact that IRA coverage had on the party. In some ways, since Sinn Féin was strongly associated with the IRA, no matter what the leaders said, this situation could be turned to the party's advantage in some instances. The leaders were faced with a difficulty when it came to clarifying their position regarding the IRA, and had strived to be careful as to how they went about distancing themselves from this image without seeming to renege on their past. They have been castigated on many occasions for their refusal to condemn the IRA or any action carried out in its name. They have also been accused of hypocrisy for claiming that they were genuine in their peace strategy yet not declaring that the so-called war was over. Republicans would no doubt contend that, even if they wished to declare that the war was over, it would not be solely up to them to do so, as there were other parties to this war besides the IRA, such as the British army and other paramilitary groups. This was made very clear in a document published by Sinn Féin in May 2003, *Who Sanctioned Britain's Death Squads?*, which states that 'British intelligence agencies and their agents are still fighting their war. They continue to undermine the peace process by mounting propaganda operations' (May 2003). Hence republicans do not believe that they should bear sole responsibility for decreeing that the war is over. In any event, there are those in the north who still believe in the armed struggle, for whom the sacrifice on the part of the volunteers who were engaged in it over the years is an important dimension of that struggle, and who would resent any statement that could be seen as a renunciation of that past. Thus, a declaration that the war is over would have to take into account positions which are highly emotionally charged; such a declaration would have to be very carefully worded. The inescapable fact of the matter is that armed struggle is still very much part of the culture of the movement as a whole. Nevertheless, there are other ways in which the leaders might try to convey this message. In October 2002, Martin McGuinness made quite a bold statement on a BBC programme, when he stated: 'My war is over. My job as a political leader is to continue to ensure a political set of circumstances which will never again see British soldiers or members of the IRA lose their lives as a result of political conflict' (*IT*, 31 October 2002).

For years, republican leaders have publicly justified the armed struggle and have praised the Volunteers who gave their lives and their freedom

for the cause of Irish reunification. To be seen to deny this would be tantamount to treason for many supporters of the movement, even if, by and
large, they have accepted that the days of the armed struggle are over.
Sinn Féin Chairperson Mitchell McLaughlin admits that the continued
existence of the IRA is inhibiting the party's progress to an extent, but
retains the view that no purpose would be served by simply walking away
from the IRA. 'These things take time', is how he puts it (McLaughlin,
interview, 2003). In the meantime, the leadership strives both to reassure
its own supporters that it has not sold out on its major principles, and
to refute any connection with the IRA. It is a subtle balancing act, one
which is difficult to maintain. In April 2002, as the Republic was about
to enter into a general election campaign, Sinn Féin organised an event in
a suburban Dublin hotel to commemorate the IRA Volunteers who had
died throughout the conflict. Gerry Adams delivered a speech in front of
some 2,500 relatives of IRA members who had died during the conflict,
and, to mark the occasion, a memorial listing the names of the IRA dead
was unveiled. Praising their courage and their dedication at a time when
the elections in the Republic were looming might have seemed like a
perilous exercise. Adams did not mince his words, paying tribute to the
'extraordinary calibre' of IRA volunteers, and stating that 'there would
be no peace process if it were not for the IRA' (*IT*, 15 April 2002), a bold
statement which could have easily been countered by his detractors who
would contend that there would have been no need for a peace process
if it had not been for the IRA. Politicians from other parties, such as Brid
Rodgers (SDLP), remarked that there was nothing glorious about the
armed conflict, and that its 'horrid' reality for those involved should not
have become the object of mystification: 'What was glorious about the
murders of innocent civilians in Belfast, London or Claudy? What was
glorious about the murders of workmen on their way home from work?'
(*IT*, 15 April 2002).

In another light, however, the event might also have served the purpose
of signalling the end of the military phase. Therefore, the memorial could
be seen as epitomising the closure of the conflict, as if no more names
would need to be added to the list. In some way, it could be the signalling
of the end of a difficult chapter and the beginning of a period of collective
mourning, not only within republican ranks but outside of them as
well. It was not the long-awaited declaration that the war was over,
but perhaps this was a skilfully staged event that had the effect of both
showing sympathy to the volunteers' families and signalling the end of an
era.

There is a contradiction in the manner in which the party upholds
the view that it does not have direct control over the IRA, and therefore
refused to comment over some of its actions, while at the same time
accepting to be seen to be playing an intermediary role when the occasion

is deemed important enough. One such case was the announcement in April 2002 of the second decommissioning act. For the occasion, a press conference chaired by Gerry Adams was organised in the Belfast offices of Sinn Féin. The party went to great lengths to explain that the decommissioning act and the electoral campaign in the Republic were totally unrelated, and was keen to dissociate the two, accusing those who made that link of political cynicism: 'This issue is too deadly serious . . . to become a mere election stunt', said Adams (*IT*, 9 April 2002). Yet the presence of the party's Louth candidate, Arthur Morgan, beside the Sinn Féin President, served to undermine what was supposed to be a coincidence. Indeed, announcements made by the IRA are often greeted in some quarters with a degree of cynicism, and the timing and motivation behind them have raised a number of questions (although not all as far-fetched as that of Ulster Unionist MP Martyn Smyth, who saw the timing of this announcement as beyond contempt 'at a time when large sections of the community are focused on the funeral of the Queen Mother' (*IT*, 9 April 2002)). Nevertheless, it may be argued that these types of coincidences, if such they are, suit the needs of the party quite well.

But although the IRA does not always necessarily generate negative publicity, on the whole these are rare occasions, as there are many more stories that tend to tarnish the image of the party. The arrest of three men in Colombia in August 2001 on charges of training the FARC guerrillas (see Chapter 5) reflected quite badly on Sinn Féin's credentials as a peaceful political party, and were damaging to its image not only within Ireland but also in the USA. Similarly, the announcement by the IRA in April 1999 of its intention to play its part in the retrieval of the remains of the disappeared (see Chapter 6), when the party was about to embark on the EU election campaign, could have been construed as a manner in which to raise the profile of the organisation. But as the searches for the bodies dragged on, one of the party's candidates to the European election, Seán Crowe, felt it necessary to explain that it was not 'an electoral issue', adding: 'we have tried to explain that we do not believe the information given about the location of the bodies was deliberately wrong. I do not believe it will damage our vote' (*IT*, 8 June 1999). Mitchell McLaughlin went one step further, specifying that this was 'an outstanding issue of human rights and justice that could and should be resolved in the context of resolving other outstanding issues' (*IT*, 31 May 1999), which prompted other parties to denounce a type of rhetoric that attempted to turn the issues around and to make republicans come across as the victim of human rights.

There are other stories which are potentially quite embarrassing for the party, such as those relating to less savoury activities of punishment beatings or vigilante-type tactics. Sinn Féin's response to these allegations is somewhat ambivalent. In the past, the IRA sought to establish a repu-

tation for being forthcoming by admitting responsibility for its own operations, and it was often left to Sinn Féin spokespersons to deal with the
public relations damage that some of these entailed (Moloney, 1991: 15).
Since the IRA ceasefires, however, this has become a much more fraught
exercise: any comment on an action attributed, rightly or wrongly, to the
IRA would implicitly mean that the IRA is in breach of its own ceasefire
and would raise the question as to whether Sinn Féin is fully committed
to the peace process. The discursive strategy that seems to dominate this
type of situation is one whereby Sinn Féin spokespersons maintain a certain
distance from these stories while seeking to avoid casting the IRA in a
negative light. They say as little as possible on the matter, yet try to demonstrate a willingness to have the matter discussed. One instance of such a
strategy was the interview with Gerry Adams about the latest developments in the recovery of the disappeared (see Chapter 6) on the RTE radio
programme, *Morning Ireland*, on 2 September 2003. Adams reminded his
listeners that the IRA stated that it was not responsible for the murder of
Gareth O'Connor, from Armagh, who had gone missing in May of that
year, implying therefore that it should be taken at its word (see also *IT*, 2
September 2003). This is problematic, above all for Sinn Féin, as it cannot
be taken for granted that Irish public opinion and political leaders alike
will accept the IRA's word. Republican leaders are therefore obliged to try
to play down any allegations that will inevitably tarnish the image of the
party. They resort at times to denial, but more often tend to divert attention to another issue. Thus, one of the arguments frequently used consists
in accusing the media and politicians of putting the spotlight on Sinn Féin
in order to divert the public's attention from more deeply unsettling stories
such as the different financial scandals that have tarnished the reputation
of prominent politicians since the late 1980s. Another tactic used consists
in deliberately situating the debate within a climate where Sinn Féin can
claim that it is still being treated unfairly, be it by the media or by politicians, and that it is being vilified in order to be ostracised. This enables
spokespersons not to answer directly the questions that are put to them.
Such was the case when Martin Ferris, Sinn Féin's candidate for North
Kerry, was arrested during the 2002 election campaign for alleged links
with vigilantism (see below). For Gerry Adams, the explanation for this
was quite simple. Martin Ferris had been a member of the IRA for some
years, and never denied this past, but there was still, in Adams' view, some
individual policemen who had crossed his path in his former life and had
a personal vendetta against him. Although this argument might have
sounded lame in the face of the allegations made against the North Kerry
councillor and, subsequently, TD, they enabled the party not to answer
embarrassing questions too directly while not appearing to refuse to
answer. Ultimately, this type of prevarication is a double-edged strategy,
as it undoubtedly raises more questions than it answers.

The campaigning party

Sinn Féin's latest motto, 'A party of equals', is the archetypal image with which the party seeks to be identified. This is quite a departure from the previous catch-phrase that was regularly invoked when mentioning Sinn Féin and which, for years, seemed to encapsulate what Sinn Féin was about. It came up in a speech pronounced by Danny Morrison, then Director of Publicity, at the 1981 Ard Fheis. 'Who really believes that we can win the war through the ballot box? But will anyone here object if, with a ballot paper in this hand and an Armalite in this hand, we take power in Ireland?' (*AP*, 5 November 1981). The expression was so catchy that it captured the imagination of journalists and republicans alike and was to become the very definition of Sinn Féin's strategy for years to come. As journalist and writer Eugene McEldowney put it, 'the phrase was a Madison Avenue advertising executive's dream' (*IT*, 13 November 1997). It was indeed a perfect sound-bite, one that rapidly took on a life of its own. It was never an official slogan but it overshadowed all other attempts at putting forward a new image. The slogan translated the party's confidence, and managed to speak to both supporters of the armed struggle and those of the political option. Down the years the phrase has been used repeatedly, in different guises, by journalists when evoking Sinn Féin's electoral strategy. Indeed, a word search on the *Irish Times* website between 1996 and 2002 reveals that the phrase is mentioned in sixty-nine different articles, although the IRA was on ceasefire for most of that period.

With the peace process, this phrase lost its currency in republican discourse. Indeed, it has possibly impaired the party's efforts to present itself as the 'party of equals'. But achieving recognition for its work as the party of 'the man of no property', to use James Connolly's expression, was going to take more than a slogan. Other, more pragmatic, strategies were used to establish Sinn Féin's credentials. In the 1980s new expressions started to emerge, and were included in Sinn Féin's repertoire, such as 'community work', 'people empowerment' and 'local democracy'. These concepts were soon to become the cornerstone of the strategy on which Sinn Féin was to successfully widen its appeal. In order to implement it, the party was to use to its advantage what had been perceived until then as an obstacle to its aspiration to become a relevant political party: its marginalisation from the mainstream political process. Indeed, Sinn Féin had gathered invaluable experience in working in an alternative political mode, by getting involved on the ground, setting up its own network of clinics and advice centres, and creating links with the voluntary groups that were emerging in the 1980s in Northern Ireland.

Sinn Féin's goal was to foster participative democracy; in other words, to bring power back to the people. This philosophy was exposed in a policy document published in 1998, *Putting People First*, which outlined the party's commitment to devolving the decision-making process to local communities, because 'to do otherwise merely leaves intact the structures, which inevitably recreate economic and social inequalities and the continued exclusion of communities from decision-making which affect their lives' (1998: 1). Its experience as a campaigning party was something that it could draw upon to put this vision into practice, since it enabled Sinn Féin activists to present themselves as the people who got things done. Its long tradition of street protest, inherited from years of being less a political party and more a machine to mobilise supporters, proved to be a powerful asset when it came to entering the electoral arena. Thus, the party was able to implement lessons learned from campaigns that were very different in scope but similar in strategy. Some of these were highly successful, such as the hunger strike campaign which, at its height, mobilised thousands of people across the island. Others were more modest, but they also used the same techniques of marches, petitions, demonstrations and fund-raising events, such as the Stop the Strip Searches, or the anti-extradition campaigns in the mid- to late 1980s. All had a common feature, which was retained in future campaigns: they emanated from groups which were close to the party but which kept a level of independence, and which were created with one specific aim and one specific demand. The National H-blocks Armagh Committee was set up by relatives of the prisoners and was not, strictly speaking, a Sinn Féin-led movement. The distinction was deemed important by republicans. Although few doubted that these groups were fronts for Sinn Féin, and although some people even condemned the manner in which they were exploited by Sinn Féin, they maintained sufficient distance from the party to enable those who were not entirely comfortable with the ideas or strategies associated with the republican movement to get involved in the campaigns. Thus, when the parades issue came to the fore in Northern Ireland in the mid 1990s, several residents' associations were put in place. A closer look at the composition of these associations would tend to show that, on the whole, their spokespersons were affiliated to Sinn Féin in one way or another (see Chapter 6). Sinn Féin's political opponents spoke of manipulation, but the distinction for the party was important, since it saw its role not as the promoter of the campaign but as the supporter of the issues at stake.

Therefore, by putting local interests and campaigns to the fore of its strategy, Sinn Féin gradually started to occupy a political space that it had identified as being overlooked in Ireland, and it presented itself as the party best equipped to carry out this type of work. In the mid 1990s a National Campaigns Department was created, headed by Jim Gibney, the main functions of which were to identify key issues and to plan and resource campaigns (Gibney, interview, 2003). Republicans were keen not to rely solely on the media or elected forums; what they sought to convey was that it was in local communities' best interest to get involved in the issue that concerned them, that a level of 'participatory democracy' could yield more immediate results than relying on institutions and authorities. The potential benefit to be gained from this strategy was significant, increasing the popular appeal of the party while enabling it to retain its specific identity, one which differentiated it from other political parties. But there was another fundamental dimension to this strategy. With the increasing importance of Sinn Féin's involvement in elections, and the consequent work undertaken within the institutions, be they local or national, Sinn Féin perceived a danger of 'institutionalisation'. Until recently, this word was anathema in the republican repertoire, as it recalled historical precedents such as that of Fianna Fáil who, in the words of leader Seán Lemass, had become by 1928 a 'slightly constitutional party' and progressively lost sight of its essential purpose according to Sinn Féin. Moreover, the party is keen to retain its radical edge, a dimension which, in the republican analysis, would inevitably become diluted if it were to work exclusively within the confines of its electoral mandate. Thus, it was essential to find alternative ways of getting involved in mainstream politics, if only to show its detractors that it was possible to work pragmatically with the institutions without necessarily seeing them as the panacea for all political problems.

As the campaigns on these different issues started to gather momentum, it was decided to decentralise the strategy, since the party's resources were being progressively overstretched. Each Cúige, or regional body, was given individual responsibility for putting in place campaign plans. This would, according to Jim Gibney, enable them to identify issues as they came to the fore and respond to them. It also fitted with the wish of the party to be seen as a democratic and decentralised structure which favoured bottom-up initiatives. On a more pragmatic level, it is obvious that not all campaigns have a national appeal: for instance, the 'bin charges' campaign has more echo in central Dublin than it does in the north or west of the country. This strategy was seen as a logical step in the drive to empower local communities. It also brought undeniable political advantages, as Jim Gibney conceded. The more people participate in solving their own problems, the more empowered they feel, and thus the more active they become. Sinn Féin sees itself as a sort of facilitator, which brings issues to the fore and lends its strong logistical support and manpower to different campaigns. TD Aengus Ó Snodaigh admits that it might not be in the best interest of the party to do things instead of the people concerned. At most, he sees his role as mediator, with the most important aspect being the readiness of local communities to get directly involved (Ó Snodaigh, interview, 2003).

One local campaign in which Sinn Féin was involved, the anti-drugs campaign, generated significant media coverage. It started in the streets of Dublin in the early 1980s and gathered momentum in the 1990s. Indeed, the number of drug-related deaths rose sharply throughout the decade, from 7 in 1990 to 119 in 2000 (EMCDDA, 2002: 38). Sinn Féin quickly understood the potential benefits of taking part in such a campaign, as not only was it born in the constituencies where it was hoping to make its first major breakthrough, the working-class communities of the inner cities, but it also offered the possibility for Sinn Féin to get involved in an issue not associated with Northern Ireland. Local communities, feeling disempowered and let down by the police forces and local authorities, started setting up their own organisations, such as the Coalition of Communities Against Drugs, in which Sinn Féin members were said to be prominent. The campaign rapidly became tarnished with the suspicion that these groups were using heavy-handed and illegal means to reach their goals: the public naming of allegedly known drug users and pushers, and, in some cases, their forced evictions from their areas. Vigilantism was seen as an inherent part of the campaign, and showed its ugly and disturbing face in 1996 when, on 10 May, Josey Dwyer, an alleged drug dealer who was suffering from AIDS, was beaten to death in Dublin's inner city. Some commentators cast their suspicion on the IRA who, according to *Irish Times* security correspondent Jim Cusack, had been attempting to take control of certain areas, but had also interfered with witnesses of crime, in some cases threatening to shoot or kneecap[2] them (*IT*, 31 May 1996). Although these stories were difficult to corroborate, they generated a feeling of unease, and Sinn Féin was accused of exploiting the campaigns for its own ends. The party repeatedly refuted the allegations that it had any links to vigilantism. Far from denying that its members were part of the campaign, however, it explained that, as local residents affected by the drugs problems, they were getting involved in the same manner as they would in unemployment or housing campaigns. Gerry Adams exclaimed: 'You're telling me that these are all Sinn Féin members, well maybe that's because the other political parties are doing nothing' (*IT*, 30 September 1996). Sinn Féin members were indeed prominent in the marches that were organised to highlight the issue, such as the one on 27 September 1996 that drew a crowd of 3,000. The debate centred not so much around the presence of politicians (after all, Independent TD Tony Gregory also attended these marches) as around the methods used against alleged drug users and dealers. Indeed, the threats proffered against the latter were seen to be effective only insofar as they carried some weight, since they conjured up, in the minds of the potential victims, the image of armed gangs, possibly from the IRA, intervening to enforce these very threats. Anti-drugs organisations justified the presence of Sinn Féin members among their ranks by insisting that they were also members of the local communities, but were careful to stress that Sinn Féin was not behind the movements.

The discourse of Sinn Féin leaders on this issue was ambivalent. On the one hand the party was striving to present a respectable public image, so it naturally condemned any action of vigilantism, to which it professed being opposed. On the other hand, individual representatives barely concealed their support for the communities who resorted to measures which could have been deemed extreme. Gerry Adams argues that the needs of local communities are not heard enough. 'What are people to do if the agents of the state are not prepared to uphold the rights of citizens?' (Adams, interview, 2004). Therefore, although the party wants to distance itself from direct action, it also expresses a level of understanding when people take such steps. One such instance occurred in the city of Sligo in February 1999 when posters carrying the names of four alleged drug dealers were put up. The Gardai asked for the posters to be removed, since they felt their presence could hinder their own investigations. Sinn Féin Mayor Seán McManus, while stressing that Sinn Féin had 'absolutely nothing' to do with the posters, none the less empathised with such actions given what he cited as the 'lack of action against drug dealers in the town' (*IT*, 23 February 1999). This type of ambivalent response undoubtedly fed the suspicions hanging over Sinn Féin regarding its alleged role in vigilante-type attacks.

The issue came to the fore in North Kerry, when a woman was arrested coming out of Sinn Féin's office in March 2001 after having handed back stolen property. As the local Sinn Féin councillor Martin Ferris explained, a businessman had approached his office regarding the theft of his mobile phone, after having also notified the Gardai. Since the identity of the thief was known, it was possible to reclaim the phone and hand it back to its owner. This prompted the Department of Justice to order a report on Sinn Féin's activities in 'crime-solving'. A heated debate ensued, in which the Minister John O'Donoghue strongly condemned what he described as the blatant intimidation techniques used by Sinn Féin members, while Martin Ferris insisted that it was the duty of elected representatives to act on the public's behalf in tackling crime, within the legal requirements. When visiting and picketing houses to retrieve property, Sinn Féin claimed it was acting within the law. John O'Donoghue countered that, by taking the law into their own hands, Sinn Féin members were subverting law and order, and undermining the work of the Gardai (*IT*, 25 August 2001).

North Kerry Sinn Féin remained in the limelight for its alleged links to vigilantism. In November 2001, a family reported having been intimidated and threatened, and although no member of Sinn Féin was identified as actually having voiced the threats, the name of Sinn Féin had apparently been linked with this incident. In another incident, in December 2001, a man was abducted in front of his 7-year old daughter and beaten up, while his car was burnt out. A group calling itself the

Concerned Parents Against Drugs claimed responsibility for the attack, and although Sinn Féin denied having any link with them, North Kerry Sinn Féin's Director of Elections James Sheehans was arrested on 2 March 2002 as part of the investigation into the December attack. Two days later, seven men were arrested, five of them members of Sinn Féin, although they were later released without charge. When the candidate for the constituency, Martin Ferris, was himself arrested on 12 March, Sinn Féin expressed its indignation at what it viewed as a campaign of vilification aimed at scaring people away from republicans. TD Ó Caoláin spoke of 'gross interference in the democratic process' and estimated that it was no coincidence that such intimidation took place in a constituency where Sinn Féin was poised to win a seat over the Fianna Fáil candidate (*IT*, 12 March 2002). Martin Ferris was released overnight, and continued justifying Sinn Féin's role along the same line of argument. Ferris stresses that Sinn Féin does not encourage people to take action, but also admits that people come to him, sometimes out of frustration because they know the identity of the drug pushers or those who have stolen from them, but they do not know what to do. 'Victims of crime, when they know who is responsible for the crime, are frustrated' (Ferris, interview, 2003). He insists that he has always worked within the strictest legality, putting out public statements, meeting with detectives and superintendents, and calling for more Gardai resources to be made available to tackle issues of delinquency.

However much the party has denied its links to vigilantism, there is still a perception, among the media at any rate, that the IRA is directly involved in criminal activity. A programme on RTE Television, *Gangland*, broadcast on 3 November 2003, alleged that the IRA had been responsible for a number of drug-related deaths since the mid-1990s. The programme also contained an interview with a former IRA member who came to Dublin from Belfast in the 1980s and who openly admitted having taken part in activities including killings. It is difficult to verify these types of allegations, but they are nevertheless potentially damaging for the party as a whole.

Sinn Féin's policy on drugs, and its vision of the role of the community in combating this problem, has shifted since the mid-1990s. Its only policy document on drugs, *Empowering Local Communities*, was issued in October 1996, at the height of the anti-drugs campaign. It hailed movements such as Concerned Parents Against Drugs of the early 1980s as 'fine examples of local democracy at work'. The decline of such groups was due, according to this document, to the smear campaigns mounted against them by the media, the authorities and political parties, who sought to portray them as groups of 'vigilantes' and as 'Provo fronts' when, according to Sinn Féin, they were only taking their problems into their own hands. Sinn Féin did not seem to have a problem with this, but it has also reassessed its role and the methods used in the campaigns of the early 1980s. Ken Fitzgerald, a member of Concerned Parents for many years and also a member of Sinn Féin, told a local Dublin newsletter in 1996: 'we were wrong in the 1980s and so were other groups. We carried out forceful evictions. We refused Gardai access to public meetings back then. We viewed statutory authorities with suspicion and alienated sections of the media. We suffered from bad press' (*Liberty News*, March 1996). The result of Sinn Féin's reassessment of its position during the anti-drugs campaign was evident in its 2002 election manifesto, where the drugs issue, although still prominent, was tackled slightly differently, with more emphasis being put on the need for treatment and for increased resources for the police. As Adams recognises, there was a 'move from defensive neighbourhood campaigning to a political campaign which is both progressive and benevolent, in that it recognises that some drug addicts who in turn become pushers need help' (Adams, interview). This was a departure from the more extreme, less understanding views held in the 1997 manifesto. But although the issue of vigilantism brought bad publicity for the party in terms of how it was depicted in the press, it did not necessarily decrease the popularity of its North Kerry candidate. Not only was Martin Ferris elected to the Dáil in May 2002, he topped the poll in his constituency. He also attracted quite a lot of attention from the media. A Belgian reporter claimed that the international press found this part of the campaign far more exciting and newsworthy than any other aspect of the general election (*IT*, 16 May 2002). Martin Ferris concludes that 'people still vote for us. They are no longer convinced by an agenda that tries to discredit us' (Ferris, interview).

The fastest growing party in Ireland?

For campaigns to be effective, a political party needs to rely on a substantial number of volunteers willing to dedicate their time to work on the ground, work which may not always prove that rewarding. In order to sustain its campaigns, Sinn Féin needed to increase the number of constituency workers and members. The party was aware that people's political involvement, particularly in the Republic, tended to find expression not so much in political parties as within community groups. More generally, Adams admits that the appeal of Sinn Féin to potential supporters had tended to centre around key events and had, therefore, been relatively short-lived (in 1969, after internment and Bloody Sunday, during the hunger strikes). Furthermore, this type of involvement was not necessarily ideologically motivated, and as the party had not clearly identified structural roles for members to play, a lot of them left. 'We are now recruiting members on a more structured and methodical basis' (Adams, interview).

Sinn Féin sees itself, first and foremost, as a party of activists. The commitment expected from its members is quite high, as they are supposed to sell the newspaper, distribute leaflets, get involved in local campaigns and organise fund-raising and publicity events. A typical Sinn Féin member needs, therefore, to be quite dedicated, and particularly so because, before reaching this activist stage, he or she will have followed seven two-hour training sessions on issues ranging from republican principles and ideology to socialism, feminism, media awareness and historical analysis. The member's guide is a lengthy document giving the facilitators of each class quite detailed guidelines on how to approach each topic and what the learning outcome should be. It also clearly states what Sinn Féin expects from its members: activism, which translates into leafleting, postering, canvassing, attending meetings, and picketing; analysis and education, that is, reading, analysing and keeping in touch with current events; and comradeship and appropriate behaviour. In brief, potential members are supposed to acquire an 'understanding of being a republican in the community' (*Members' Guide*). Nevertheless, this commitment is probably in relatively short supply, and the party is now looking at ways of making membership less daunting and more flexible by offering the possibility of affiliate membership, or of some part-time involvement that would still give the party the manpower it needs to carry out its local and electoral campaigns.

It is difficult to establish the exact membership of Sinn Féin, as there are no statistics available, although some party spokespersons put the figure at 3,000 (Bhreatneach, interview, 2003). The party's national organiser, Pat Treanor, talks of 'approximately 5,000 members' (*AP*, 8 January 2004). Michael Pierse, who is in charge of the Membership and Education Department, points to the increase in the number of sections that have been set up in recent years throughout the island, and more specifically in areas that would have had no Sinn Féin presence before, such as Mayo or Roscommon (Pierse, interview, 2003). All cumainn send two delegates to the annual conference (Ard Fheis), which has indeed grown in size over the past decade. Nevertheless, Sinn Féin's assertion that it is 'the fastest-growing party in Ireland' is difficult to assess in the absence of hard figures. The Fine Gael leader, Enda Kenny, claimed in May 2003 that his party had gained 8,000 new members in the year since the general election (FG, PR, 6 June 2003). These figures would undeniably put Fine Gael in the position of contender for that particular title.

While growth in Sinn Féin membership is hard to assess, it would seem that support for the party has indeed increased quite substantially in the Republic over the past decade. This is measured not only in terms of the votes that Sinn Féin obtained in the May 2002 general election (see below), but also in the results of the opinion polls which show a constant growth in the number of people declaring their intention to vote for Sinn Féin. Indeed, the support for Sinn Féin in the local elections went from 3.5 per cent in 1999 to 8 per cent in 2004. A similar rise in the share of the first preference vote occurred for the European elections, the party's vote going from 6.3 per cent in 1999 to 11.1 per cent in 2004. On the other hand, the approval rating of its leader is fluctuating. Credited with an approval rating of 56 per cent when he was first measured in this type of barometer of party leaders in January 2002, Gerry Adams' rate of satisfaction had dropped quite substantially to 43 per cent in September 2002. However, Adams' popularity ratings increased to 54 per cent in February 2004, making him the leader with the highest popularity rating at the time.

Opinion polls reveal an interesting profile of Sinn Féin voters. More than twice as many men as women are likely to vote for Sinn Féin, which, for some observers like former Taoiseach Garret Fitzgerald, is hardly surprising, given that 'most women are more queasy than men about anything associated with violence' (*IT*, 3 November 2001). There may be another, more pragmatic explanation for this, namely that women identify less with Sinn Féin because it is still perceived as a male-dominated party. However, the party's efforts to enhance its profile in the field of gender equality in the last decade of the twentieth century might contribute to alter this perception (see Chapter 4). But the other dominant characteristic of Sinn Féin voters is that a substantial proportion of them are young. One survey, carried out in Dublin South West in April 2001, showed that, among those who were intending to vote for Sinn Féin, 27 per cent were among the 18 to 24-year-old group, and 29 per cent were aged between 25 and 34 (in national terms, the 19 to 34 age group represents 25 per cent of the population (*IT*, 21 April 2001)). These findings were consistent with those of a survey carried out in July 2000, which showed that, out of the 447 young people interviewed as part of the Decode Youth Lifestyle Research Programme, 22 per cent stated they would vote for the government parties, and 14 per cent for Sinn Féin (*IT*, 27 July 2000). The following year, a survey in January showed that support for Sinn Féin among young people had risen to 22 per cent, while Fianna Fáil was still ahead in their voting intentions with 34 per cent. These figures raise a number of questions. Why would young people who had grown up in the years of the Celtic Tiger be attracted to a party strongly associated with working-class politics? Why would a party with such a strong tie to the north and its conflict have any appeal to a generation who had grown up quite removed from that experience? According to *Irish Times* columnist Fintan O'Toole, it is precisely because they did not 'remember the vicious mass murders. . . . Gerry Adams and Martin McGuinness are not apologists for sickening atrocities but calm, reasonable, earnest men who talk about peace' (*IT*, 13 January 2001).

Such a statement, however emotional, did seem to convey that the new image which the party was seeking to put across was increasingly successful. But there are perhaps other explanations. Sinn Féin's involvement in local communities, and particularly with the drugs issue, responded to the preoccupations of young people, who quoted that particular problem as their primary concern, along with crime and suicide (*IT*, 11 January 2001).

Sinn Féin's appeal to the younger generation of Irish voters led, in 1997, to the creation of a section of the party dedicated to the 16 to 27 age group. Obviously, Sinn Féin is not the only party to have a specific youth branch. This group was initially set up by Eoin Ó Broin, who had closely studied the Basque Youth Movement, and saw the potential for giving youth a platform and a voice. It also drew from the experience of the 1997 general election in the north, where the strategy of the 'youth canvass' had been put into practice, consisting of targeting young people at the doorsteps during election campaigns. From the data gathered, it became apparent that there was an important number of first-time voters who would get involved in politics if they had the right organisation to join. From then on, a 'Winter School' was organised in Belfast, with workshops on mural paintings, banner- and stencil-making, press and publicity skills, to give the younger activists training and hands-on experience. But there was also a radical edge in this youth movement, articulated by Eoin Ó Broin at the first national conference in November 1997: 'The leadership, whether at a local or national level, must realise that the time when young people can be told what to do is over' (*AP*, 13 November 1997).

Sinn Féin Youth's links with the party were formalised at the 1998 Ard Fheis, although it kept a degree of autonomy, viewed as crucial by the youth leaders. The following year it adopted its new name, Ógra Sinn Féin, and strongly advocated a link between 'personal independence and national independence', the personal element having a strong appeal for those at the crossroads between adolescence and adulthood. Ógra Sinn Féin has a representation of fifteen delegates at the Ard Fheis and has a member on the Ard Comhairle. It campaigns on issues such as anti-racism and drugs, which, while not necessarily linked to traditional republican themes, are seen as essential to sustain young people's interest in politics. However, it would appear that the movement has not been capable of maintainig its initial momentum. According to a study carried out by the *Irish Times* in October 2003, the number of Sinn Féin members in third-level institutions has dropped. This survey contradicted the view expressed by the party's headquarters that numbers were growing, but the findings were confirmed by student union leaders, who stated that 'campus Sinn Féin membership is dropping and [that] the party's visibility is greater than its activities deserve' (*IT*, 28 October 2003). As Sinn Féin does not produce definitive figures regarding its membership, its claim to be 'the fastest-growing party in Ireland' is difficult to corroborate.

Breakthrough? The 2002 general election

Sinn Féin entered the 2002 general election campaign with a high level of enthusiasm, a large number of hard-working activists, and relatively low expectations (at least according to public statements). Having only one incumbent TD seeking re-election, any seat gained would be portrayed, and possibly perceived, as a victory. Indeed, the party's president was quite modest in his objectives, talking of the possibility of winning only three seats, and jokingly adding that, obviously, five would be even better. This public reticence may well have been a deliberate electoral strategy.

The manner in which the candidates were chosen for the 2002 general election campaign, and the constituencies in which they were fielded, were carefully decided upon following a close study of the potential Sinn Féin vote, based on the previous election performance. Some constituencies are traditionally sympathetic to republican ideals, such as the border counties (Louth and Monaghan being the most obvious examples) and some regions in the west, such as North Kerry. The second biggest bastion of Sinn Féin voters is the cities, and specifically the working-class areas. Some constituencies were therefore targeted to receive more intense campaigning: North Kerry, where local councillor Martin Ferris had come close to winning a seat in 1997, and Dublin South Central, where a by-election in October 1999 gave the Sinn Féin candidate 8.3 per cent of the vote. In all, thirty-seven candidates were fielded, eight of whom were local councillors and one of whom was already sitting in the Dáil. Being a relatively recent contender in national elections, Sinn Féin is at a disadvantage when it comes to gaining media attention for its candidates, as they do not benefit from the high public-office profile of candidates in other parties. For instance, out of Fianna Fáil's 106 candidates, only seven were not office-holders. Of the 463 candidates put forward for election, ninety-seven were first-time candidates (Gallagher *et al.*, 2003: 41). A closer look at Sinn Féin's candidates also reveals a gender imbalance: only 19 per cent of them were women, which was in keeping with the national average, but which rated poorly when compared with the Greens (29 per cent) and the PDs (30 per cent) (Gallagher *et al.*, 2003: 50).

The bulk of the campaigning, as with other parties, was carried out by local activists, and, given the fact that Sinn Féin's work is very much community-based, this undoubtedly gave the party an advantage over its adversaries. But the unique feature of the party's campaign was that its best-known leaders were not candidates in the election. Indeed, Gerry Adams, who is the undisputed leader of Sinn Féin, was fighting an election in which he had no individual stake. This gave him, as well as Martin

McGuinness and other northerners who regularly came in to support the candidates, an advantage, insofar as they were not directly answerable to the constituencies in which they were canvassing. Furthermore, Sinn Féin was the only party, apart from the Greens, not to have any government experience, and was therefore able to maintain quite a dogmatic line on essential issues, free from the burden of having to prove their track record. In other words, the campaign was typically that of an opposition party that was not seeking – and was not likely to gain – power for the immediate future.

The outcome of the election was better for Sinn Féin than had been predicted, and the results were reasonably in line with what the polls had been forecasting in the previous months. Sinn Féin obtained 6.5 per cent of the national vote, and five of its candidates were elected, two in Dublin, one in North Kerry, and two in border counties (Louth and Monaghan). Of these five candidates, three topped the poll, which added to the general feel-good factor among republicans. Furthermore, the overall result was considered promising for the party's prospects in future elections. Four of its unsuccessful candidates won more than half the quota of first preference votes, indicating, in those constituencies (Dublin North West, Dublin Central, Meath and Sligo/Leitrim) a strength and a potential that could be built upon.

Exit polls confirmed that the bulk of Sinn Féin voters were to be found in two categories: the young (18 to 24 years old), of which 14.5 per cent had voted for the party (its single biggest cohort), and the working class, of which 10.3 per cent had voted for Sinn Féin, just behind the Labour Party (with 11.9 per cent). Nevertheless, these two particular groups are slightly problematic as there tend to be more abstentions among their ranks, with 59.5 per cent and 45.7 per cent respectively (Gallagher *et al.*, 2003: 151). Indeed, a poll carried out for the National Youth Council of Ireland in October 1999 showed that two-thirds of first-time voters did not vote in the 1999 European and local elections, the main reasons quoted being that they were not registered, too busy or not interested (*IT*, 28 October 1999). The exit polls also showed that there were boundaries that Sinn Féin had not yet managed to cross: only 4.5 per cent of middle-class electors had voted for its candidates, and only 2.4 per cent of farmers had given their first preference to Sinn Féin, which would tend to show that the party is still very much an urban phenomenon, although Martin Ferris insists that Sinn Féin has 'strong support across the whole spectrum, rural and urban' (Ferris, interview). Although this indicates that the short-term strategy of the party seems to be to build on its existing strength, it also points to the limitations in the Sinn Féin vote and to the necessity for the party to rethink both its strategy and possible ways of optimising its vote. Moreover, the issues that were quoted by the electorate as being decisive for voting Sinn Féin were quite limited in their scope. The drugs issue was at the top of the list (16.3 per cent), followed by housing (11.7 per cent). At the other end of the spectrum were broader concerns such as the economy (5.3 per cent) and the cost of living (6.1 per cent) Based on these findings, Sinn Féin still has some work to do in order to convince a larger audience that it is an alternative to the major parties, and that it is not simply a party restricted to local and specific issues, however important these are to the people most affected by them. In the 2004 local elections, Sinn Féin succeeded in increasing its share of the first preference vote, which indicated that the results of the 2002 general election were not simply a transient phenomenon. The party's gains could quite obviously be measured in terms of seats, as the party more than doubled its representation on local councils, going from 23 seats in 1999 to 52 in 2004. But equally important perhaps were the lessons that could be drawn from such results. According to some estimates, those votes, if repeated in a Dáil election, would have translated into 14 or 15 seats for Sinn Féin, a scenario which would undoubtedly present a major challenge for the Republic's main parties. Sinn Féin's gains were in great part obtained at the expense of Fianna Fáil. However, as Secretary General Robbie Smyth conceded, 'they have been thinking long term, almost as long term as we have. They were ready to weather this storm. They have been saving a war chest' (*IT*, 14 June 2004).

The party occupies a unique position in Republic of Ireland politics, in that it is competing on two different levels with two different political parties: it is fighting for the republican vote, which, until recently, has been almost exclusively associated with Fianna Fáil, and for the socialist vote, traditionally represented by the Labour Party. But one of the biggest problems facing Sinn Féin in this battle is the transfer of votes. The results of the 2002 general election indicated that most transfers from Sinn Féin candidates tended to benefit both Fianna Fáil and the Labour Party, but the opposite was not the case. Therefore, this raises the question as to whether Sinn Féin has reached a ceiling in its potential growth. The Labour Party, while admitting that Sinn Féin inflicted some damage in the last election, taking two of its safe seats, one in North Kerry and one in Louth that will be 'difficult to take back', is confident that this trend will not continue. 'For the time being, they have done us as much damage as they can' (Finlay, interview, 2004). The next general election will undoubtedly show whether Sinn Féin can find new ways of making inroads into an electorate which still seems hesitant to place its confidence in a party that is still seen by many as being only 'slightly constitutional'.

4   The equality agenda

'Equality is the most important word in the republican vocabulary.' This priority, articulated by party President Gerry Adams at the 2003 Ard Fheis, could be seen as a departure for a party that was, for decades, focused on the national question and reunification which constituted the main dynamics behind Sinn Féin's struggle. Although these objectives were linked, in republican rhetoric, to the achievement of a just and equal society, the mechanisms by which they would be attained were, for years, not thoroughly spelt out or thought through. But in the twenty-first century Sinn Féin's focus has been altered, and the party strives to be seen as a truly socialist organisation.

Socialist republicanism

Republicans contend that inequalities persist in the Republic of Ireland, in spite of the recent economic boom that was baptised the Celtic Tiger. They attribute the main cause of this to the economic model that underlies the prosperity, one which is thought to be unsustainable. Justin Moran, parliamentary assistant to Sinn Féin's Dublin South West TD Sean Crowe, considers that 'the type of jobs that are being created by multinational corporations, who will leave when the situation is no longer profitable, are not unionised' (Moran, interview, 2003). Republicans also sharply criticise the failure of successive governments, be they Fianna Fáil- or Fine Gael-led, and with or without the collaboration of the Labour Party, to make the fight against poverty and destitution a priority. Sinn Féin goes even further, estimating that inequalities have worsened since the newly achieved prosperity of the nation (Sinn Féin Manifesto, 2002: 1). Its policy document, *No Right Turn: Sinn Féin's Call to Action Against the Privatisation of Ireland*, identifies this trend in Ireland as 'an agenda [which] represents a very negative development in Irish politics and will exacerbate the problems of gross inequality and injustice that exist in the State already' (*No Right Turn*, 2003: 3). The economic indicators that placed Ireland at the top of the league of EU countries at the end of the millennium are not sufficient evidence, according to Sinn Féin's analysis, of the economic success of the country. On the contrary, the fact that in spite of the spectacular growth rates which have been achieved over the last decade of the twentieth century,[1] the gap between rich and poor has increased, poverty is rampant and the number of children living beneath the poverty line has also increased, is ascribed to the missed opportunities on the part of successive governments to correct injustices. When launching his party's electoral manifesto for the 2002 general election, Adams enumerated what he viewed as the main social problems in Ireland. Those were: a quarter of children and one-fifth of adults living in households with half the average income; the crisis in the healthcare system; the most unequal distribution of wealth of all industrialised states outside the USA, and the over-representation of women among those on minimum wage and part-time work (Adams, PR, 23 March 2002: 4). One of the party's objectives is to 'eliminate poverty', which is analysed as a 'persistent condition associated with unfettered market economies. It also arises out of the failure of the state structures to plan development' (*Eliminating Poverty: A 21st Century Goal*, 2004: 2). The recommendations listed in this policy document include more spending on social inclusion, higher powers given to the Equality Commission and a human rights approach to the combat against poverty. Sinn Féin's analysis is totally incompatible with that of the Progressive Democrats, one of the parties in the Fianna Fail-led government elected in 2002: Minister for Justice Michael McDowell contended, on the contrary, that 'A dynamic economy like ours demands flexibility and inequality in some respects to function', adding that such inequality 'provides incentives' (*IT*, 28 May 2004).

Sinn Féin points to the state of the public sector, and particularly that of the health services, as proof of the failure of the state to tackle issues that affect, primarily, the most vulnerable sections of society. Indeed, state investments in the newly achieved prosperity have been sparse. A study of the Celtic Tiger points to the fact that Ireland was the only state in the EU whose public expenditures were less than 40 per cent of the GDP, and concludes that 'successive administrations in Dublin drew away from providing public services and public welfare in the 1990s in favour of providing tax breaks that favoured the richer segments of Irish society' (Coulter and Coleman, 2003: 48). In Sinn Féin's view, only a complete overhaul of the economic and social structures will lead the country forward on its road to equality. This means opposing all attempts at privatising public services such as transport or health. The proposals of the party in this regard are quite straightforward: massive state investment in essential public services to make them accessible to all; free healthcare, free education and a better distribution of wealth through an overhaul of the current taxation system. This, obviously, is at odds with the policies of the Irish government, which has maintained tax cuts and low expenditure as the key to economic success. It is thus not surprising that leaders such as Progressive Democrat Mary Harney sharply criticise these proposals: calling Sinn Féin's economic proposals 'extremely left-wing policies that have been abandoned by others', she forecast that 'their economic policies would destroy the country and the economy and create huge unemployment again. They are very anti-foreign investment, they want huge corporate taxes' (5 June 2001).[2] Sinn Féin General Secretary Robbie Smyth replies that his party has 'no problem with foreign investment, but there needs to be more interaction with the host communities, and the investors need to be made aware of their responsibilities' (Smyth, interview, 2003).

Sinn Féin criticises its main rival on the left, the Labour Party, for what it perceives as its increasing shift to more liberal policies: 'in a move to capture working-class votes, Labour has ceased to be a campaigning party. In the last election, as it had a realistic opportunity to overtake Fine Gael, it moved to the right. In this process, it has lost votes and even seats to Sinn Féin in many working-class areas' (Moran, interview). The type of socialism that is advocated by Sinn Féin does not belong to any particular school, the main reference being to James Connolly and to a native historical line that goes back to the 1916 Proclamation. In some way, socialism is presented as being synonymous with republicanism, and therefore there is no perceived need to theorise or to have any external references. But if the avowed aim of Sinn Féin has been, since the early 1960s, the establishment of a thirty-two-county socialist republic, the party's relationship with that particular ideology has been, over the past forty years, somewhat ambivalent. There were several reasons why socialism was not, per se, the ideology that best suited the nationalist struggle waged by republicans. First and foremost, any analysis of the northern conflict in terms of class struggle was seen as divisive, and could in itself jeopardise the ultimate aim of reunification. This is precisely what most divided Officials and Provisionals in the 1969 split. Early day Provisionals considered sectarianism to be the main divisive factor and saw little merit in the Official objective of uniting the working class. This type of rhetoric was even deemed counterproductive as it was seen as comforting the partitionist analysis. To some extent, the type of socialism advocated by those who sought to unite the working class beyond the sectarian divide was seen almost as revisionist and counter-revolutionary, since it proposed to correct inequalities through the state and its institutions. Furthermore, socialism was far from being a consensual ideology in a movement which brought together people from very different cultural, social and economic backgrounds. In an interview with the magazine *Hibernian* in 1979, Gerry Adams was careful to point to the fact that Sinn Féin was not a Marxist organisation, although he recognised the same year that 'we must ensure that the cause of Ireland becomes the cause of Labour, a cause neglected since Connolly's time' (*AP*, 23 June 1979). Finally, there was a fear among republicans that socialism would jeopardise the military option by taking first place in the republican objectives. This was based on the numerous experiences within the movement which had seen the IRA cast aside when the socialist analysis prevailed, particularly in the 1960s, when the Officials identified one of the main factors which prevented the ultimate objective of unifying the proletariat as being, precisely, armed struggle. Reliance on IRA campaigns, however, led to a neglect of politics, making Sinn Féin come across as an apolitical grouping whose focus was mainly, if not exclusively, on direct action.

Although the objective of the Provisionals was the establishment of a thirty-two-county socialist republic, socialism was not a term that was used frequently in the 1970s and 1980s. Former chief-of-staff Seán MacStiofáin's vision of socialism was quite blunt:

> Certainly as revolutionaries we were automatically anti-capitalists. But we refused to have anything to do with any communist organisation in Ireland; on the basis of their ineffectiveness, their reactionary foot-dragging on the national question and their opposition to armed struggle. We opposed the extreme socialism of the revisionists (Officials) because we believed that its aim was a Marxist dictatorship, which would be no more acceptable to us than British imperialism or Free State capitalism.
>
> (MacStiofáin, 135)

MacStiofáin could have been considered more reactionary than other fellow travellers such as Ruairí Ó Brádaigh and Daithí Ó Conaill who were undoubtedly more forthcoming in their espousal of socialism. Nevertheless, the analysis of the 1980s still prioritised the national question and positioned socialism in the background. Tom Hartley, then General Secretary, was pragmatic in his approach, stating that 'you limit your appeal if you base it on socialism. You have to prioritise what is required to get rid of partition. We want to bring the struggle to a conclusion. Will you do that on a socialist basis or on a broader basis?' (Hartley, interview, 1987). Gerry Adams had already answered that question in 1986: 'I don't think that socialism is on the agenda at this stage, except for political activists of the left. What's on the agenda is an end to partition. You won't get near socialism until you have national independence. It's a prerequisite' (*IT*, 10 December 1986).

The discourse in the following years shifted more progressively to the left, and Sinn Féin started to affirm more confidently its commitment to socialist ideals. More than that, it sought to present itself as the only real left-wing party in Ireland. Sinn Féin had identified a niche on both sides of the border and was seeking to occupy it. This probably corresponded to a change of dynamics within the party which meant that socialism was now an acceptable credo. But the peace process also made more tangible the conviction that the end of partition was in sight and that the time for socialist policies had, indeed, come.

There is little doubt that the end of the armed struggle and the IRA ceasefires paved the way for a more openly socialist-based view. Nowadays, republican leaders and thinkers are confident enough to put forward a class analysis. Republicans insist that Sinn Féin must retain its working-class focus and identity if it is serious about delivering equality to those it represents. 'We can't change to attract the middle-classes. Forty per cent of those who didn't vote [in the 2002 general election] were from working-class backgrounds. We can attract them' (Moran, interview).

Sinn Féin presents itself as a party well equipped to combat social injustices. Its reasons for doing so are both ideological and pragmatic. Its self-avowed lack of political cynicism is expressed in statements such as that made by Adams when presenting O'Caoláin's candidacy to the 2002 general elections. In a nutshell, Sinn Féin is not concerned with the 'trappings of office or politics of self interest' (PR, 23 March 2002) and is thus combating injustices in an almost selfless capacity. To support this, republicans quote the reputation that they have earned throughout their constituencies, that of hard-working, dedicated and earnest politicians (Ó Broin, interview, 2003). However, republican representatives have a tendency, at times, to project their party as the only one doing work on the ground and showing an interest in local or deprived communities. According to Martina Anderson, the party's All-Ireland Coordinator, 'no one has a strategy of targeting the most deprived and areas of disadvantage. There is no evidence of any other party going into the community and working with them, going around, knocking on doors, outside of election times' (Anderson, interview, 2003). Sinn Féin's presence within the communities and the visibility that its representatives have been able to maintain on the issue of drugs has indeed been seen as one of the main factors which explain its electoral successes, according to Fianna Fáil Dublin South-West TD Brian Lenihan (interview, 2003). But this does not mean that Sinn Féin is the only party involved in local issues. For instance, during the 'bin charges'[3] campaign that took place in Dublin in October 2003, the most visible politicians on the ground were not only from Sinn Féin; those who were actually imprisoned alongside their constituents for refusing to pay the bin charges were from the Socialist Party, which would tend to indicate, as former French presidential candidate Valéry Giscard d'Estaing eloquently put it to his socialist adversary François Mitterrand in a televised debate in 1974, that Sinn Féin does not have 'the monopoly of the heart'.

Nevertheless, Sinn Féin does see itself as the party of the oppressed, and it has forged an image of itself as the political organisation in Ireland which has suffered most from discrimination and oppression. The fact that the party has, in some respects, not only survived against difficult odds, but also overcome this oppression and achieved a degree of political, social and cultural recognition at home and abroad, testifies in the republican analysis to the resilience of Sinn Féin and to its capacity to combat the oppression of others. Because of this perceived experience, Sinn Féin sees itself as the champion of those fighting against all types of injustice, no matter what their nature may be. This is stated bluntly in Sinn Féin's policy document on gays, lesbians and bisexuals:

> republicans are only too well aware of what it means to be treated as second-class citizens. Our politics are the result of decades of resistance to marginalisation and discrimination. Self-determination is our core demand, not only as a nation, but also as diverse communities within that nation. When confronted with experiences which are similar to our own (such as those of ethnic minorities, Travellers, women etc) it should be automatic for us, as republicans, to understand and actively express that understanding through solidarity. The denial of justice from one section of this nation is a denial of the rights of us all.
>
> (*Moving On*, n.d.)

Nevertheless, this type of rhetoric is problematic, since minorities do not necessarily share the same experience when it comes to discrimination. As the Editor of the Dublin weekly *Gay Community News* puts it, 'my experience as a middle-class, Dublin homosexual has nothing in common with that of a Northern nationalist' (Finnegan, interview, 2003).

Another important reason why Sinn Féin deems itself well equipped to fight inequalities is that it claims to be the heir of a long line of democratic and egalitarian thinkers. It therefore frequently goes back to its history and to its forefather, Theobald Wolfe Tone, in order to justify its credentials as the party of equals. Former Campaigns Coordinator Jim Gibney states that what distinguishes republicanism from other ideologies, and from unionism in particular, is that it is 'a democratic, open tradition'. He refutes the argument that the very presence of the IRA within the history of republicanism contributed to cast a shadow on this democratic lineage: 'the IRA have made a significant contribution to try and establish a democratic tradition on this island. Catholics and nationalists would still be treated as second-class citizens if it wasn't for the IRA' (Gibney, interview, 2003).

But resorting to this type of rhetoric may not be sufficiently convincing to those who doubt Sinn Féin's democratic and socialist pedigree. The fact that it saw the role of the republican movement as that of defending one minority in the north does not necessarily make this transfer to society at large as clear-cut as presented by Gibney. Furthermore, these credentials seem flawed to those who see Sinn Féin as a party that has had no record, until recently, of fighting injustices, and for whom armed strategies are inherently contradictory with democratic and equalitarian politics. The most acerbic criticism comes from those who see the republicanism embodied by Sinn Féin not as a socialist ideology, but as a confederacy of nationalists and populists. This is how the former leader of the Progressive Democrats Des O'Malley described them: 'Sinn Fein is certainly nationalist on political matters. But it is decidedly socialist on economic matters. It seems to me that the party could be described as embracing what might be called national socialism. They hate those who disagree with them' (O'Malley, 2000: 3). Going one step further, Ian Paisley warned that the final objective of republicanism was 'the triumph of fascism' (*IT*, 5 July 2000). But while this type of rhetoric is not unusual emanating from the DUP leader, it is also to be found in some left-wing quarters. Former SDLP MP for West Belfast, Joe Hendron, talked of Sinn Féin being 'a fascist organisation' (*IT*, 29 May 1996). In the run-up to the 2002 general election in the Republic, former Labour Party leader Ruairí Quinn attempted to link Sinn Féin with extreme-right parties such as the French National Front. In an interview with the *Observer*, Quinn stated that 'they are an extreme nationalist party. They are not a socialist party and a vote for men like Ferris is like a vote for Le Pen,' adding that Sinn Féin's nationalism was 'part of the extreme European tradition which has given us civil wars, international wars and xenophobia' (*Observer*, 12 May 2002). However, for journalist Niall Stanage, this argument did not hold much sway: 'the attack failed, largely because it was seen as absurd. Sinn Féin is supportive of asylum seekers' rights, for example – a stance that has contributed to containing the growing racism of recent years' (*Guardian*, 21 May 2002). Therefore, a closer scrutiny of the party's track record on the fight for gender equality and against racism can contribute to assessing to what extent the party is genuinely committed to egalitarian policies or whether this is a façade in its strive for legitimacy.

Gender and nationalism

Gender equality is defined as a fundamental principle within Sinn Féin's republicanism. Indeed, it is probably the issue that comes up most regularly, and that triggers the most passionate debates within Sinn Féin when discussing the broader context of equality. The party is keen to be seen as moving actively on this issue and taking what it sees as the necessary steps in order to become a gender-balanced party, both in terms of policies and structures and in terms of membership and leadership. At the 2003 Ard Fheis, for instance, the Constitution was amended in order to introduce a measure of positive discrimination, reserving four seats on the governing body, the Ard Comhairle, to women. A system of quotas had been in place up until then, but this only allowed women to be co-opted and did not automatically guarantee them a seat on the Ard Comhairle.

The manner in which Sinn Féin has dealt with women's issues throughout the years is both common to other political organisations in Ireland and particular to its own history. On the one hand, the legacy of colonialism and nationalism has had an impact on the overall attitude to women, which has resulted in a tendency towards a patriarchal model of society (Meaney, 1991: 5). This has contributed to the sidelining of women's issues and of their participation in the overall political process. On the other hand, the fact that republicanism went hand in hand with armed struggle, which was, for most of its history, an area dominated by men (but does not mean that women did not play an active part in that struggle), has led to some structural imbalances and to a skewed perception of the role of women within the movement as a whole. In the early 1980s, however, Sinn Féin started embracing women's issues, which corresponded to a growing grassroots demand for equality and a recognition that emancipation had to encompass the struggle for gender equality. This trend was not particular to Sinn Féin, as academic Jon Lovenduski noted; in the early 1980s, feminist and women's organisations began to reconsider the importance of mainstream politics and to become more actively engaged within political parties. This, in turn, led political organisations to expand their programmes 'to include policies on equal opportunities and reproductive rights, as well as to revise traditional party positions on family policy to take into account new understandings of gender and power' (Lovenduski and Norris, 1993: 2).

Women have played a significant role within the Republican Movement, but they were not portrayed as being at the forefront of the national struggle. For years, the IRA had a women's component, Cumann na mBan, which was organised separately but came under the orders of the Army Council. Women took part in the 1916 Rising and in the Civil War, they experienced incarceration and went on hunger strike. The politics of this organisation were, at times, 'radical', as former IRA prisoner Ella O'Dwyer would choose to describe them (O'Dwyer, 2003: 3), or 'intransigent', the term preferred by academic Bowyer Bell. Indeed, 416 of its members voted against the 1921 Treaty as opposed to sixty-three in favour (Bowyer Bell, 1983: 55). Cumman na mBan then embarked on a pamphlet-writing campaign in the late 1920s which aimed to subvert the loyalties of the Free State Army and police. This group was eventually incorporated into the mainstream of the IRA after 1977,[4] and from then on, women volunteers operated alongside their male colleagues in the Provisional IRA.

The role of women in republican history was nevertheless obscured by the more publicised and more obvious role that men played. As O'Dwyer notes, 'the Republican movement, like all other microcosms of society, reflects the kind of gender inequality that has restricted women's political participation over generations' (O'Dwyer, 2003: 2). The names of some heroic feminine figures are quoted by the party to underline the essential contribution of women over the years. One such figure was Constance Markievicz, who was the only woman in the First Dáil, and was also Minister for Labour from 1919 to 1921.[5] Nevertheless, there is no record of any woman in a commanding position within the IRA. In the public perception, women were often relegated to more traditional roles, that of being the so-called backbone of the struggle. When the armed campaign was at the forefront of the movement's strategies, Sinn Féin was the forum where women could play a role. Indeed, the party can even boast to have been the first political organisation in Ireland to have had a woman president, in the 1940s, when the Republican Movement was going through what was probably its darkest period in history. Margaret Buckley, who had taken part in the 1916 Rising and had acted briefly as a judge in the Republican courts established by Dáil Éireann, took over the leadership of the party. Former Sinn Féin President Ruairí Ó Brádaigh conceded that it was not much of a party. In fact, 'Mrs Buckley was Sinn Féin' (Ó Brádaigh, interview, 1985). Her contribution was short lived, since when the party was reorganised in 1948, she stepped down. Before her, Mary McSwiney, sister of dead hunger striker Terence McSwiney,[6] had played an important role within the ranks of republicanism, being one of the only spokespersons of the movement in the late 1920s and 1930s, albeit strongly disapproved of and eventually isolated within her own organisation.[7] It was not until the 1970s that another woman came to a position of prominence within Sinn Féin, when Maire Drumm, wife of veteran republican Jimmy Drumm, became Vice-president of the party from 1970 until she stepped down in 1976.[8] Sinn Féin follows a well-documented pattern within Irish politics, where access to the political sphere for women is still strongly linked to their family connections. According to the National Women's Council of Ireland, 'almost 45 per cent of all serving women TDs come from families where male relatives had previous experience as TDs, senators or local councillors' (NWCI, 2002: 4). Nevertheless, the contribution of these women to the movement's past and recent history is beyond doubt, although their role was overshadowed by that played by their male relatives.

It was the prison protests and the hunger strikes that substantially highlighted the role that women had been playing within the ranks of the Republican Movement. They were no longer seen only as the backbone of resistance, providing the logistical and emotional support to the struggle on the ground; they were fighters in their own right, taking chances, willing to risk their freedom and their lives for the same cause. Three women prisoners went on hunger strike in Armagh Prison in October

1980. Former prisoner and hunger striker Lawrence McKeown wrote his Ph.D. thesis on the issue of the prison struggle. His conclusions on the gender issue are quite startling. According to him, women who ended up in prison were deemed doubly guilty – 'not only had they broken the laws of the state but they had also gone against their feminine gender roles as defined by society' (McKeown, 1999, available online). The role of women was also highlighted by the campaign they waged outside the prison in support of the prisoners' demands. When the women in Armagh announced that they would go on hunger strike, they received a lukewarm response from their male counterparts. Some of them found it difficult to let the 'wee lassies' embark on such a protest, while others thought that playing on the kind of stereotypical images linking women and physical weakness could garner more support and thus bring a more rapid conclusion to the protest. According to McKeown, 'discussion on the issue, however, had raised questions about just what role women should or could play within the struggle, what relations men had with those women in the struggle and what relations men had with their female relatives, be they mothers, sisters, wives, partners' (McKeown, 1999). In some way, the prison experience meant that men started questioning not only their perception of women, but more fundamentally perhaps, their masculinity and the role that they had assigned themselves within the struggle, and they seemed more prepared, some at least, to challenge fundamental notions such as power and authority. Classes in women's studies were organised and attended by a sizeable portion of the male prisoners. 'The results of my study showed that the course had been a tremendous success and that it raised more questions than answers – which is what most men attended for. It put a focus onto masculinity and the role that it played in our lives in an all-male society and in our relations with women' (McKeown, 1999).

While the prison experience certainly played an important role in raising awareness among a number of inmates, it is probably more difficult to extrapolate this process to the Republican Movement as a whole. There were other factors that contributed to bringing women's issues to the fore, and that changed the perception of women as being, at best, a support group to the struggle, but at worst, simply invisible. Indeed, the issues which faced women in Northern Ireland were intricately linked to the conflict: 'women have suffered from political neglect, poverty and violence, and have had to deal with three areas: bread and butter issues, political stalemate and violence and, finally and whenever possible, doing what was good for them' (in Roulston and Davies, 2001: 20). Rooney identifies two main reasons for women's invisibility in the political sphere. First, they have often been characterised as being apart from the conflict, in that they were not seen as playing an active part in it. Furthermore, the feminist agenda was often overtaken by the divisive nature of the political situation. Therefore, 'the dominance of masculinity, and masculine meanings and material power and advantages over women, are not on the mainstream negotiating agendas in the north of Ireland' (in Roulston and Davies, 2001: 176).

Within Sinn Féin, the notion of putting women's issues to the fore was met by a level of resistance in some quarters. There was a traditionalist and probably even patriarchal tendency within the movement, which coexisted, on the other end of the spectrum, with a radical voice which was seeking change and recognition. These potential conflicts were compounded by the belief that any issue that was not directly linked to the national question was a diversion from the struggle and thus had to be set aside, at least until the main objective had been achieved. Nevertheless, the contradiction that this inevitably entailed did not escape leaders and members alike, who progressively started recognising that self-determination could not only be limited to a territorial or institutional aspiration. It had to embrace all sections of the population, and women's demands were an important dimension of this process.

The 1980s saw the emergence of women's centres, mainly in working-class urban areas of the main cities (Roulston and Davies, 2000: 14). Parallel to this development, Sinn Féin established a Women's Department in 1982, in order to promote the role of women within the movement and society at large. This was in reply to an increasingly militant rank and file among women, who were working closely, especially in the north, with other women's groups and organisations. It was around this time that the links between progressive and until then parallel struggles were identified, and mergers sought between feminism and republicanism. For a long time, feminists, especially in Northern Ireland, saw the two struggles as separate. To embrace the cause of republicanism was, for them, to rein force the divisions that were already fuelled not only by the influence of the Church but by the sectarian nature of the state. This was deemed not to serve women's interests, which were seen primarily as the achievement of equal status within society, in terms of equal pay and equal opportunities, and contraception. As the issues that concerned women were similar across the dividing line of sectarianism, feminism was seen as a vehicle for cross-community cooperation and possible unity. For this reason, there was at times a clash between the support for women's causes and that for republicanism. This came to the fore during the campaign to stop the strip searches in Armagh Prison in the mid-1980s, where women inmates were submitted to thorough and degrading body searches on their way to and from visits. Although the issue was clearly identified by Sinn Féin as constituting an infringement of women's rights and a violence enacted upon their bodies, feminists found it difficult to get involved (Roulston and Davies, 2000: 177).

This perception gradually began to change, as some feminists saw the exclusion of republicanism from feminism as damaging to women's causes. One such thinker was Geraldine Meany who wrote in 1991:

> Instead of increasing the isolation of republican women and pushing them further into a ghetto where violence is the only form of political expression left, there is an obligation to enter into some kind of dialogue. Instead of lecturing Republican women on their political and moral failings as women, we might pause to listen. Perhaps they could teach us to address those women for whom the myth of Mother Ireland is still a powerful enchantment.
>
> (Meany, 1991: 13)

Although she conceded that 'feminism has reason to fear hijacking by nationalist and republican groups', she added that 'it cannot allow that fear to paralyse it'. On the republican side, some changes were also beginning to emerge, with republican women seeking a merger of their agenda with that of feminism. In 1994, the first umbrella group of republican women organised a conference that was attended by both feminists and republicans, Clár na mBan (A Woman's Agenda for Peace), which began as an informal gathering and was founded largely in response to the fear that the peace process would sideline women. Nevertheless, the philosophy of a specific women's group ran contrary to the republican belief that women's emancipation could come about only if explicitly linked to the overall struggle. According to one of the leading voices of Clár na mBan, Claire Hackett, 'for women the attempt to reach an area where we can all agree and unite is understandable as an effort to find a strong voice in an oppressive society. But it is ultimately destructive because it leads to the suppression of difference' (Hackett, 1995: 112). She warned that both struggles could not be mutually exclusive, because 'neither struggle is complete if it ignores the claims of the other. However, we still have to fight for the legitimacy of our priorities not only in Irish society generally but also within the women's movement and the broad republican movement.' Indeed, the advent of such an agenda within the Republican Movement attracted the criticism of some, because of the well-established fear that any issue not directly connected to the national agenda could prove divisive, but also because 'feminists challenging the republican movement from within are often seen to be disloyal, to be breaking ranks which need to be solid in order to be strong' (Hackett, 1995: 113).

It had indeed emerged a few years previously that the area of women's demands could prove a divisive one, as it highlighted the internal contradictions of the movement and its somewhat heterogeneous composition. In this regard, no issue illustrated better the opposing views of republicans than that of women's right to choose in the case of abortion. The ambivalence and contradictions that emerged when the debate was first launched, and that were still not entirely resolved some twenty years later, brought to light the difficulty for the party to adopt a policy that would be both progressive and acceptable to the more conservative section of its rank and file.

Abortion is unconstitutional in Ireland. The first legislation on this matter was passed in 1861 when abortion was made illegal. It was only in the latter part of the twentieth century that the issue came to the fore again, partly as a result of a growing demand on the part of feminist circles and of the legislation passed in neighbouring EU countries. But equally important was the campaign mounted by the anti-abortion lobby, which sought an absolute ban on abortion, one which would prevent either courts or legislature from liberalising or repealing the 1861 law. The Eighth Amendment of the Constitution approved by referendum in 1983 (the first of several on this specific issue) recognised the right to life of the unborn.[9] This amendment was voted by 66 per cent of the electorate, with a 50 per cent turnout. In the wake of this referendum, pro-life groups turned their attention to the information women were still able to obtain in some family planning centres or women's clinics regarding abortion abroad, mainly in Britain, and successfully lobbied the government and the courts to close down information centres and counselling services. In 1986, the High Court ruled that the provision of information to women seeking abortion was in breach of article 40.3.3 of the Constitution, and this judgment was upheld by the Supreme Court.

This issue divided Ireland between those who claimed that the life of the unborn must be preserved at all costs (the biggest organisation in that field being SPUC, Society for the Protection of Unborn Children), those who campaigned for the right to choose, and a more moderate opinion which sought to preserve the right to information while not necessarily advocating the right to choose. Most of the political parties at the time of the referendum and in the following years tried to remain as remote as possible from the controversy, since it was one which could prove potentially divisive within their own ranks. Interestingly, Sinn Féin decided to take a clear stance when, at the 1985 Ard Fheis, the delegates voted in favour of a motion which recognised, simply, that 'women have the right to choose' (Clár, 1985: 99) This radical departure not only from previous policies within the party but from the general consensus within Irish society was surprisingly progressive given the tensions that the abortion debate was generating in Ireland at the time. However, the motion was not supported by the then Ard Comhairle, which voted against it as a group. Some of the delegates who spoke against the motion warned of the dangers of division that such a policy would entail. Some also argued that this went against the ethos of their party, while advocates of the right to choose underlined the importance for a party which fought for self-determination to extend that concept to women and their bodies. The debate raised a high level of discomfort and discontent, and the passing of this resolution was ascribed by some to the fact that the vote had taken place at the end of the conference, when a sizeable number of delegates, some of whom were from rural areas, had already left.

The extent to which this particular policy was unpopular among the rank and file of the movement was made obvious at the following year's Ard Fheis, when delegates from all over Ireland reported how they had been challenged by their own members and supporters for having allowed such a motion to be passed. This was revealing of the tensions that existed within the movement between its self-avowed inclination towards more progressive and revolutionary politics and its ill-defined alliance with a more conservative, Catholic constituency which represented a sizeable fraction of its members.[10] Therefore, the consensus at the following Ard Fheis, among the leadership, but also even among some who had spoken forcefully in favour of the proposal, was that the previous year's vote had been a hasty decision which did not serve the interests of the movement, as it was too divisive, too controversial and, ultimately, too damaging. The new wording that was inserted into the party's constitution was that 'we are opposed to the attitudes and forces in society that compel women to have abortions. We are opposed to abortion as a means of birth control' (Clár, 1986: 47). Such wording could have appeared lame, and seen as a U-turn from the position held the previous year. Yet the ultimate guideline on the position that Sinn Féin would take seemed to be the level of acceptability of that policy within the movement. One of the advocates of the right to choose conceded at the time: 'we gradually found that this was damaging the overall struggle, which was more important. . . . If it damages our struggle, then it will have to wait' (Johnson, interview, 1988). It thus seemed that whatever could get in the way of the nationalist aspiration was immediately cast aside, and the women's struggle was no exception.

Nevertheless, the 1983 referendum, as forecast by many of the opponents of the amendment, did not in any way address the question of unwanted pregnancies in a satisfactory manner, as was reflected by the number of women going to Britain each year to have an abortion.[11] The issue came to the fore once again in 1993, with an individual case that shocked and greatly disturbed Irish public opinion, the 'X' case, when a 14-year-old-girl who had been abused and raped by a neighbour was refused permission to travel to Britain for an abortion. That decision was upheld by the High Court but partially overruled by the Supreme Court which decided by a majority of four to one that travelling for abortion was permissible if the mother's life was in danger. This led to a second referendum on this issue, in the autumn of 1993, when the Irish electorate approved the right to travel to procure an abortion as well as the right to information on abortion, and rejected an amendment that would have ruled out the risk of suicide as a reason for abortion.

Once again, however, this left the issue largely unresolved. The Fianna Fáil government announced in December 2001 its proposal for a new amendment to the Constitution, which was decided upon by the Irish electorate in February 2002. What was put to the vote this time was whether to retain the 'suicide' clause in the Constitution as a reason for permitting abortion, and whether to retain the right to information and to travel. The wording was quite confusing, and the No camp had opposing views as to the reasons for campaigning against this new amendment. For the most extreme pro-life campaigners, this amendment did not do enough to protect the life of the unborn, whereas for pro-choice campaigners, it represented a step back without addressing the issue as a whole.

Sinn Féin unambiguously called for a No vote. Opening his party's campaign against the amendment, Monaghan TD Caoimhghín Ó Caoláin said that:

> the Constitution is not and has never been the place to deal with the complex issue of abortion. Whatever the outcome of the referendum, we as a society, and legislators in particular, will still have to deal with the reality that some 6,000 women every year leave Ireland to have their pregnancies terminated.
>
> (PR, 20 February 2002)

However, the party's campaign for a No vote was not waged in defence of abortion as a right, but on the basis that measures should be put in place to assist women with crisis pregnancies. For the pro-choice campaigners, the shortcoming of this analysis is that it only takes into account external reasons for abortions, such as financial hardship and lack of family support, but does not consider the woman's ultimate right to make a decision. In other words, Sinn Féin's analysis on this theme is quite progressive, in that it calls for an end to the criminalisation of women who are compelled to have an abortion, but it falls short of recognising women's right to choose as far as their own bodies are concerned.

Nevertheless, Sinn Féin's Joan O'Connor, who was in charge of her party's campaign on this occasion, strongly defends the current policy. 'In terms of our own constituency, there are huge divisions within the party on this issue. The position we have at this moment in time is one of the most progressive of all political parties. It's the position that our party members sign up to' (O'Connor, interview, 2003). Sinn Féin's policy document, *Women in an Ireland of Equals* (2002), does not mention the issue of abortion or reproductive rights, although it deals with most issues that are recognised as being of major importance to gender equality, such as education, childcare, violence and employment. However, in its discussion document *Rights for All*, Sinn Féin states that 'Everyone has the right to bodily and psychological integrity', including, among others, the right to 'make decisions concerning reproduction' (*Rights for All*, 2004: 8).

But while Sinn Féin might be seen to be sitting on the fence regarding this particular question, it has taken steps in other areas to promote gender equality and to redress the gender imbalance that exists within the party. In order to do so, an Equality Section headed by former Secretary General Lucilita Bhreatnach has been set up. One of its first tasks was to carry out an internal audit in 2001 to collect information on women's demands, on their status within the party, on means of making political power more accessible, and on ways to increase the female membership by responding to their needs. Although the results of this survey are 'confidential', some general trends seem to have emerged, related to processes of decision-making and empowerment, which are not specific to Sinn Féin. Women do get involved in local issues, and seem to be more visible on the ground, such as in the Bins Campaign, the anti-drugs movements or at elections times in the north. However, this involvement and visibility tends to decrease higher up in the hierarchy of the party (Bhreatnach, interview, 2003). Therefore, Sinn Féin applied to the Equality for Women Measure of the Department of Equality and Law Reform and obtained funding for its project to 'correct a significant gender imbalance in the decision-making process in political party structures and in the peace process' (*Annual Report*, 2001: 42).[12] Although the process of upskilling women is in areas such as negotiations or communications skills, the work carried out by Sinn Féin in the area of gender equality is deemed 'constructive' by the NICW, which quotes, in particular, the introduction of positive discrimination, the engagement of leaders and equality officers with women's organisations, and the work being carried out at grassroots level (NICW spokesperson, interview, 2003).

One of the aims of the party is to develop the visibility of women outside of its own structures, by increasing the representation of women during election campaigns. One of the difficulties the party faces is that its representation at a national level is still male-dominated. All five Sinn Féin TDs are men, as are three out of four Westminster MPs. This is not typical of Sinn Féin, as women do not fare much better in other political organisations. In the 1997 general election, women totalled 19.8 per cent of the candidates for the Dáil (ninety-six), of whom twenty were elected, representing 12 per cent of the total of TDs (Galligan, 1998: 296). These figures increased somewhat in the 2002 general election to 13 per cent (NWCI, 2002: 6) which led the National Women's Council of Ireland to conclude that 'at this rate, it will take 370 years for the percentage of women in the Dáil to reach 50 per cent' (NWCI, 2002: 4). The problem which Sinn Féin faces is not only that of presenting women candidates, but of succeeding in having them elected. Of the thirty-eight candidates it fielded in the 2002 general election, six were women (representing 18 per cent of the total), none of whom were elected. On average, they obtained around 5 per cent of the first preference vote, below the party's national average of 6.51 per cent.[13] Bhreatnach acknowledges that the candidacy of women has to be looked at and that a gender proofing of electoral guidelines is needed which has to be holistic, 'from the beginning: the planning of elections, the choice of ideal candidates, the overall constituency, the electoral convention, the analysis on the number of seats and the ones that are winnable' (Bhreatnach, interview). In order to redress this imbalance, Sinn Féin nominated two women candidates out of five for the 2004 European elections: Mary Lou McDonald for Leinster and Bairbre de Brún for Ulster, both of whom were elected. De Brún had a high profile not only within her movement but among the public at large, having served as a minister in the executive and having been part of the negotiating team during and after the Good Friday Agreement. McDonald was less well known beyond her party supporters, which probably, at least partly, explained the efforts made by Sinn Féin to make her more visible whenever the opportunity arose. Therefore, she was seen alongside Gerry Adams on TV news reports after the announcement of the 2003 Northern Ireland assembly results, although she had had little to do directly with that campaign. This type of tactics makes some sneer at what they see as 'window dressing'. One such critic was Brid Rodgers of the SDLP, who openly scorned the presence of Sinn Féin women as being simply a show put on by the party. 'I've never seen the Sinn Fein leadership appear in public without being flanked by women. But with one exception [Bairbre de Brún], I've never heard any of them allowed to speak. They're always conscious of the need for PR, but the reality is Sinn Fein is as male-dominated as any other party' (*IT*, 6 November 1999).

Nevertheless, in Northern Ireland, women have made more visible inroads into the representation of the party, both at local and national level. At the 1998 assembly election, Sinn Féin fielded sixty-nine candidates, of whom nineteen were women, representing approximately 27 per cent of the party's candidates. Out of a total of eighteen elected MLAs, five (28 per cent) were women, which showed a good correlation between the choice of the constituency and the chances of winning the seat. This trend was confirmed at the 2003 assembly election, when Sinn Féin fielded a total of thirty-four candidates, of whom nine were women (25 per cent). Seven were elected, making Sinn Féin female representation more than one-third of the total feminine contingent in the Assembly (with a total of eighteen women, five for the SDLP, two for the DUP, Alliance and UUP respectively). Moreover, Sinn Féin and the UUP are the only parties with a woman MP: Michele Guildernew (Sinn Féin) and L. Hendron (UUP).

Although Sinn Féin's equality department seems to concentrate largely on the gender issue, there are other areas that the party has addressed within the broader agenda of equality. One such area is homosexuality. The party's policy document, *Moving On: A Policy for Lesbian, Gay and Bi-Sexual Equality*, sets out to rectify the 'denial of equality of rights and opportunities' that gay, lesbian and bisexual people (GLB) suffer from 'in the social, political, economic or cultural spheres'. In order to achieve this objective, it proposes three broad areas of initiative: legislative reforms, internal education and campaigns. However, a closer analysis of the document reveals that the party still has some way to go before it may be seen as a serious defender of GLB rights.

The main problem of the document is that when accessed on the Sinn Féin website in April 2004, it was outdated. For instance, it seeks the introduction of the Employment Equality Act (1998) and the Equal Status Bill (1999), when both of these legislations have been enacted since the document was put together. This lack of updating makes the policy less credible and the exact extent of the party's commitment to such issues is left open to question considering that it does not seem to keep abreast of latest developments in Irish society. Director of Publicity Dawn Doyle admits that this is problematic, and is, in her view, 'part of the problem of a growing party. Policies are being updated, we're going as fast as the party can, while trying to coordinate that on an all-Ireland level' (Doyle, interview). The reforms suggested by Sinn Féin strongly support action to correct the social exclusion and poverty that affect the GLB community. Regarding internal education, Sinn Féin pledged its organisation to embark on a training programme of all members at all levels. Campaigning, finally, means encouraging members to get involved in campaigns such as Gay Pride or HIV/AIDS Day. The document also suggests that *An Phoblacht* 'establish links with lesbian and gay newspapers and organisations in order to keep informed of the current issues affecting GLB' (*Moving On*: 2). However, according to Brian Finnegan, Editor of the Dublin-based weekly magazine *Gay Community News*, there has 'never been any connection with Sinn Féin in either GCN or GI, the main two publications' (Finnegan, interview).

For Finnegan, the main problem of the Sinn Féin policy document is that does not mention one of the most pressing demands articulated by the gay and lesbian community: the need for partnership legislation. This indicates, in his view, that Sinn Féin, 'like the rest of the parties, is sitting on the fence' by failing to deal with an issue that is still considered contentious (Finnegan, interview). According to him, this has been deliberately left out of the policy programme. Nevertheless, when interviewed by the magazine *GI* in April 2002, Gerry Adams clearly stated that 'I think men and women of marriageable age including those of the same gender should have the equal right to marry and to found a family. Some people might find this offensive or find that isn't for him or her. That's fair enough – we are not asking them to do it' (*GI*, 2002: 64). Finnegan considered Adams' interview with *GI*, which was part of a series of interviews with political leaders, as 'the more honest, and the more inclusive'. However, Adams conceded that there were pragmatic choices to be made, such as the decision to attend the St Patrick's Day parade in New York, which excludes gay and lesbian marchers. 'You have to make tactical decisions – was the most important thing to not go because of the gay protest or to go, having stated your position, because the Irish cause in terms of the whole peace process was better served? There was not intent to offend and I explained my position' (*GI*, 2002: 67).

Sinn Féin's policy on GLB is seen by Finnegan as 'well-meaning, but wishy-washy'. According to him, 'all parties pay lip-service to the issue, but the Sinn Féin policy document is not even that' (Finnegan, interview). He admits that a number of members from the GLB community would be inclined to vote for Sinn Féin, because of its discourse on poverty and social exclusion, and because of its role in the Northern Irish peace process, but not necessarily for its views on GLB. Consequently, it would seem that Sinn Féin's commitment to gay and lesbian rights, as reflected in this particular policy document, is not yet fully credible to those who are primarily affected by the issues at stake.

Republicanism and multiculturalism

Multiculturalism is often described as a recent phenomenon in Ireland, one which started in the early 1990s with the arrival of asylum seekers and migrant workers in the country.[14] The absence of sizeable foreign ethnic minorities until then led to a vision of Ireland as a relatively homogeneous state, a vision endorsed by unionist leader David Trimble: 'contrast the United Kingdom state – a vibrant multi-ethnic, multi-national liberal democracy, the fourth largest economy in the world, the most reliable ally of the United States in the fight against international terrorism – with the pathetic sectarian, mono-ethnic, mono-cultural State to our south' (*IT*, 11 March 2002). This remark triggered some vivid comments from political quarters. Taoiseach Bertie Ahern reciprocated tersely by saying: 'we do not have the Drumcrees or the Garvaghy Roads of the north. Thankfully we don't have that kind of sectarian divide down here.' This exchange was interesting in that it epitomised the manner in which the Taoiseach and the First Minister viewed each other's jurisdiction. But more particularly, it encapsulated to a great extent the content of the debate on racism, ethnic minorities and asylum seekers that has gathered momentum in the past decade on both sides of the border. The arrival of asylum seekers and migrant workers from faraway or nearby countries has significantly altered the social and cultural landscape of the island with new issues and new media arising, as well as new debates on inclusivity, racism, and cultural and religious diversity.

Until recently, Ireland was seen, and saw itself, as relatively free of racism. In a statement made to the European Parliament Committee of Inquiry into Racism and Xenophobia in 1990, an Irish MEP explained:

Ireland is a racially homogeneous country with no ethnic minority groups. As a consequence there are no racial problems of the kind experienced in countries with such groups. Neither is there a large presence of foreigners . . . the position could alter if the influx became sustained . . . there is however a minority group of travelling people giving rise to some of the problems associated with racism.

(in O'Connell, 1997: 1)

The argument ascribing racist attitudes to the presence of a substantial ethnic minority is problematic, as it tends to shift the blame for racist attitudes on to the very victims of racism, i.e. the ethnic minorities. But as the above comment suggests, racism was present in Irish society before the arrival of immigrants and asylum seekers. The travellers' community has indeed been the object of discrimination for decades, on both sides of the border.[15]

In Northern Ireland, the debate on racism possesses specific characteristics. First, it is situated in the context of sectarianism. These two phenomena, although not totally symmetrical, have inextricable correspondences. Because religion is the dividing line between communities in the case of sectarianism, it has been rejected in some quarters as being a form of racism. In a report carried out for the Office of the First Minister, researcher Paul Connolly explains that although an analysis linking both phenomena undoubtedly has some merit, 'in legal terms, the Race Relations (NI) Order 1997 precludes such a definition as it does not list religion as a basis upon which a "racial group" can be identified' (Connolly, 2002: 7). Moreover, the Macpherson report[16] defines institutional racism as 'the collective failure of an organisation to provide an appropriate and professional service to people because of their colour, culture or ethnic origin' (Connolly, 2002: 8). Nevertheless, the manifestations of racism and sectarianism can be quite similar, and both are seen by the organisation NICEM (Northern Ireland Council of Ethnic Communities) as having overlapping characteristics. 'Racism in Northern Ireland can be understood in the context of the extension of the sectarian divide and the generalised lack of democratic accountability' (NICEM, 2000: 4). According to this view, to which Sinn Féin subscribes, just like in the case of racism, sectarianism has led to institutional, economic and social discrimination and inequalities that are still in the process of being corrected in Northern Ireland. Therefore, the sectarian dimension is seen to play a part in the analysis of racism and in the response given to this phenomenon.

The prevailing view of Irish identity in the national discourses, to which Sinn Féin was no exception, was one in which 'Irishness and citizenship have been correlated with whiteness and Catholicism, both of which implicitly acted as the measure against which difference was constructed' (in Coulter and Coleman, 2003: 89). Over the years, Sinn Féin tended to negate difference in favour of a relatively homogenous concept of the Irish nation, both from a historical and a cultural point of view. This process of amalgamation was perceived as essential in order to justify the ultimate objective of reunification. One of the characteristics of the Irish identity that was put forward by Sinn Féin was that it was defined mainly in opposition to another identity, the British. Until recently, no Sinn Féin policy document mentioned the existence within the territory of ethnic minorities, particularly that of the travellers, although this dimension was also, by and large, ignored by other major political parties. Some speak of 'invisible racism', insofar as people are not aware that racism does exist.[17]

Sinn Féin's policy on racism, *Many Voices, One Country*, dates from 2001, and consists of a comprehensive document which reads like an anti-racist pledge. The views adopted on issues regarding asylum seekers seem to correspond broadly to the recommendations of the Irish Refugee Council, such as the elimination of the direct provision system,[18] the abolition of what is termed 'forced' dispersal,[19] the revision of the appeals procedure and the recognition that 'policy on asylum seekers and refugees is primarily about their treatment, not their right to exist or their numbers' (*Many Voices*: 5). Regarding migrant workers, Sinn Féin does not seek to establish a quota, but gives the figure of 200,000, which was also the figure considered necessary to sustain the growth of the economy.[20] One of the most original ideas put forward by Sinn Féin is the suggestion that recruitment should be linked to the work of the ministry responsible for overseas development, in order to ensure that potential immigrants from developing countries are given equal treatment. This is obviously not in line with the manner in which visas are being granted. The vast majority of migrant workers come from non-African and non-Asian countries, which indicates 'a systematic racialisation of work permits by the state [which] can be seen in terms of a straightforward attempt to regulate internal ethnic and religious diversity' (Coulter and Coleman, 2003: 80). Furthermore, the main criterion for the granting of work permits seems to be that of qualification, in order to fill the existing gaps within the economy, as is the case with the nursing sector where recruitment takes place in targeted countries such as the Philippines.

The manner in which Sinn Féin explains the rise of racism in Ireland is consistent with its overall analysis of the political and social situation that is still viewed as a postcolonial one. 'Colonisation and its legacy are important dynamics in the promotion and perpetuation of racism. The colonisation practised by a handful of countries, over many centuries, has left a lasting impression on our lives' (*Many Voices*: 3). From this analysis follows the view that sectarianism and the consequent discrimination against the nationalist community in Northern Ireland is a by-product of racism. 'As colonialism has used racism as a device to divide and conquer many nations, so sectarianism in Ireland has always served British colonial interests. Therefore, the issue of religious equality in Ireland should be integrated into broader projects against racism and promoting racial equality' (*Many Voices*: 9). The party insists on the quasi-endemic nature of this phenomenon in a postcolonial context that has not yet been totally overcome. As long as the institutions and the states linked to partition continue to exist, the issue of racism, and that of inequalities in general, will not be totally resolved. It is possible to put in place some immediate and medium-term plans of action, but the underlying causes of discrimination, whoever it might target, are ascribed to the partition of the island and to the residual colonial nature of both states.

This analysis applies primarily to the Northern Ireland situation. According to Sinn Féin's line of reasoning, the state being, by definition and by its very nature, sectarian, discrimination is unavoidable. Racism is, above all, of an institutional and political nature, and is fed by institutions and parties alike. The discourse that the party has developed regarding the nationalist community is transposed to ethnic minorities, who are the victims, like nationalists, of the discriminatory practices of the state and its agents (police force, social services, legal system), but also of loyalist organisations. When commenting on the racist attacks in South Belfast in January 2004, Alex Maskey stated that it was 'very clear that there is now a campaign in loyalist areas of South Belfast to drive members of the ethnic minority community out' (PR, 5 January 2004). In this context, refugees and asylum seekers are discriminated against by the legal system (arbitrary detentions, appeal procedures not always fully respected, unsatisfactory processing of their applications). They are seen as the target of the police's prejudices. Indeed, in his report for the Office of the First Minister, Paul Connolly indicated that ethnic minorities tend to take the view that the police fail to take racial crimes seriously, although he also noted a substantial rise in the number of such crimes (over 400 per cent between 1996 and 1999) (Connolly, 2002: 72). Sinn Féin draws a parallel between the situation of ethnic minorities and that of the community which the party purports to represent, which leads it to give similar responses to what are perceived as similar problems. Interestingly, one of the actions taken by Sinn Féin on a practical level is to assist those asylum seekers who are detained when entering the UK without a visa (approximately 15 per cent of those who apply for asylum in the north) and placed 'on remand'. This is an area in which Sinn Féin can draw on its vast experience of the prison system, which enables its representatives to advise ethnic minorities on issues such as prisoners' rights and to organise a support network. According to Sinn Féin's policy adviser on multiculturalism, Caroline Coleman, it is only natural that ethnic minorities should turn to Sinn Féin to solve this type of problem:

'We have the experience, we've been through this, we know how to deal with the prison authorities and what the prisoners are entitled to' (Coleman, interview, 2003).

The work undertaken by Sinn Féin Mayor of Belfast Alex Maskey was an interesting experience as far as the party's engagement with multiculturalism was concerned. Following on from his pledge to be the mayor of the whole city, irrespective of community or religious backgrounds, Maskey undertook to open up City Hall to all ethnic communities and to invite their representatives to make representations on behalf of their constituents on a monthly basis. He also pledged support to the building of a mosque in Belfast. Another plan for the construction of a mosque on the outskirts of Craigavon, on land which belonged to a Muslim businessman Mohammed Ashraf, and financed by a group of local Muslims, had created controversy. The local council of the town, predominantly unionist, blocked the planning permission on the grounds that the roads to and sewage at the site were not adequate. Sinn Féin dismissed this argument as being disingenuous, pointing to the statement of UUP councillor Fred Crowe, a former Mayor of Craigavon, as indicative of the prejudices on which this decision was based. Indeed, the unionist politician explained that residents believed their way of life would be threatened if the mosque was built, and claimed the development could pave the way for an al Qaeda cell in the area, adding that the residents would be kept awake by 'noisy chanting and wailing' (*AP*, 30 January 2003). Sinn Féin local councillor John O'Dowd welcomed David Trimble's reprimanding of this type of statement and pledged to find a compromise on this issue. Nevertheless, the Muslim community decided subsequently to delay the building of the mosque, as they did not wish to do it against the wishes of the local community (BBC, 13 October 2003).

Sinn Féin's engagement with ethnic minorities can be measured by its work with the travellers. Because of a general tendency, until recently, to consider travellers as an 'invisible community', a phenomenon which was all the more obvious in Northern Ireland where it did not seem to fit in within the sectarian divide, political parties showed little interest in the welfare and rights of the travelling community. According to Paul Noonan, spokesperson of the Travellers Resource Centre in Belfast, because the community in Northern Ireland is quite small from a numerical point of view (some 1,600 people, although the numbers fluctuate depending on the period), there is no electoral benefit in defending them (Noonan, interview, 2003). Connolly's research showed that travellers in the north fare very poorly in the fields of employment (with 53 per cent 'economically inactive'), education (with 50 per cent having no formal education and 1 per cent having third-level education) and health (estimates have placed the life expectancy of Travellers as 20 per cent lower than that of the general population). Until recently, no Sinn Féin document mentioned their situation, although they were the targets of discriminatory practices on both sides of the border, and although their 'indigenous' status would situate them within the nationalist community, which partly explains the total lack of concern, and at times overt hostility, of unionist politicians towards them (Noonan, interview). However, before the suspension of the institutions in October 2002, Sinn Féin ministers engaged with the travellers' community, according to Noonan, both being accessible and prepared to take into account their demands (Noonan, interview). Sinn Féin also actively canvasses the travelling community at election times, encouraging them to vote and ensuring that they are registered on the electoral lists.

In the Republic, the response of organisations such as Pavee Point, an association which promotes the travelling community's cultural and civil rights, to the work undertaken by Sinn Féin is also quite positive. At a national level, republicans have taken a strong stance on some issues such as the law voted by the Dáil in July 2002, the Housing (Miscellaneous Provisions) Act, 2002, which makes it an offence to occupy land without the consent of the owner (excluding by-roads). Pavee Point described this law as 'racist', as it targeted the travelling community directly, and considered that it made nomadism a criminal offence. Sinn Féin TD Aengus Ó Snodaigh echoed these criticisms when he stated that:

> the only way to interpret this law is that it makes Traveller culture illegal. As such, it violates Travellers' human rights and equality rights that the Government is legally bound to protect. . . . The law also does not serve settled communities well, as it stands to increase tensions between the Traveller and settled communities.
>
> (PR, 23 July 2002)

A few days later, he also condemned the proposal by the Vintners Federation of Ireland to impose a blanket ban on travellers as discriminatory, 'completely unjustified and abhorrent' (PR, 9 August 2002). Some local Sinn Féin representatives are actively engaged with travellers. One such person is Larry O'Toole, Sinn Féin councillor in Finglas (North Dublin), who sits on the Travellers Accommodation Committee. O'Toole started working with travellers in the early 1980s, and has been proactive in ensuring that the issue of their rights and entitlements features regularly on the agenda of his party's Ard Fheis. As evidence of Sinn Féin's engagement with travellers' issues, O'Toole argues that there are more members of that community in Sinn Féin than in any other party, a fact that is corroborated by Martin Collins from Pavee Point. Whether this translates into immediate gains is not easily verifiable. Travellers may tend to join Sinn Féin more than any other party, but the numbers are still, according to Collins, relatively low. The benefits in terms of votes is also, probably, quite minimal, although this is difficult to assess with some accuracy. It is undeniable that individual members of Sinn Féin are committed to working on the ground and are recognised by travellers' organisations as being genuine in their commitment. Whether this can be extrapolated to the whole of the party remains to be seen, as there is little doubt that it is not immune to the prejudices that run deep in Irish society regarding the travellers' community. Globally, however, the party's policies are deemed positive by the Pavee Point representative, who indicates that Sinn Féin is perceived as the party that 'gets the job done' (Collins, interview, 2003).

The work carried out by Sinn Féin with ethnic minorities in the Republic, however, is harder to assess, as it does not seem yet to have fully engaged with them on the ground. Dublin South-Central TD Aengus Ó Snodaigh concedes that the party and its constituency offices would not be an obvious port of call for individuals seeking advice or help, primarily because there are a number of NGOs which cater more specifically for them, but also because Sinn Féin workers are not totally conversant with the legislation and entitlements regarding asylum seekers (Ó Snodaigh, interview, 2003). Sinn Féin's policy on multiculturalism was not a top priority in the 2002 general election. When launching his party's manifesto Gerry Adams listed nine priorities; none referred to the ethnic minorities or the anti-racist agenda (PR, 29 April 2002). The party's seventy-one-page manifesto dedicated only one page to the issue of immigration, which was situated within the context of racism, implicitly linking the two issues. Sinn Féin also tends to ascribe racism to structural causes and to concrete problems such as the waiting lists for hospitals or social housing, which put the asylum seekers in direct competition with a section of the population that has been left behind by the general economic policy of the state. The explanation given by the Sinn Féin President to the rise of racism, one which seems to have been adopted by most of the party's spokespersons, seems to show a willingness to be as neutral as possible on this issue. 'It is important to state that racism does not grow by accident. Everywhere it has taken hold it is because unscrupulous people in politics and other spheres of society have nurtured it for their own cynical interests' (PR, 14 May 2002). This analysis tends to ascribe responsibility and blame from above, and, while it does recognise the attitudinal dimension of the phenomenon, tends to minimise it. When asked to expand on the meaning of this particular sentence, North Kerry TD Martin Ferris quoted the case of one local Cork councillor during the general election campaign who voiced racist comments. Ferris concluded that this has to be combated by 'being brave, not facing down, even if we lose votes' (Ferris, interview, 2003).

Nevertheless, a study commissioned by the Africa Solidarity Centre and published in November 2003, *Positive Politics: Participation of*

Immigrants and Ethnic Minorities in the Electoral Process, revealed some important gaps within the six main political parties regarding their integration policies, and Sinn Féin was no exception. According to the findings of the study, none of the parties surveyed had introduced specific measures to encourage membership of ethnic minorities. Only one party, the Greens, had selected a candidate from an ethnic minority for the 2004 local elections, where non-nationals are entitled to vote. The party took a firm anti-racist stance in its 2004 local election manifesto. In the section on Multiculturalism, it explained that 'All Sinn Féin candidates have been to anti-racist training facilitated by the National Consultative Council on Racism and have individually signed an anti-racist pledge' (2004 Manifesto: 35).

Sinn Féin pledges to combat racism and to 'give political leadership'. This translates into three different levels. Not surprisingly, it promotes an all-Ireland approach, with legislation on a thirty-two-county basis and the integration of the Equality Authority with the Equality Commission in Northern Ireland. It also undertakes to use the voice of its representatives in the Dáil and in the Northern Ireland assembly to raise the issue whenever relevant. This has indeed been the case on various occasions in the Republic, but also in Northern Ireland. On 13 February 2001, for instance, Conor Murphy (MLA) proposed the following motion: 'that this assembly notes with concern the report by the Secretary of State on the detention of asylum seekers and calls upon the government to develop an alternative to detaining asylum seekers and to devise methods of expediting the application process' (Assembly debates, available online). The motion was passed, although not unanimously, given the nature of politics in Northern Ireland; Roy Beggs (UUP) admitted that he agreed with much of the motion, but because it originated from Sinn Fein he could not vote for it.

The third level, that of the community, could prove more problematic to tackle. Sinn Féin is still in the process of establishing its place within the Irish political landscape, on both sides of the border, as the party of the oppressed and the most vulnerable in society. If there is, in its eyes, an inherent logic in taking on the fight of ethnic minorities as the new symbols of social injustice and discrimination, there is also a price to pay in terms of votes. The party's electoral successes are to be found primarily in deprived areas and working-class districts, where voters might also be those who are most vulnerable to the populist discourses that blame inequalities on immigrants. Sinn Féin is thus cautious in its approach in order not to antagonise its own constituents. It thus:

> recognises the tensions and difficulties that arise from large numbers of asylum seekers being 'dumped' in particular areas, often the poorest and least resourced working-class areas of Dublin or small

and under-resourced rural communities. Community concern is sometimes dismissed as racism but there are other more complex dimensions to this. In particular, communities that saw their own children forced to emigrate, have been hit by the irresponsible press coverage.

(*Many Voices*: 6)

However, when Minister for Justice Michael McDowell announced the holding of a referendum on Irish citizenship, aimed at amending the article of the Constitution granting citizenship to anyone born in Ireland, Sinn Féin unambiguously campaigned for a No vote. Gerry Adams stated that 'there should be none of this negativity, locking the doors, claiming that there's no room in the inn' (*IT*, 10 June 2004).The party acknowledges that there is an imbalance between the policies advocated by the leadership and the feelings of some of its members who, according to Mitchell McLaughlin, display the same type of prejudice as the population at large when it comes to ethnic minorities and travellers (McLaughlin, interview). Indeed, the citizenship referendum was passed by an overwhelming majority of 79.2 per cent against 20.8 per cent. In the run-up to the referendum, opinion polls were showing a support ranging from 54 to 57 per cent for the amendment, as opposed to 23 to 24 per cent against it, the rest of the electorate being undecided. Interestingly, the Sinn Féin voters were in line with the rest of the Irish voters, in spite of the leaders' advocacy of a No vote, as 56 per cent declared their intention to support the amendment against 32 per cent (*IT*, 24 May 2004). Nevertheless, Sinn Féin could find itself in a position where it will have to make a choice between retaining a broader appeal and thus watering down its policies on ethnic minorities, and a more radical approach whereby it decides to part with those members who, according to Ó Snodaigh, might have impeccable republican credentials in what they have done for the national question but display prejudices that are no longer acceptable (Ó Snodaigh, interview). The manner in which Sinn Féin constructs and pursues a policy that is truly radical could be the litmus test of its ideological commitment to the defence of the most vulnerable, and evidence that the traditional discourse on Irish identity is no longer relevant in a multicultural Ireland.

5   The international dimension

Cuba, Turkey, South Africa, Spain, the USA. . . . These are just five of the many countries that Sinn Féin representatives have visited on a number of occasions since the mid-1990s. Although the common thread between these destinations may not be immediately obvious, the logic behind Sinn Féin's foreign policy is driven by two factors: the peace process and solidarity with what the party terms 'peoples in struggle'. As a party fighting for self-determination, Sinn Féin supports what are perceived to be similar struggles throughout the world. As a socialist party, it establishes links with regimes that are considered revolutionary. Finally, as a participant in the resolution of the Northern Irish conflict, it seeks to promote abroad the peace process and the eventual reunification of the island, primarily, but not solely, in the USA. This policy can be risky, because demonstrating solidarity with one particular country might jeopardise the level of support that can be garnered in another country. Nevertheless, Sinn Féin has strived, in the past, to pursue both dimensions of its strategy and to keep on board governments and pressure groups that play an essential role in the peace process while not overlooking its affinity with struggles akin to its own, even if this position can lead to contradictions.

The effort to ensure that Ireland's quest for self-determination features on the international agenda is not new. Such a policy was already one of Dáil Éireann's first priorities. On 21 January 1919, the day of its inauguration, the newly convened Irish assembly approved, alongside the Declaration of Independence, a 'Message to the Free Nations of the World' which called on 'the civilised world, having judged between English wrong and Irish right, [to] guarantee to Ireland its permanent support for the maintenance of her national independence' (Lyons, 1983: 401). Dáil Éireann appointed three delegates to attend the Versailles Conference, and dispatched an envoy to Paris to gain their admittance to the peace talks, but this was to no avail. In the following decades, Sinn Féin retreated into an isolationist position and tended to focus on the internal dimension of the struggle.[1]

Lessons from abroad

For decades, Sinn Féin's foreign policy was confined to the creation of links of a rather aspirational nature with selected organisations across Europe, and to the establishment of support networks in countries such as the USA, Australia, Germany and France. The party's stated interest in foreign policy in the 1970s was limited to expressions of empathy towards self-determination movements in Brittany, Wales, Scotland or the Basque Country. The Provisionals' policy document, one that was regarded as official policy until the early 1980s, *Éire Nua*, contained no mention of the international dimension. At best, there was the expressed 'support for those throughout the world engaged in struggles for national liberation and [we invite] their explicit support for the struggle in Ireland' (Clár, 1976).

In the mid-1980s, however, the Ard Fheis passed a motion asking the 'incoming Ard Comhairle to create a committee of Ard Comhairle members to monitor and promote Sinn Féin foreign affairs policy' (Clár, 1985), which led to the creation of a Foreign Affairs Department in 1985. However, Sinn Féin's efforts to forge links with political organisations abroad were hampered by the campaign of the IRA. Sinn Féin recognised at the time that armed struggle was unacceptable within the European context, which made it next to impossible for any political party to have formal relations with Sinn Féin. While republicans had been keen to dissociate themselves and the IRA from groups which were clearly not fighting for national liberation and self-determination, such as the Red Brigade, Action Directe or Baader Meinhof, the amalgam that was drawn by the public and political parties alike between those organisations and the Republican Movement was recognised by Sinn Féin itself as being detrimental.

Sinn Féin's involvement in the peace process contributed to promoting the party beyond the shores of Ireland. Among the main characteristics of the process, those which were seen as potentially transferable to other conflict resolution scenarios were its inclusivity, the ceasefire and the progressive disarmament of the paramilitary organisations as well as the establishment of institutions paving the way for power-sharing and increased collaboration between the two parts of the island. To this must be added a number of confidence-building measures, such as the amendment of the Irish Constitution and the repeal of the 1920 Government of Ireland Act, the early release of prisoners, the reform of the police, as well as the establishment of safeguards regarding human rights. This model was all the more attractive given that no party could claim to have won but, equally importantly, none had lost. Each side had successfully made and obtained compromises.

What made Sinn Féin's role particularly relevant was its successful transition from a party which had shown a level of inflexibility in the

manner in which it presented its objectives, to one capable of accommodating other views of the conflict. Moreover, this transition was
apparently achieved without causing major upheavals within the
Republican Movement. From the signing of the Good Friday Agreement,
McGuinness, Adams and others members of the leadership of the
Republican Movement became world players on the conflict resolution
scene and embarked on several international tours to speak about the
manner in which they had approached the peace process, both within
their organisation and in their interaction with other players.

Sinn Féin insists that it cannot be prescriptive in the advice it offers
to other movements or organisations, since it maintains that there is
no model of conflict resolution as such which could be transferable
from one situation to another. However, there have been numerous
instances of 'borrowing', to use John Darby's phrase, between different
peace processes (Darby and McGinty, 2002). The Northern Ireland peace
process borrowed heavily from South Africa, where some formulas were
tried out successfully and then transferred. These include the notions of
sufficient consensus and of transitional institutions. Sinn Féin is keen
to acknowledge its debt towards the ANC, whose experience it used
both as a model and as a way of legitimising its own choices in the eyes
of its supporters. The anti-apartheid struggle was the epitome of a just
cause, one that was described by Gerry Adams as an 'inspiration to
humanity', in his first visit to South Africa (*The Militant*, 3 July 1995).
In this respect, the fact that Nelson Mandela hailed Sinn Féin as an
'old friend and ally' (*IT*, 3 October 2001) was certainly very significant
for republicans. The links between Sinn Féin and the ANC have been
successfully explored by republicans to highlight the parallels between
the two struggles. A mural portraying Nelson Mandela appeared on the
streets of West Belfast as early as the mid-1980s. The charismatic stature
of Mandela and of his organisation carried considerable weight among
the rank and file of the organisation, and in the aftermath of the signing
of the Good Friday Agreement, Sinn Féin invited an ANC delegation to
Ireland to promote the Agreement among republican supporters. The
ANC former chief negotiator, Cyril Ramaphosa, addressed a gathering
of republican supporters in Belfast, conveying a straightforward message:
'There were times when people thought it would be better to go back to
the armed struggle. But even as they went through all these emotions
and doubts, we knew that there was no alternative to negotiations'
(*IT*, 29 April 1998). The following day, his colleague, the Minister for
Transport Mac Maharaj, called for unity and reason to prevail over
emotion. Although the South African representatives stressed that the
situation in their country was very different to that in Northern Ireland,
they pointed to the fact that there were also similarities and lessons to be
learned.

Sinn Féin was not the only party to seek advice from South Africa. A number of inter-party delegations, including representatives of the unionist parties, visited the country on several occasions. Nevertheless, over the years, close links were forged between the ANC and Sinn Féin, which were presented as legitimising Sinn Féin's choices both to its own supporters and to the outside world. Gerry Adams' first visit to South Africa aimed to 'convert those lessons to our country' (*The Militant*, 3 July 1995). Undoubtedly, the fact that one of the weapons inspectors was Cyril Ramaphosa helped the leadership to convince its own grassroots that the IRA was not surrendering by putting some weapons beyond use. To the outside world, the relationship between Sinn Féin and the ANC suggested that the republican position was legitimised by those who successfully brought the process forward in South Africa. Indeed, in late September 2001, when Sinn Féin's role in the peace process was under intense scrutiny after the failure of the IRA to decommission and the arrests of three men in Colombia (see below), and when its relationship with the US administration and, to an extent, with Irish America, was described as frosty by many observers, Gerry Adams visited South Africa for the third time. The occasion was the unveiling of a sculpture to the 1981 hunger strikes in Robben Island, where Nelson Mandela had spent twenty-seven years in prison. The dedication read: 'To political prisoners who suffered and died as a result of hunger strikes in prison in Ireland and South Africa.' Clearly, the parallel established between the two struggles was highly significant.

There were many lessons that Sinn Féin learned from the South Africans, which in turn guided the republican leadership throughout the process, both in their public and private dealings. At the heart of these was the fact that compromises and risks were an integral part of any conflict resolution. The road that republicans embarked on in the early 1990s was presented by the leadership as a difficult one, fraught with dangers and possible setbacks, and inevitably leading to compromises. The leaders have, time and again, stressed the risks that were involved, collectively and individually, such as that of dividing their own ranks and being outmanoeuvred by their adversaries. Personal risks were also taken, according to republicans, particularly in the early years of the process when Sinn Féin members were potential targets of loyalist attacks and at times paid with their lives for their involvement. Nevertheless, what emerged from the republican discourse was that its experience over the thirty years of conflict had given it the necessary resilience to see through the resolution of the conflict. This was predicated on a number of qualities deemed fundamental, such as patience, something which republicans claim to have unlimited reserves of due to the long years of 'hardship' that they have experienced.

Another important lesson that republican leaders learned from the ANC was, according to Martin McGuinness, that 'the most important constituency you will negotiate with is your own' (McGuinness, interview, 2003). In other words, it was fundamental to keep the rank and file on board. In their discourses, republican leaders have been careful to stress the fact that the process has to be a bottom-up one, in which leaders have remained close to their base and have strived not to bypass their own constituents. The danger of sidelining the grassroots has been highlighted by Lederach, in his peace building model (1996), where he states that 'grassroots is the tier at which many of the symptoms of conflict are manifest – social and economic insecurity, political and cultural discrimination, human rights violations, but lines of ethno-national conflict are drawn vertically rather than horizontally'. This in turn creates:

> two inverse relationships. Those at the top have the greatest capacity to influence the wider peace building process but are least likely to be affected by its consequences on a day-to-day basis. Those at the bottom will have limited access to the decision-making process and a narrower view of the process and a narrower view of the wider agenda which may demand bargaining and compromise.
> (quoted in Knox and Quirk, 2000: 24–25)

Since one of the words of the utmost importance within the republican vocabulary is 'empowerment', it was essential for the party to establish a collective responsibility for the process, whereby the people are its guarantors. In that respect, its failure or success rests in their hands as much as it does in the hands of the political leadership. This notion of collective responsibility is significant. Moreover, there is a delicate balance between the short-term and long-term objectives of a peace process. In the republican agenda, the short-term gains were the early release of prisoners and the establishment of institutions. On a longer term basis, reunification is at the centre of this vision. There is a constant need to be seen as moving forward while justifying necessary compromises without relinquishing the ultimate objective. This is, according to Sinn Féin's spokesperson on international affairs, Joan O'Connor, one of the lessons that was learned from the South Africans, which gave the party 'a sense of the difficulties of conflict resolution and particularly of how dangerous the transition can be' (O'Connor, interview).

Republican leaders insist that they have, by and large, kept their constituents on board. According to Conor Murphy, Sinn Féin group leader in the assembly, 'we have constantly engaged, right through these last few years, with our own base on a very regular basis. This is vital to ensuring that our support base and the party stay united and we all understand where we're going' (Murphy, interview, 2003). The constituency he represents, South Armagh, is frequently portrayed in the media as critical, and at times even hostile, to the peace process. Murphy rejects this view, suggesting that:

> when the media want to see where the difficulties are, where these are more likely to arise, they go to South Armagh because South Armagh provided the stiffest resistance. They think they'll be more sceptical about the peace process. It's not necessarily the case. I have done meetings in South Armagh on many occasions over the last 5 years, I've done meetings as far away as Wexford, I get the same questions arising in most places, the same doubts, the same support, the same optimism, the same determination to stick with the process.
>
> (Murphy, interview)

Arguably, it could be said that the electoral results which Sinn Féin obtained in the November 2003 assembly elections are evidence of the continuing support for the manner in which Sinn Féin has managed the peace process. However, some criticisms have been voiced within the party which reflect an uneasiness about the hierarchical nature of decision-making within the party. At the 2003 Ard Fheis, a motion from North Belfast urged 'that this Ard Fheis considers it a priority that the communication mechanisms linking all levels of the structures are in immediate need of improvement, especially where decisions may lead to a shift in direction or policy change' (Clár, 2003: 31).

Another crucial lesson learned from the ANC related to the importance for the movement or party involved in negotiations to have a 'communicator', someone like Nelson Mandela who enjoyed a level of respect not only within his own constituency but on an international level. This, combined with the raising of awareness and the mobilisation of international public opinion, was an essential ingredient to the success of the South African process. The Sinn Féin negotiating team is made up of many members, but Martin McGuinness and Gerry Adams have certainly been centre-stage. It was important that Sinn Féin leaders were seen to command respect within their own ranks, to achieve international standing and to have had direct experience of the conflict, in order to achieve the necessary credibility both within and outside their movement to engage in negotiations.

The lessons learned from the ANC were fundamental, and enabled Sinn Féin to become, in turn, a party whose advice on conflict resolution is sought by what republicans perceive are liberation movements, and sometimes even by governments. It has thus, according to Joan O'Connor, been approached by a number of countries such as Burundi or Sri Lanka (O'Connor, interview). O'Connor talks of a 'conflict resolution industry', with numerous delegations visiting Ireland and examining the Good Friday Agreement. Their reason for approaching Sinn Féin is, according to her, because they see us as being successful. You don't go and seek advice from those who you perceive to have failed. We would be quite critical of ourselves in terms of what we have achieved, but once you step outside of Ireland, in an international context, the perception of Sinn Féin is very positive. People view Sinn Féin as having achieved its goals.

(O'Connor, interview)

However, the fact that Sinn Féin did contribute to the situation of the IRA ceasefire cannot be disregarded, even if Sinn Féin prefers to project the image of a successful political party, or more precisely, a 'conflict resolution party'. Indeed, Sinn Féin has played the role of facilitator in at least one case, that of the Basque Country.

In September 1998, for the first time in its thirty-nine-year history, ETA, the Basque separatist organisation, declared a ceasefire. A few days later, Gerry Adams was given a statesman's welcome in the Basque capital Bilbao by a delegation of politicians from most of the region's parties and cheered on by thousands who had lined the streets, waving the Tricolour next to the Basque flag. This visit seemed somehow to represent the recognition of Sinn Féin's strategy as well as its leader's own achievements and personal charisma. But beyond the media attention that surrounded this event, Gerry Adams' one-day trip was the continuation of a bonding process between Basque separatists and Irish Republicans that had been ongoing for some years.[2]

The peace process in Ireland paved the way for closer collaboration between Sinn Féin and Batasuna. In the early 1990s, Basque representatives started to visit Ireland on a regular basis in order to study the situation in Northern Ireland, taking some of its key points on board, such as the necessity for dialogue and inclusivity. Sinn Féin hosted delegations travelling on 'fact-finding missions' and invited to Ireland leaders such as the Batasuna spokesperson Arnaldo Otegi. From their different visits, the Basque delegates put together a strategy to embark on a course of action similar to that of the northern parties. On 20 June 1998, an Irish Forum was formed in the Basque Country. The discussions that took place throughout that summer culminated in the signing, on 12 September 1998, of the Lizarra Agreement, a document clearly inspired by the Irish peace process and by the Belfast Agreement.[3]

The strength of the Lizarra Agreement was that it involved all sectors of Basque society, constituting, in the words of O'Connor, a 'lock-in'. As John Darby has noted, the 'pan-nationalist front' combining Sinn Féin, the SDLP, the Irish government and Irish America inspired the 'third space' which performed a similar function for Basque constitutional and revolutionary nationalists (McGinty and Darby, 2002). The borrowing from the Irish peace process was thus quite striking, in that it facilitated the emergence of a united front that in turn put forward an alternative to the armed conflict and placed negotiations at the heart of the process. But it could be argued that there were also instances of 'negative borrowing', such as the resumption of the ETA armed campaign after fourteen months of ceasefire.

When asked if it has failed in its role as adviser to the Basque separatist movement, Sinn Féin shifts the responsibility of the collapse of that peace process on to the Spanish authorities. Nevertheless, it does acknowledge that neither the two movements nor the two situations had reached the same stage of development. The Basque situation, it claimed, was reminiscent of that in which republicans found themselves in the late 1980s. Sinn Féin believes that a successful peace process is possible in the Basque Country, and still retains its links with Batasuna, although this has been made more difficult since the banning of the Basque organisation.[4] To a certain extent, it could be said that Sinn Féin is acting in the Basque Country in the same capacity as the ANC with Sinn Féin. In some way, just as the ANC's international reputation as the representatives of an oppressed people lent some legitimacy to Sinn Féin, so the image that Sinn Féin conveys on the international stage is used by the Basque separatist organisation.[5] While it is possible that the links between the two movements have positive repercussions for Batasuna, it is not clear whether the same may be said for Sinn Féin. The presence of a Batasuna delegate, Joseba Alvarez, at the 2001 Ard Fheis created some controversy in the wake of the 9/11 attacks. Sinn Féin was asked to justify why it had as a guest speaker a member of an organisation which does not condemn violence and that, to some extent, is seen as condoning it. The situation was made all the more difficult given the claim by *Irish Times* security correspondent Jim Cusack that it was through ETA that the IRA came into contact with the FARC in Colombia (*IT*, 28 September 2001). However, Sinn Féin maintained its line that Batasuna and ETA were two separate organisations, one being (at the time) legal and the other not, a rhetoric reminiscent of that used at times through the years to diffuse questions about the IRA. Interestingly, in his address to the Ard Fheis, not once did the Batasuna delegate mention ETA, choosing to restrict his speech to very general concepts on globalisation and the Basque struggle. But Sinn Féin cannot be seen to be turning its back on those whose struggle has been hailed for years as being akin to theirs, and the party is still committed, in the words of Joan O'Connor, 'to make the struggle of others our own struggle' (Ard Fheis 2001).

The continued support for organisations such as Batasuna is not without its problems for Sinn Féin. David Trimble asked for clarification on the relationship between the two parties when Batasuna was made illegal, claiming that any continued support would be in breach of the Good Friday Agreement. 'One would want to know if the party in question

[Sinn Féin] has maintained its connections with ETA and with the now illegal Batasuna party, because it would be quite contrary to the agreement for that party to maintain its connections' (*Guardian*, 9 September 2002). More generally, the relationship between Sinn Féin and the Basque movement is one that its political opponents have used at times to point to the contradictions of republicans. Former Junior Minister Liz O'Donnell, during a debate in the Dáil on a bill on neutrality tabled by Sinn Féin TDs, dismissed the proposal as being disingenuous in the light of Sinn Fein's relationship with terrorist organisations abroad. In her opinion, republicans were 'fostering ETA terrorists in a fellow EU state', which meant that their 'claimed commitment to the demilitarisation of Europe apparently excludes the tons of Semtex in republican hands' (*IT*, 20 February 2003). Hence there would seem to be a price to pay for Sinn Féin's continued solidarity with those it sees as fighting for self-determination. However, the price would probably be higher were the party to sever all links with these movements. Its continued support may be used to show its rank and file that it has not softened its position on self-determination and reunification. In the light of the unease within its own ranks on some issues arising out of the peace process such as policing and the future of the IRA, its solidarity with Batasuna is a reminder to its members and critics alike of how attached Sinn Féin still is to the basic principles of self-determination.

The peace process: the American dimension

The arrest of three Irishmen in Colombia on 11 August 2001 was bad news for republicans. For the three men, It was the beginning of a long and tortuous judicial process in a country where the human rights situation and the issue of prisons has been featuring high on the agendas of human rights organisations such as Amnesty International or Human Rights Watch. Regarding the IRA, it raised serious doubts as to the validity of its ceasefire. These doubts inevitably extended to Sinn Féin, as it is in great part held accountable for IRA actions and as its presence in the process is conditioned by the continued ceasefire. A few days after the arrests, the IRA withdrew the offer that it had made to the International Commission on Decommissioning to agree on a scheme to put their weapons 'completely and verifiably beyond use'. The stated reason for doing so was the unionist rejection of the IRA proposal, although some observers saw a direct link with the arrests in Colombia. The continued presence of Sinn Féin within the executive was under increased scrutiny. This story was most detrimental to Sinn Féin's image in the USA, and to its relationship not only with the Bush administration but also with the party's close supporters and lobbyists. America has played, in the eyes of republicans, a fundamental role in the peace process, and an equally fundamental role in the support that it garners for the party, not only logistically and financially but also politically. Any damage to that relationship would inevitably represent not only the loss of influential supporters but also a considerable financial setback for the party.

The involvement of the USA in the peace process has been crucial in many ways, but there are different interpretations of the American administration's objectives and motives. Republicans see the reason behind US involvement as the result of mounting pressure from Irish America, a group which comprises, according to Sinn Féin's representative in the USA, Rita O'Hare, first-, second- and third-generation Irish-Americans who are sympathetic to the 'nationalist plight' (O'Hare, interview, 2003). She insists that this particular group was well informed, more so than the average British public, and was therefore able to make an informed decision on its position regarding the future of the north, although the portrayal of a politically aware Irish-American community is probably not consensual.

Sinn Féin sees the role of the USA as essential, for two reasons. First, in order to take off and then to gain momentum, the peace process needed to attract international attention, and the involvement of the American administration brought Northern Ireland into the limelight. Second, republicans saw the need for a neutral party, or 'honest broker', that could guarantee the even-handedness of the proceedings. In Sinn Féin's view, neither the Irish nor the British governments could act in that capacity, as they both had vested interests in the outcome of the situation. The American administration's even-handedness has indeed been remarked upon both by participants in the process and by scholars, as it has strived to steer clear from partisan positions. Thus America was perceived by Sinn Féin to bring balance to the manner in which issues would be approached and leaders would be treated. The US involvement is thus credited by O'Hare with forcing the British and unionist politicians to move out of what she calls a 'bunker-like mentality' to a position where they had to concede that no one could be excluded from the process. To support this argument, O'Hare refers to the Economic Conference in Chicago held in 1995 which was attended by unionist and republican representatives alike, the former being given no alternative but to accept Sinn Féin's presence. This was, in actual fact, the first time that they came in close contact, at an official or public level at least (O'Hare, interview).

Furthermore, the involvement of the USA was important in the sense that, according to republican thinking, it kept the British government in check. Several examples are given to illustrate this. The fact that Bill Clinton granted a limited visa to Gerry Adams to travel to the USA in January 1994, before the IRA announced its ceasefire and when republican leaders were still banned from travelling to Britain, is seen as proof of the independent stance that the USA was to take. This decision, taken against the advice of the State Department and in spite of protests voiced by the British government, angered unionists who condemned the 'film-star' reception afforded to Adams. Nevertheless, to ensure that their voice would be heard as well, the UUP sent one of its representatives, Martin Smyth, to the USA, coinciding with Gerry Adams' visit.

However, another explanation of US involvement has been put forward by academic Paul Dixon, in whose view the USA contributed strongly to edging the Republican Movement towards a strategy in which the leaders would be able to sell the peace process to their grassroots by highlighting the benefits that could be accrued from this. In his view, the international dimension was a 'carefully choreographed' strategy which provided discourses for players. In the case of Sinn Féin, it provided them with:

> access to discourses (Europe and the inevitability of Irish unity; the end of the Cold War and anti-imperialist troubles moving into peace processes; the power of the US and pan nationalism to push the British government etc) that has been used in an attempt to persuade the rank-and-file of the necessity to put an end to the armed struggle.
>
> (Dixon, 2002: 119)

In this analysis, the public display of British anger was part of a carefully staged strategy aimed both at 'creating the illusion of the pan nationalist front in which the US played an important symbolic role' and at showing republicans 'the influence they could have', while also serving to show that the 'British government still maintained the pan-unionist unity' (Dixon, 2002: 114).

The American dimension is not only important from a political perspective; it also has considerable logistical weight. America is the most important source of funding for Sinn Féin and has contributed in great measure to the peace process from a financial point of view. In 2002, the public money contributed by the Bush administration to Northern Ireland, through the International Fund for Ireland,[6] represented, according to the organisation's annual report, $2.5 million, intended to 'encourage contact, dialogue and reconciliation between nationalists and unionists throughout Ireland' (available online). Added to this is a significant amount of private investment which, according to Richard Haass,[7] has considerably benefited the region. 'Foreign investment has created 31,000 new jobs since 1998. . . . American investment alone has created more than 20,000 new jobs since 1994' (Haass, 2002, available online).

Fund-raising for Sinn Féin is carried out in the USA by the organisation 'Friends of Sinn Féin', established in 1995. Some estimates put the figure of the amount collected at over $5 million between 1994 and 2001 (*Observer*, 19 August 2001), which would undoubtedly make the USA the largest source of funding for Sinn Féin. This is evidenced by the figures published every year by the Public Office Commission, which records all donations received by the Irish political parties, since they are compelled, under the Electoral Act (1997), to give details of donations received. The figures for 2002 showed the extent to which Sinn Féin depended on the USA for its funding. Out of a total of €365,810 received in donations, $295,740 came from the USA, which made Sinn Féin the greatest beneficiary from donations, since it took almost twice as much as the largest party, Fianna Fáil, which declared €194,615, of which none was recorded as originating in the USA (Public Offices Commission, 2002, available online). For Sinn Féin, fund-raising in the USA has only been possible since the IRA was withdrawn from the list of designated terrorist organisations which is regularly published and updated by the State Department. The presence of an organisation on this list, as was the case with the Real IRA when it was added in November 2001, 'makes it illegal for persons in the United States or subject to US jurisdiction to provide material support to the Real IRA or any of its named aliases, requires US financial institutions to block assets of the designated groups, and enables us to deny visas to representatives of the group' (State Department, Press Release, 16 May 2001).[8] The IRA was originally withdrawn from that list in 1995, although it was subsequently added after the breakdown of the ceasefire in 1996. In that year, the State Department Report described it as one of the thirteen 'major terrorist groups', being 'a radical terrorist group formed in 1969 as the clandestine armed wing of Sinn Féin, a legal political movement dedicated to removing British forces from Northern Ireland and unifying Ireland. Has a Marxist orientation. Organized into small, tightly knit cells under the leadership of the Army Council' (Patterns of Global Terrorism, available online).

For this reason alone, the case of the Colombia Three was potentially deeply damaging for Sinn Féin. The story was problematic, as it raised contentious issues. The fact that the IRA was accused of training guerrilla movements abroad, notably in Colombia, was not in itself a new development, as suspicion, whether founded or not, that these types of links did exist had been voiced previously. But the group incriminated in this particular case, the Revolutionary Armed Front of Columbia (FARC), a Marxist organisation, was designated in the 2001 State Department list as a Foreign Terrorist Organisation. The deputy coordinator for counter-terrorism, Mark Wong, described it in his statement to the House Committee on International Relations, in April 2002, as the world's 'largest terrorist organization and perhaps its richest', operating within 'the world's most terrorism-afflicted nation. In 2001, for example, 55 percent of all terrorist attacks on U.S. interests abroad occurred in Colombia' (Wong, 2002, available online). Consequently, any connection with the FARC was not only unlawful but likely to provoke an angry reaction from the American administration. Furthermore, the FARC is suspected of financing its operations mainly through drug trafficking, the fight against which ranked as one of the priorities of the American administration before 9/11.

The story that was emerging regarding the arrests in Colombia was quite disturbing. The three Irishmen were accused of having provided technical and logistical support to the FARC in exchange for finance that the Colombian organisation had allegedly raised through its drug-trafficking operations. This was deemed ironic as republicans had fought against what their party termed the 'drugs epidemic' at home. David Andrews, former Irish Foreign Minister, pointed to the contradiction between the movement's stated anti-drugs policy and a connection between the IRA and the notorious drug-smuggling organisation (*IT*, 17 August 2001). Not to mention the fact that, if the allegations were true, the IRA was in direct breach of its ceasefire, which would then raise serious questions regarding the role of Sinn Féin in the executive.

The IRA immediately published a communiqué in which it clearly stated that the three men had not been sent to Colombia by the organisation and that no official mission had been authorised. Sinn Féin stated repeatedly that it had had no knowledge of the presence of the three men in Colombia. Privately, Sinn Féin leaders talked of their anger and their astonishment at learning this news, which was potentially so damaging for their party. The three men arrested were all known to the British and Irish security forces. James McCauley was said to be the leading figure in the 'engineering department' of the IRA; James Monaghan had contributed to the development back in 1973 of such devices as the mortar and the remote control. More denials came from Sinn Féin, some from Gerry Adams, who stated categorically that 'they were not there to represent Sinn Féin. I would have had to authorise such a project and I did not do so. Neither was I or anyone else asked' (*IT*, 29 August 2001). In fact, Sinn Féin was quite indignant that it should be made accountable for the actions of men who it said were former members of the party. A few days after the arrests, the Cuban Ministry of Foreign Affairs stated that the third man, Niall Connolly, was the Sinn Féin representative on the island. It transpired a few days later that Connolly was indeed the republican representative in Cuba. The explanation provided by the Sinn Féin President was quite contorted, when he stated that a senior figure had asked Connolly to fill that role, but this so-called appointment had not gone through the proper procedures (*IT*, 23 October 2001). Which ever way Sinn Féin tried to spin the story in order to distance itself from the case, it could do little to put an end to speculation by politicians and the media alike regarding the Republican Movement's involvement with the FARC. A report from the *Observer* contended that Sinn Féin would be one of the beneficiaries of the alleged deal made between the IRA and the FARC whereby, according to security sources, the IRA would provide logistical and military assistance in exchange for considerable sums of money, as the party was in dire need of cash to pay its numerous staff and electoral workers to maintain its political clinics (*Observer*, 19 August 2001).

Undoubtedly, the story proved quite damaging to the relationship between Sinn Féin and the USA, especially in the wake of 9/11. The party's efforts to distance itself from any terrorist organisation, its repeated messages of sympathy to the victims of the terrorist attacks on New York and Washington, were in themselves insufficient to restore the confidence that had been built over the years on Capitol Hill and among the Irish-American community. Nevertheless, something needed to be done to regain that confidence, and this was delivered by the IRA on 23 October. On that day, Martin McGuinness was in Washington, meeting representatives of the US government at 5 p.m. and Richard Haass at 6.15. At 5 p.m. that day, the IRA announced its first decommissioning act. This was hardly a coincidence, but rather, probably, a confidence-building measure on the part of republicans to try to regain lost ground.

The three men arrested in Colombia argued from the outset that they were there as tourists, although they did admit to travelling on false passports and claimed to be in the country to observe the peace talks. In spite of stories that appeared regularly in the papers which seemed to cast a shadow over their innocence and prompted their supporters to talk about a trial by media, the case against the three men was not as straightforward as had been initially presented. Indeed, the evidence produced in the Washington file that was put before the House Committee investigating the links between the FARC and the IRA was not in itself conclusive. The commander-in-chief of the armed forces of Colombia, General Fernando Tapias, could not confirm that the three men had been sent on an official IRA mission (*Guardian*, 25 April 2002). Asa Hutchinson, administrator of the US Drug Enforcement Agency, stated that there was no intelligence indicating IRA involvement (*Washington Post*, 25 April 2002). However, the report also quoted British sources as suggesting that the IRA had received up to $2 million from the FARC, although it also specified that there was no hard evidence to support this (Porter, 2002, available online).

Sinn Féin maintained that it had no case to answer and that it could not be held responsible for the presence of the three men in Colombia. Gerry Adams himself was asked to attend the House Committee hearings, but he refused on the grounds that this could prejudice the forthcoming court case, and that his party had nothing to do with the cases. His refusal was seen as an indication that Sinn Féin had something to hide, which politicians such as unionist leader David Trimble and SDLP's Alex Atwood were quick to highlight. Whether or not this was the case, it is clear that Sinn Féin tried to distance itself from the case for the Colombia

Three. A campaign to release the three men was put in place immediately after their arrest, 'Bring them home', organised by Caitríona Ruane, a human rights activist who was subsequently elected to the assembly in November 2003 for Sinn Féin. The main arguments put forward by this support group were that the three men would not be given a fair trial in Colombia, as the Colombian legal system was deemed one of the most corrupt of the region, and it would not therefore be in a position to guarantee their human rights or even their safety within the prison system. According to the documentation put together by the campaigners, 612 inmates died in the space of four years in Colombian prisons (*Bring Them Home*, available online). Dublin West TD Seán Crowe was one of the most vocal supporters of the Colombia Three, and made several trips to the country to attend the court hearings. The case against the men was partially dropped in April 2004, when the Bogota Court acquitted them of training the FARC guerrillas. However, they were convicted on using false passports, and their sentences ranged from twenty-six months for Connolly to thirty-six months and eighteen days for McCauley and forty-four months for Monaghan. But an appeal lodged by the office of the Attorney General in Colombia delayed the release of the men.

The arrest of Niall Connolly highlighted another possible contradiction that Sinn Féin had to manage within its overall relationship with the USA. Building links with revolutionary movements and countries presents risks, insofar as these particular connections are frowned upon by some of its most important allies, notably the USA. This is undoubtedly the case for Cuba. For a number of years, Sinn Féin's policy consistently demanded the end of the US blockade and praised the Cuban socialist model, much in the same manner in which this had been done in the mid-1980s with the Sandinistas in Nicaragua. Sinn Féin has shown that it can be relatively independent when it comes to making foreign policy choices. Indeed, Gerry Adams announced that he would not cancel his scheduled trip to Cuba in December 2001, where he spent four days, along with a number of Sinn Féin representatives. The purpose of the visit was the unveiling of a monument to the memory of the 1981 hunger strikes. In the process, Adams met Fidel Castro, whose regime he thanked for its support during the hunger strikes and the peace process. This visit went ahead in spite of the strong criticism that it attracted from some of Sinn Féin's supporters on Capitol Hill, such as Peter King who advised the Sinn Féin President not to go to Cuba, considering it a mistake.

There are other contradictions at play within Sinn Féin's international policy and its relationship with its US supporters. These came to the fore in February 2003, with the debate surrounding the war in Iraq. Sinn Féin strongly criticised the Bush administration's policy, and was among the leading voices in Ireland in the opposition to the war. But republicans see no contradiction between their continued efforts to garner support for the peace process on Capitol Hill and their opposition to some of the policies of their American supporters. As such, there was no perceived lack of consistency between Sinn Féin's welcoming of the US administration's involvement in Northern Ireland and its opposition to the foreign policy of that same administration, as both components of the party's foreign policy are seen as separate. Therefore, in spite of the republican grassroots' involvement in the campaign against the war in Iraq and subsequent demonstrations, where Sinn Féin members kept a very obvious presence (such as in the march organised in Dublin on 15 February 2003), Gerry Adams' keynote address to the 2003 Ard Fheis did not once mention the war in Iraq or the Bush administration. Furthermore, George Bush's visit to Northern Ireland in April 2003, during the war in Iraq, could have presented Sinn Féin with a dilemma. On the one hand, the party had been actively campaigning against the war, but it could not be overtly seen as castigating the power whose efforts are deemed important to the continuation of the peace process. When a demonstration was organised two miles outside Stormont Castle to protest against the visit of the US President, Sinn Féin kept a relatively low profile, and when asked by the peace movement to shun the American President in protest against its policy on Iraq, it refused. This prompted the *Observer* correspondent Henry McDonald to conclude that:

> republican realpolitik dictates that while Gerry can fly to Havana and hug as many trees as he pleases in the end he will always opt for America. Castro might be cuddly but the pro death penalty-for-cop killers Peter King and his chums in corporate America can deliver far more in terms of finance and influence than the Cuban dictator could ever offer.
>
> (*Observer*, 6 April 2003)

Indeed, it has been suggested that Sinn Féin's socialist rhetoric is substantially toned down in the way it is presented in the USA, its strategists privileging an image centred on the role it has played in the peace process. '[Another] conflict is their packaging of their socialist agenda to a capitalist Irish-American audience. Again it is a practiced opacity that enables Sinn Féin to appeal to the Irish-American allegiance to the "cause" whilst concealing their "socialist agenda"', writes Seán McGough in his study on the marketing of Sinn Féin (McGough, 2002: 20).

Adams refutes this analysis. He points to the fact that no one has ever asked him to boycott Tony Blair when the British government was in full support of the US administration in its approach to the Iraqi crisis, although it could be argued that the parallel does not fully apply, since the roles played by the British and American governments in the peace process are not comparable. Nevertheless, the Sinn Féin President contends that his position has been consistent. Therefore, he specifies that on the occasion of the American President's visit to Northern Ireland, he gave a letter to both George Bush and Tony Blair outlining Sinn Féin's concern on the war in Iraq. He also recalls challenging Bill Clinton on the US administration's policy regarding Cuba and pressing for the cancellation of the Third World debt. But the view he takes is, ultimately, pragmatic. 'Some challenge us, some deeply criticise us, some agree. But we continue. People don't have to agree with what we do' (Adams, interview, 2004). Although the avowed objective of Sinn Féin's engagements in the USA is to win support for the peace process, this does not, according to Adams, 'prevent us from keeping our independence'. And as Rita O'Hare puts it more pragmatically, 'do you think the Bush administration really cares about what a small party like Sinn Féin thinks about its policy on Iraq?' (O'Hare, interview).

Sovereignty and neutrality

Ultimately, what guides Sinn Féin's policy on international relations can be summarised in one word: neutrality. This is seen as a key principle, one that has been inherited from history and must be retained at all costs. 'Each nation comes to neutrality from its own history. What's good about Irish neutrality is how we came to be neutral. It's our own experience as a nation and a people, of those who have been colonised, of those who have been oppressed, those who have suffered from imperialism' (O'Connor, interview). This was one of the main reasons for Sinn Féin's opposition to the Irish government's stance on the war in Iraq, it was its main objection to the Nice referenda held in the Republic of Ireland in 2001 and 2002, and it drives many of its analyses on the European Union in general. Therefore, Sinn Féin strongly condemned the Irish government for allowing US military aircraft to land in Shannon to refuel on their way to Iraq. This, in its view, was only a development within a more global governmental policy which has been gradually undermining Irish neutrality. This debate, to which Sinn Féin is not the only contributor, found its most heated expression during the campaign for the referendum of the Nice Treaty, which took place in Ireland in June 2001. Sinn Féin, alongside the Greens and the Socialist Party, fought the campaign in the No camp, mainly on the grounds that this EU Treaty contravened the neutrality and sovereignty of the Irish Republic.

The Nice Treaty was agreed by the fifteen EU member states in December 2000. Its main objective was to provide for the enlargement of the EU, with ten new member states from the former Eastern Europe, and to alter the organisation of the EU, especially at the level of decision-making. Therefore, it provided for changes in the nomination of the commissioners, which would mean that when the twenty-five-member Union came into effect, the number of commissioners would be reduced and rotate among the different member states. The European Parliament, currently consisting of 626 members, would be enlarged to 732, but Ireland's share would be reduced from fifteen to twelve Euro deputies. Finally, the qualified majority voting system, which allows decisions to be taken by majority and not by unanimity, would be extended to a further thirty-five areas.[9] The Treaty of Nice also contained a clause of Common and Foreign Policy, which provided for, among other things, strengthened security and the safeguard of common values in conformity with the United Nations charter.

Sinn Fein was opposed the Nice Treaty on several grounds. The qualified majority was seen as a move away from the EU being a 'partnership of equals' to a situation where 'a core group of states could advance ahead of the rest, as they would have a stronger say in common decisions' (Nice Manifesto, 2001). This was also seen as an erosion of the right of veto of individual states. Furthermore, the Treaty, in the republican analysis, eroded neutrality as it 'further develops the common foreign, security and defence policies of the EU', already diminished with Ireland's involvement in the EU's Rapid Reaction Force, 'an army designed for war, an army to impose by force the interests of the EU or an elite within it. There is no requirement in Nice to have a UN mandate' (Nice Manifesto). Its argument on neutrality was sneered at by the then Minister for Justice, John O'Donoghue, who asked: 'Can this, we wonder, be the same Sinn Féin that also seems quite at ease with the idea that private armies should hold on to their lethal and illegal arsenals until they themselves, in their own good time, decide otherwise?' (*IT*, 28 May 2001).

The government's campaign was centred on the need for Ireland to accept Nice, as membership of the Union carried responsibilities as well as benefits. The Nice referendum was portrayed, first and foremost, as a necessary step to facilitate integration. The fact that the Treaty would be implemented was presented as a *fait accompli*, something which might have irritated the electorate, which was seemingly asked to give its opinion while at the same being told that this opinion would, ultimately, carry little weight. Taoiseach Bertie Ahern thus warned the electorate that if they voted No, 'all we would do is succeed in marginalising our influence. . . . The rest of the Union would either find a means or legal advice for leaving us behind and going ahead without us, or alternatively we would have, like Denmark, to hold a second vote to reverse our earlier decision' (*IT*, 19 May 2001).

But more fundamentally, the main problem lay with the manner in which the Nice Treaty was presented. Indeed, as an opinion poll showed, the reasons for voting No were, primarily, to do with lack of information (39 per cent of people surveyed), and not with the issue of enlargement, which featured very little in their concerns over Nice (only 3 per cent quoted a 'refugee problem' as their reason for opposing the Treaty (Gilland, 2003). Furthermore, although the No camp's argument over the 'militarisation' of the EU certainly struck a chord among part of the electorate, an opinion poll carried out a week before the referendum showed more support than rejection of Ireland's participation in the Rapid Reaction Force, being favoured by 49 per cent as opposed to 32 per cent against and with 20 per cent having no opinion (*IT*, 2 June 2001).

The Treaty of Nice was rejected by 53.9 per cent of the voters, with the lowest turnout (34.8 per cent) ever registered for a referendum concerning the EU.[10] The results were all the more surprising given that all three major parties (Fianna Fáil, Fine Gael and Labour) had campaigned in favour of the Treaty. This was not necessarily a reflection of the support for the political organisations that had opposed it. It was more, according to the *Irish Times* foreign correspondent, 'a reaction against the smug assumption of domestic and European leaders that the electorate here will do what it is told and that there is no need to knock on doors or give time for a proper debate' (*IT*, 11 June 2001), an analysis that was shared by many commentators.

The Nice referendum was put to the vote again, in February 2003. In the meantime, some changes were sought and obtained by the Irish government. One concerned the introduction of new structures at the level of the Oireachtas, whereby ministers had to appear before the legislative committee before and after attending the European Council. The government also secured, at a European Council in Seville in June 2002, a declaration that was added to the Nice Treaty and which stated that 'Ireland's participation in the EU common foreign and security policy does not prejudice its traditional policy of military neutrality'. Therefore, Ireland was not bound by any mutual commitment and would not be a party to any plans to develop a European army (Department of the Taoiseach, 2002: 14). The Seville Declaration introduced the concept of a triple lock preceding any European rapid response force participation: it had to have a UN mandate as well as Cabinet and Dáil approval.

However, the Seville declaration was not an integral part of the Treaty of Nice. This was going to be one of the main arguments of the No campaign, and particularly of Sinn Féin, which saw the document as 'political statements, not protocols and so do not alter a word of the Treaty' (*AP*, 10 October 2002). Sinn Féin's campaign was fought along similar lines as for the previous referendum, based on three key concepts: neutrality, sovereignty and the danger of a two-tier Europe. To this was added the fact that the holding of a second referendum on the same Treaty was undemocratic, as it implied that the government was ignoring the original decision of the electorate. Some of the party's critics pointed to the fact that the choice of terminology of republican leaders, such as the word 'superstate', was reminiscent of that of the British Eurosceptics, academic Bridgid Laffan concluding that 'if the issue was not so serious, it would be amusing to see the president of Sinn Féin taking his political cue from the Tory right' (*IT*, 10 September 2002). Sinn Féin's position was scrutinised by journalists and politicians alike. Paul Gillespie, *Irish Times* Foreign Editor, pointed to what he saw as a contradiction between Sinn Féin's attitude to sovereignty, stressing its inviolability, and the 'experimental approach to sharing sovereignty exemplified by the Belfast Agreement' (*IT*, 21 September 2002). The SDLP's Seán Farren warned of the dangers of a second No vote which would isolate both sides of the island, especially given the fact that the north had benefited from Europe's Peace Programmes, and stressing that Sinn Féin's position was not in line with the sentiment of the nationalist community which was, by and large, pro-European (*IT*, 19 August 2002). Martin Mansergh, adviser to the Taoiseach during the all-party negotiations, urged Sinn Féin to reflect on its own argument on the unionist veto when condemning the end of the unanimity rule for a number of decisions at European level, arguing that 'vetoes should only protect the most vital interests, not block progress unreasonably' (*IT*, 13 September 2002).

Most pro-Nice observers insisted upon the role that Europe had played in normalising relations between Ireland and the UK, putting an end to what Mansergh called the 'claustrophobic relationship' between the two islands. In that sense, Sinn Féin's European policy was deemed difficult to comprehend. However, Sinn Féin does not overtly reject membership of the European Union. The key concept that it puts forward, according to Marylou McDonald, Sinn Féin EU candidate for the June 2004 election, is one of 'critical engagement' (McDonald, interview, 2003). Sinn Féin registers its 'profound concerns', such as the 'transfer of political and economic sovereignty to largely unaccountable European institutions', the 'economic centralisation and the peripheralising of regions like Ireland', and the abandonment of Irish neutrality. It stresses the positive impact of the structural funding, acknowledging the progress made in developing infrastructures and in facilitating an 'all-Ireland economic network'. However, Sinn Féin, like other parties campaigning against the Nice Treaties, was criticised by the Yes camp for seeking an 'à la carte' membership.

One of the elements that featured more prominently in the second Nice referendum was the issue of the accessing countries. Some voices within the No camp sought to focus part of their campaign on the allegation that enlargement would entail so-called 'floods' of immigrants into the country. Sinn Féin was castigated by the then Minister of State Tom Kitt for keeping silent on these allegations. However, this particular accusation is not supported by any evidence. Indeed, the different press releases and statements made throughout the campaign by Sinn Féin spokespersons not only sought to dissociate the party from such rhetoric, but emphasised that immigration 'was not an issue in the last referendum campaign and Sinn Féin is opposed to its introduction as an issue in this one' (*AP* 15 August 2002). Sinn Féin further stated on various occasions the similarities between the accession countries and Ireland, both being considered peripheral countries, and emphasised that it welcomed enlargement and opposed the concept of a Fortress Europe. Indeed, some in the No camp criticised Sinn Féin for its particular stance on the accession countries. The Secretary of the No platform, Anthony Coughlan, in a letter to TD Seán Crowe, affirmed that 'if Sinn Féin in particular had adopted a more critical attitude to the government's "own goal" in agreeing to a different immigration policy for Ireland from most of other EU states, it could have increased the No vote further in working class communities' (*IT*, 28 October 2002).

The second Nice referendum was approved by the Irish electorate by 62.8 per cent votes to 47.2 per cent. The success of the Yes campaign was due in great part to the fact that it had been a vigorous contest, contrary to the first referendum. The fact that the pro-Nice parties prioritised the campaign was shown by the overall spending which was nine times more than that of the No camp. Moreover, the Seville Declaration and the triple lock guarantees over the issue of neutrality had probably been sufficient to sway a large part of the electorate. However, for Sinn Féin, this did not mean that the debate was over; on the contrary. The controversy surrounding the issue of neutrality in the wake of the war in Iraq showed indeed that this issue has the potential to mobilise the electorate. A few days after an anti-war demonstration in Dublin that brought together 100,000 people on 15 February 2003, Sinn Féin introduced a Private Member's Bill in the Dáil, the first to be tabled by republicans since they started participating in the institutions of the Republic. The Bill sought to enshrine neutrality in the Irish Constitution, by introducing a new article that would have read. 'Ireland affirms that it is a neutral state. To this end, the state shall, in particular, maintain a policy of non-membership of military alliances.' Moreover, the proposal sought to amend the clause of the constitution on the declaration of or participation in war, by adding that the state 'shall not participate in any war or other armed conflict, nor aid foreign powers in any way in preparation of war or other armed conflict, or conduct of war or other armed conflict, save with the assent of Dáil Éireann'. This was clearly set against the backdrop of the debate on whether the government should allow US military aircraft to refuel in Shannon, thereby, in the eyes of Sinn Féin and other critics, effectively helping the USA in its preparation of the war on Iraq. The Bill was easily defeated, as 100 TDs (both Fianna Fáil and Fine Gael) voted against it and thirty-five TDS (Sinn Féin, the Greens and independent TDs) in favour (the Labour Party abstained). Sinn Féin's Bill was seen by the

Minister of State for Foreign Affairs as a 'blatant attempt to confuse the issue, to spread doubt or misinformation, and to portray this government as somehow "soft" on the question of Irish neutrality' (*IT*, 19 February 2003). However, on a more pragmatic level, the Bill was a significant move on the part of Sinn Féin TDs. Not only did it show that it could capture the mood of the country on important issues and bring support to the party (according to Sinn Féin Press Officer Dawn Doyle, the Nice campaign greatly contributed to raising the party's profile in the Republic), but also because issues such as neutrality showed, according to Gerry Adams, the potential for a realignment to the left within Irish politics.

Sinn Féin led a vigorous campaign for the 2004 European election, fielding a candidate in all five European constituencies (four in the Republic and one in Northern Ireland). Its efforts at raising the profile of its Dublin candidate, Mary Lou McDonald, in a constituency that was from the outset targeted as a 'winnable seat', meant that she appeared on various television programmes, in newspaper articles, and travelled with her election team in a 'Sinn Féin' bus, relaying the message that Sinn Féin was not anti-European but for a Europe of Equals. Its potential MEPs were set ambitious tasks in the party's electoral manifesto, *Campaigning for Full Equality*, as they would, for instance, campaign for 'full equality', champion workers' rights, work towards the elimination of poverty, and defend human rights and civil liberties. Some of the party's adversaries viewed this type of programme as more rhetorical than practical and criticised the candidates' lack of concrete knowledge of the European Union. However, the message that Sinn Féin chose to put forward obviously found an echo among the electorate. The party's four candidates in the Republic of Ireland obtained a total of 11.1 per cent of the first preference votes, putting them slightly ahead of the Labour Party (with 10.6 per cent). Mary Lou McDonald won the Dublin seat with 14.3 per cent of the vote, and her colleague Pearse Doherty came second in the North West constituency, only 1,200 first preference votes behind the independent candidate who topped the poll (although Pearse was eliminated on subsequent counts). In Northern Ireland, Bairbre de Brún took the seat on the first count, being 7,000 votes ahead of the quota. In spite of the repeated calls from Minister of Justice Michael McDowell to reject Sinn Féin on the basis of its connection with the IRA, the republican vote was strengthened on both sides of the border, which not only vindicated Sinn Féin's political and electoral strategists, but also showed that, in the words of Martin McGuinness, the vote for Sinn Féin was not a 'transition thing' (*IT*, 14 June 2004).

6 The legacy of the conflict

When Gusty Spence, former UVF member and prisoner, announced the loyalist paramilitaries' ceasefire in October 1994, the tone employed was unusually compassionate: 'in all sincerity, we offer to the loved ones of all innocent victims over the past twenty-five years abject and true remorse. No words of ours will compensate for the intolerable suffering they have undergone during the conflict' (Taylor, 1997: 348). The loyalist organisations' plea for forgiveness was not immediately echoed by the IRA, since according to republican thinking, the 'war' as they saw it was justified, and they operated within this logic. Although some Sinn Féin leaders had sought at times to distance themselves from certain actions, republicans in general were reluctant to embark on an introspective process and reassess their own past. This was compounded by the fact that they tended to cast themselves and their organisation as soldiers, but also as victims. Researcher Mary Smyth talks of a culture of victimhood within the republican and loyalist paramilitary groups, without which 'their violence becomes politically inexplicable and morally indefensible' (Smyth, 1998: 6). Nevertheless, there was a gradual shift within the IRA away from the perception of victimhood towards one where it was accepted that it had also been a perpetrator.

Reconciliation

Acknowledging the past was to be a fundamental principle on the road to peace and reconciliation, in a context where perceptions differed so utterly that there was no agreement even on the terminology used to describe the conflict. Thirty years of what Queen Elizabeth called 'civil unrest and terrorism' (*IT*, 13 April 2000) on her first ever visit to Northern Ireland in March 2000, or of what the IRA would have described as a war, have deeply scarred Northern Irish society on a number of levels. The cost of the Troubles is high, particularly when set against the population of Northern Ireland.[1] Some 3,601 people have died, of which a disproportionate number were civilians (1,868), often referred to as the 'innocent victims' of the conflict.[2] Moreover, there have been, proportionally, more casualties within the nationalist minority than in the unonist community, the death ratios being 2.5 per 1,000 as opposed to 1.9 per 1,000 (Fay *et al.*, 1999: 164). A further 40,000 to 50,000 people are estimated to have been injured, which translates into a large number of 'secondary victims'.[3] This relatively high level of violence has strengthened the sense of division that already ran deep in Northern Ireland.

In that respect, any agreement reached by all parties participating in the discussions could not focus only on the political or institutional dimensions. It had to tackle the crucial issue of how to deal with the past, and to study what mechanisms could be put in place in order to work towards the goal of reconciliation. None of the previous agreements aiming to resolve the conflict in the north had placed any great emphasis on this issue. The Sunningdale Agreement, in 1973, was fundamentally a political solution as to how power could be devolved to Northern Ireland, while reflecting the different communities that compose it, but failed to analyse the human impact of violence. Similarly, the Anglo-Irish Agreement of 1985 did not include any specific measure aimed at reconciling the divisions through the recognition of the traumatic experiences of the population, although it did stress the importance of promoting reconciliation and respect for human rights. But the central questions underlying these preoccupations were those of cultural and military cooperation rather than the establishment of mechanisms to redress past injustices. In that respect, the Belfast Agreement of April 1998 added a new dimension: that of the necessity of building a bridge between the two communities not only by demanding respect for the 'different traditions' that compose Northern Ireland, but also by accepting that both communities shared a traumatic past, even if this violence and the trauma that ensued were subject to different, and in some instances antagonistic, interpretations.

Facing the past in the Northern Irish context presents several problems. In a society where identities have been largely shaped by history, which is re-enacted periodically through marches and parades, the past is never one-dimensional, and is more likely to divide than to bring together. First, none of the agents of violence would agree on the reasons for the violence and its nature. The majority of republicans would see the conflict as a situation of war between the security forces and the IRA, and would view the state and its representatives as responsible for a substantial part of the suffering. But only the supporters of the IRA and, to a much lesser extent, part of the nationalist community, would agree to qualify the conflict as a 'war'. On the other hand, a significant section of the unionist community would tend to consider that the violence was a matter of 'terrorism' and that their community was unilaterally wronged by this violence. This perception had an important effect on the manner in which the peace process was viewed. According to Robin Eames, Church of Ireland Archbishop of Armagh, 'perhaps the most significant emotion to emerge within the Protestant community as details of the "small print" of the Peace process began to emerge was hurt' (Eames, 2000: 14). Indeed, the DUP strongly believes that the Agreement has rewarded those who perpetrated the violence, whereas victims have been ignored, and it seeks to 'oppose terrorists and their organisations who would seek to promote their fellow travellers as victims' (DUP Manifesto, 2003). Therefore, this party holds the view that republicans are to blame for the past violence. Ian Paisley Jr. said in 1997:

> our whole community, indeed our whole country, has been the victim of the IRA for over 30 years. We have been victims of their war, and we are now victims of their proxy war involving the parading issue. If we are not careful we will be made victims of an IRA peace.
> (Northern Ireland Forum Debates, 4 July 1997, available online)

Nevertheless, this is not an accurate picture. Republican paramilitaries were responsible for 55.7 per cent of all deaths, loyalists for 27.4 per cent, the British army 8.9 per cent, the RUC 1.5 per cent and the UDR 0.3 per cent, the remaining 6 per cent being attributed to 'others' (Fay *et al.*, 1999: 169). The Women's Coalition representative Pearl Sagar proposed a definition of victims that was far more far-reaching and generous. According to her,

> the costs of the conflict in Northern Ireland are often measured, quite properly, in terms of lives lost, human beings maimed and property destroyed. It is our view that there are many other costs that must be acknowledged and recorded, including people imprisoned and their families, those who lost their lives in controversial circumstances, those unjustly imprisoned and those harassed and abused by members of the RUC and the British Army. All such people and their relatives are entitled, as a minimum, to have the truth of what happened acknowledged.
> (Northern Ireland Forum Debates, 6 December 1996)

In the run-up to the Good Friday Agreement, the sense of resentment running through all levels of civil society was high. The majority of the deaths were deemed 'random' and unjustified. Forgiving as part of the mental process of reconciling memories was thus complex, all the more so given that Northern Ireland is a very small territorial entity. Consequently, there is a geographical proximity between 'victims' and 'perpetrators' that does not allow for much anonymity. As one mother explained when the early release of prisoners was announced, it was likely that she would find herself in the street one day face to face with the killer of her son. Notwithstanding these difficulties, the peace process acknowledged early on the importance of dealing with the issue of victims. The Secretary of State Mo Mowlam announced in 1997 the establishment of a Commission 'to look at possible ways to recognise the pain and suffering felt by victims of violence arising from the Troubles of the last 30 years, including those who have died or been injured in the service of the community' (Bloomfield, 1998: 8). The Chairperson of this Commission, former civil servant Kenneth Bloomfield, had himself survived an attempted assassination in 1988. However, he sought to reassure all parties as to his impartiality in the matter, specifying that 'any individual's involvement in unlawful activity does not lessen the grief and loss of the family who mourn him or her. . . . We need to remember that our society does not attribute guilt by association.' He thus defined victims as 'the surviving injured and those who care for them, together with those close relatives who mourn their dead' (Bloomfield, 1998: 14). In his report *We Will Remember Them*, Bloomfield explored different ways of dealing with past traumas in order to find consensual ways of remembering the past and of compensating victims. The recommendations ranged from the setting up of appropriate structures to deal with victims to the building of a memorial. However, some criticised what was perceived as a strong focus on victims of paramilitary violence, to the detriment of victims of the security forces.

The compromise reached in the Agreement attempted to reconcile both individual and collective dimensions of the legacy of the conflict. A section was dedicated to the 'Reconciliation and Victims of violence', which stressed that 'it is essential to acknowledge and address the suffering of the victims of violence as a necessary element of reconciliation' (GFA, 1998: 21). Many initiatives were subsequently taken to address the issue of victims. The Secretary of State nominated Adam Ingram as Victims Minister in the NIO,[4] and a Victims Liaison Unit was established, which aimed to provide assistance to victims' support groups, fund the Northern Ireland Memorial Fund and implement the findings of the Bloomfield report.[5] The Human Rights Commission established under the Agreement has also tackled the issue, and has set out four conditions under which it aims to work: the right to information about the incidents of violence in question; the right to adequate compensation; the right to have someone held to account for the violence inflicted on them; and the right to be treated equally with other victims of violence (NIHRC, 2003).

The issue of prisoners, although it did not, strictly speaking, come under the section dealing with victims, was also tackled during the multi-party talks, being an important element of the healing process. In April 1998, there were almost 500 prisoners in Northern Ireland, the UK and the Republic of Ireland, who belonged to republican and loyalist para-military organisations. Under the Agreement, those whose organisation was committed to and maintained a ceasefire were to be released by May 2000. This was a fundamental point, one which greatly helped both the Republican Movement and the loyalist parties to sell the Agreement to their rank and file, but it also revealed a willingness on the part of participants to come to terms with violence and to start to forgive its perpetrators. The two communities reacted differently to this measure. The nationalists seemed to accept this as part of the overall agreement, whereas the unonists found it more difficult to deal with. A poll carried out a week before the May 1998 referendum showed that the main reason for voting against the Agreement among the Protestant community was precisely the early release of prisoners (45 per cent of No voters). This proportion was substantially higher than the number intending to vote No on the basis that the Agreement represented the 'beginning of a move towards a united Ireland' (18 per cent) (*IT*, 15 May 1998). Their essential belief was that many prisoners, no matter what group they belonged to, were getting off lightly and that whatever time they would have spent in prison would not sufficiently reflect the seriousness of their crime. This measure was also seen as lending political legitimacy to those considered to be, quite simply, terrorists. Yet it was a fundamental move, not only because of its political implications, but because it gave society the oppor-tunity to collectively forgive those whom it had held responsible for the suffering.[6]

In total, 429 prisoners have been released in Northern Ireland and forty-five in the Republic since the signing of the Good Friday Agreement. Of these, approximately 225 were republicans. However, this process was not without its problems. For instance, the announcement in June 1999 that Patrick Magee, who was responsible for the 1984 Brighton bomb which killed five people, was to be released, prompted the unionist leader David Trimble to call for the resignation of the Northern Ireland Secretary Mo Mowlam. Nevertheless, the high security prison of Long Kesh, specif-ically built in 1975 to host paramilitary prisoners, closed its gates on 28 July 2000. From then on, only five men whose organisation was on cease-fire and who had been convicted prior to the signing of the Agreement remained imprisoned, in Castlereagh, in the Republic of Ireland. Those five men had been sentenced for the killing of Detective Garda Gerry McCabe in Adare, on 7 June 1996. The dispute that ensued focused on the Republic's interpretation of eligibility under the GFA. According to Sinn Féin, the early release provision applied to the five men as they ful-filled the conditions set out in the Agreement: their crime was related to the conflict, and their organisation was on ceasefire. However, the Dublin government has taken a different view, considering that the crime, not immediately acknowledged by the IRA as being carried out in its name, was related to the robbery of a post office and therefore should not be treated in the same manner as the crimes for which the remaining republican prisoners had been released. This issue presents an obvious dilemma. On the one hand, the authorities' position did not seem to be wholly consistent, as it had supported the early release scheme as part of the overall mechanism for reconciliation in Northern Ireland, but was excluding this particular case on the grounds that it was not, strictly speaking, covered by the Agreement. On the other hand, the killing of Garda McCabe, although not in itself planned, contravened the IRA's own rules of not attacking military or police personnel in the Republic, and is seen by the public more as a criminal than a political act. The controversy surrounding the killing of Gerry McCabe resurfaced in May 2004, when Gerry Adams revealed that the Irish government had agreed to release the men if a deal had been brokered in October of the previous year on decommissioning and the reinstatement of the institutions. Bertie Ahern explained to the Dáil that such a move would 'happen only in the context of acts of total completion', that is, 'arms decommissioning and an end to all forms of paramilitarism by the IRA' (*IT*, 13 May 2004). The prisoners took their case to the Supreme Court, which ruled, at the end of January 2004, that their early release was at the discretion of the Minister for Justice. This decision infuriated Martin Ferris, who exclaimed:

> The Irish government cannot preach to others about their obligations in relation to the peace process when they themselves are not willing to live up to their responsibility, and it is certainly not good enough that these men's rights under the GFA are left to the whim of a vindictive and anti-republican Minister for Justice.
>
> (PR, 20 January 2004)

Sinn Féin's position is consistent with its overall stance on the issue of prisoners. As it campaigns for the early release of these men, it sees no contradiction in having the bodhran – Irish traditional musical instruments – that are made by these prisoners sold in its different shops. One Sinn Féin local representative, David Cullinane, candidate for the 2004 local elections in Waterford, clearly stated that although he personally 'repudiated' the killing of Gerry McCabe, 'for a long number of years Sinn Fein supported IRA prisoners and we always support republican prisoners. They are part of an armed organisation that is on ceasefire for the last eight years and is committed to the Peace Process. It's an organisation I hope will be disbanded in the long term' (*Waterford News*, 26 September 2003).

Prisoners, or ex-prisoners, are seen by republicans as being part of the victims of the conflict.[7] Coiste na n-Iarchimí, the umbrella organisation that was launched in 2000 to coordinate all groups and individuals working for the reinsertion of republican ex-prisoners, assessed the figure of republicans imprisoned during the conflict at 15,000.[8] These men and women encounter well-documented problems of reinsertion, as it is estimated that they constitute, for example, about a quarter of the unemployed in West Belfast alone. Coiste highlights some contradictions in the legislation, for instance, the fact that ex-prisoners are ineligible for employment in the Civil Service, yet one of the Northern Ireland ministers in the power-sharing executive from 2000 to 2002, Martin McGuinness, was himself an ex-prisoner.

Prisoners have always played a significant role in republican history. They were seen as having paid a huge tribute to the cause, and there is undoubtedly a sense of debt that the movement as a whole feels towards those who gave up their freedom. Therefore, the early release of prisoners was considered essential in bringing the rank-and-file members to accept the agreement. When a special Ard Fheis was organised on 10 May 1998 to discuss and eventually adopt the document, four high-profile prisoners, the Balcombe Street Gang,[9] were granted parole by the Irish government to attend the debate. As Gerry Adams recalls, 'the huge spontaneous outpour of welcome when they entered the Ard Fheis was a measure of the love and respect in which they were held' (Adams, 2003: 373). Their very presence was proof of the fact that there was much to gain from endorsing the Agreement, although this public display was criticised by Democratic Left leader Proinsias de Rossa: 'Triumphalist parades through ranks of cheering Sinn Féin members of those convicted of appalling crimes is not conducive to a spirit of reconciliation' (*IT*, 12 May 2004). But the presence of former prisoners at the 1998 Ard Fheis also sent the message that the leadership was not betraying those who symbolised, on the one hand, an attachment to the more militaristic approach, and on the other, the values of dedication and abnegation that republicans ascribe to prisoners. Many members and leaders of Sinn Féin have spent some time in prison. Some wrote about their experience in the form of journals (Bobby Sands, Gerry Adams, Danny Morrison) or more academic essays (Lawrence McKeown). What clearly came out of these writings was the feeling of common purpose and the strong sense that prison, far from being anathema, was an accepted part of the republican struggle, in spite of the hardship and difficulties conveyed by these writings. The prison experience is therefore still very much part of the culture of contemporary republicanism. Although there is no longer a POW department as such, Sinn Féin still has a spokesperson on prisons, Gerry Kelly, who deals with issues concerning 'ordinary prisoners'. Consequently, when incidents involving loyalist prisoners broke out in Maghaberry Prison in January 2004, Kelly observed that the prison authorities were imposing 'communal punishment' on prisoners who 'do have rights, and these rights must be respected' (PR, 29 January 2004).

Revisiting the past

Acknowledging the past has also meant revisiting some of the darkest episodes of the Troubles and shedding new light on them, in order to put an end to the bitterly contested version of events that had officially prevailed until then. One such instance was, quite obviously, the case of the inquiry into the events of Bloody Sunday, when, on 31 January 1972, fourteen civilians were killed during a peaceful Civil Rights march in Derry. The inquiry that followed, chaired by Lord Widgery, produced a report as early as April 1972, which, in the eyes of the nationalist community, simply absolved the British paratroopers of any responsibility, by alleging that some of the dead had been handling bombs or guns, even though there was no evidence of this. This led to an even greater suspicion and resentment on the part of the nationalist community towards the Northern Irish and British institutions as a whole. In this respect, the new official inquiry into the events of Bloody Sunday announced in January 1998 was crucial in the attempt to restore a degree of confidence in the institutions among one section of the population.

Bloody Sunday, together with the introduction of internment without trial on 9 August 1971, are regarded in republican collective memory as significant turning points in the history of the conflict. These two events, which came within a few months of each other, were seen as specifically targeting the nationalist community, making the war against the British forces not only justified but also acceptable within that community. This was a time when the ranks of the IRA started swelling, as armed struggle was seen as a legitimate way of vindicating the rights of the people that republicans sought to represent. These two events are commemorated every year, yet neither pertains directly to the history of republicans exclusively; internment overwhelmingly targeted the nationalist community, but many of the people initially detained had no links to the Provisional IRA,[10] while Bloody Sunday was the consequence of a demonstration organised not by republicans but by the Civil Rights Association. Nevertheless, both of these events have been integrated into republican mythology and they have become assimilated into the history of oppression and resistance that characterises the manner in which republicans represent their own past.

Therefore, it was seen as important that light should be shed on the events of Bloody Sunday in order to heal the resentment and distrust that this incident had generated. When announcing the establishment of a new tribunal of inquiry,[11] to be chaired by Lord Saville, British Prime Minister Tony Blair explained: 'I believe that it is in everyone's interests that the truth be established and told. That is also the way forward to the necessary reconciliation that will be such an important part of building a secure future for the people of Northern Ireland' (Parliamentary Debates, 28 January 1998). The inquiry was seen not only as a means of making public a version of the incident that was officially silenced at the time, but also as a way of testing British credentials in the peace process. The capacity of the British authorities to produce a fair and honest response was seen as a measure of their willingness and good faith in the negotiations in general.

One of the highlights of the hearings of the tribunal was undoubtedly the much-awaited testimony of Martin McGuinness. Republicans have been unrelenting in their calls for the truth to be made public as, according to McGuinness, 'the British have to acknowledge that the people killed were innocent' (McGuinness, interview, 2003). Although he is somewhat critical of the Saville inquiry for what he perceives is its lack of independence, he made a written deposition in 2001, but initially refused to come forward and testify. When he eventually did, in November 2003, McGuinness admitted to having been second in command of the Derry Brigade in 1972, having initially joined the Official IRA and then switched to the Provisionals some months later. His testimony was important in that this was a high-ranking Sinn Féin leader who was publicly admitting his past involvement in the IRA. This was a significant departure, according to the Sinn Féin leader, as it meant that he was willing to come to terms with his own past: 'me talking about what I was doing on Bloody Sunday is a good start . . . when is everyone else going to start?' (*IT*, 5 November 2003). Nevertheless, McGuinness was criticised for refusing to answer some of the questions that were put to him regarding the location of 'safe houses' and arms dumps in Derry at the time. McGuinness justified his refusal by explaining that 'for me to give the location of these buildings and in doing so identifying the people who own these buildings would be a gross act of betrayal and I just cannot do that' (*IT*, 5 November 2003).

Bloody Sunday is not the only file that nationalists want to have reopened and reinvestigated. Several other events are still deemed unresolved, either because the cases were not impartially or fully investigated, or because the truth about the cases has not been fully established. Among these cases are the killings of two solicitors by loyalist paramilitaries: Pat Finucane, who was shot on 12 February 1989 and Rosemary Nelson, who was killed by a car bomb on 15 March 1999. An inquiry was initially established in 1989, led by the Commissioner of the Metropolitan Police Service John Stevens, to report into allegations of collusion between loyalist paramilitaries and security forces regarding the murder of Finucane and Brian Adam Lambert, a student shot on 9 November 1987, when he was mistakenly targeted in revenge for the IRA's Enniskillen bombing. After fourteen years and three reports, the overview and recommendations of the inquiry were published on 17 April 2003. In its opening page, the author stated that 'My enquiries have highlighted collusion, the wilful failure to keep records, the absence of accountability, the withholding of intelligence and evidence, and the extreme of agents being involved in murder. These serious acts and omissions have meant that people have been killed or seriously injured' (Stevens Inquiry, 2003: 3). The report further talked of obstruction that he had encountered throughout all three inquiries, concluding that this was 'cultural in its nature and widespread within parts of the Army and the RUC' (Stevens, 2003: 13). The third inquiry, begun in April 1999, was the largest ever undertaken in the UK, leading to 144 arrests and ninety-four convictions. It concluded by pointing to the fact that both murders could have been prevented, and that 'informants and agents were allowed to operate without effective control and to participate in terrorist crimes. Nationalists were known to be targeted but were not properly warned or protected' (Stevens, 2003: 16).

The Stevens inquiry also brought to light the fact that informants within the IRA were used by the security forces in order to gather intelligence on the organisation. One such informant, who was wanted by the inquiry for questioning, operated under the code name of Stakeknife. He was alleged to have personally overseen the murder of at least a dozen informers during the Troubles, which effectively meant that the security forces were prepared to turn a blind eye to his activities in order to protect him. Stakeknife's identity was revealed in April 2003, causing major shock within the Republican Movement but also major embarrassment for the British security forces, as it highlighted further instances of collusion.

Allegations of collusion were also investigated by retired Canadian Judge Cory, who was appointed by the British and Irish governments following the negotiations at Weston Park in 2001. The reports that were initially published in December 2003 only dealt with collusion between the Garda and the IRA for the murders of Lord Justice Gibson and his wife in April 1987, and for those of two RUC officers, Harry Breen and Bob Buchanan, in March 1989. While, in the first case, the report concluded that there was 'simply no evidence of collusion upon which to base a direction to hold a public inquiry' (Cory, 2003, *Gibson*: 44), the Canadian judge recommended establishment of an inquiry in the case of the RUC officers, as 'the documents reveal evidence that, if accepted, could be found to constitute collusion' (Cory, 2003, *Breen*: 48). The reports into the deaths of Rosemary Nelson, Pat Finucane, Robert Hamill and Billy Wright[12] were published in April 2004. The main recommendation was that 'in each of the four cases the documented evidence indicates that these are matters of concern which would warrant further and more detailed inquiry' (Cory, *Finucane*, 2004: 3).

Republicans have been consistent in their calls for the British and Irish authorities to shed light on these and other events,[13] and view this as essential for the process of reconciliation and for building confidence in the new institutions, especially the police force.

However, as was acknowledged by Gerry Adams early on in the process, all parties to the conflict have a part to play in the process of healing past grievances and recovering the truth. Addressing the unionists at his party's Ard Fheis in 1996, he stated:

> I'm not going to ask you to forget the past nor to forgive republicans for the pain we have visited on you. At the same time I don't expect nationalists or republicans to forget what you inflicted on us. However the wrongs of the past must not paralyse us. We must not be trapped in a web of suspicion and doubt about each other.
>
> (Adams, Presidential Address, 1996)

Republicans, therefore, have their part to play in the process of reconciliation. The darker episodes of the conflict cannot be attributed exclusively to the state forces; they are also to be found within the republicans' own organisation, and this was an issue that needed to be addressed. In July 2002, the IRA issued a statement of apology, addressed to all relatives of 'non-combatants' killed in the course of its operations. The date chosen for this was the thirtieth anniversary of Bloody Friday, when twenty-seven bombs were detonated in the centre of Belfast, killing nine people of whom seven were civilians. In offering its condolences, the IRA acknowledged that 'the future will not be found in denying collective failures and mistakes or closing minds and hearts to the plight of those who have been hurt. That includes all of the victims of the conflict, combatants and non-combatants' (*AP*, 18 July 2002). Nevertheless, apologies are seen as insufficient by those who have been directly affected by republican violence. Sections of the unionist community are asking for more clarity over some events. For the DUP, the official inquiries that have been opened, at great expense in its view, are proof of the fact that the peace process is one-sided and favours nationalists. That party is also demanding for the truth to be brought to light regarding some events, and it lists a number of what it calls 'atrocities', for which it wishes to see public inquiries: Enniskillen (1987), Shankill (1993) or Kingsmill (1976).[14] All three incidents relate to actions carried out by the IRA in which a high number of civilians, for the most part Protestants, died. McGuinness' reply to the request of the DUP is one of bafflement. 'There were official enquiries, by their own police force, the RUC. I've never heard anything about questioning how they were carried out' (McGuinness, interview). This view is echoed by Alex Maskey, who sees no objection to inquiries being held although he sees little merit in these particular instances (Maskey, interview, 2003).

However, the debate surrounding these episodes of the conflict where civilians were killed, on either side, and the repeated demand for truth on the part of both communities, obviously raise the question of the pertinence of a Truth Commission along the line of the experiences of South Africa or Guatemala. Some consideration has been given to this, by researchers as well as by political parties. However, no one seems to be in a position to give a definitive answer on this issue. Researchers agree that some mechanism has to be found to uncover the truth, but warn against the danger of such a process increasing already deep-seated antagonisms by pointing the finger of guilt. Others have indicated that a full process is next to impossible as it would involve the British government accepting to play its part. Finally, there is the fact that 'perpetrators', for the most part, refuse to admit that 'they did anything wrong or that their action (or inaction) was complicit in perpetuating the conflict' (Hamber, 1998: 2).

Sinn Féin's approach to this issue is mixed. In its discussion document published in September 2003 entitled *Truth*, the party recognised that 'some formal collective examination and acknowledgement of the past is necessary for them [victims and survivors] to find closure' (*Truth*, 2003: 1). The Sinn Féin document is guarded as to the effectiveness of a Truth Commission, on the grounds that the evidence of whether it works or not is inconclusive; it also stresses that in the short term it can be somehow counterproductive, since it raises expectations that can inhibit rather than enhance reconciliation. However, the party is not averse to the idea, provided that its format follows a certain number of principles, such as being victim-centred. Furthermore, according to this document, all parties should agree to full cooperation and disclosure, there should be no hierarchy of victims and it should be politically neutral, which means that any panel must be international and independent. Finally, this type of process should not be restricted to combatant groups, and must include other institutions such as the media or the judiciary.

Republicans have been urged repeatedly to revisit their past and to be truthful on one particular issue that could be regarded as one of the most sensitive and difficult of their recent history, that of the 'disappeared'. A BBC news headline in June 1999 captured the significance of this issue when it stated that the disappeared had returned 'to haunt Ireland's conscience' (BBC, 7 June 1999). Indeed, the topic that made the news for those few weeks was the story of those people who had been 'disappeared' in the course of the conflict. According to the figures most commonly quoted, fourteen people have disappeared in Northern Ireland during the Troubles, mostly in the 1970s. The IRA only admitted to having 'disappeared' nine of these. The INLA admitted responsibility in one case, that of a man abducted and murdered in Paris in 1986. No one seems to be ready or willing to come forward to speak about the fate of the four remaining people, but in 1999 the issue was finally reviewed, after years of campaigning from relatives and pressure groups. The IRA accepted in March of that year to disclose the location of the bodies of the nine people it admitted to having killed. After years of silence, republicans yielded to the pressure emanating from governments and non-governmental organisations alike.

The Bloomfield report had dedicated one section to the 'special predicament' of the 'poignant category of the disappeared'. More specifically, the author made a plea to whoever was in possession of information to disclose it, suggesting that 'cast-iron arrangements could be made, if necessary through trusted intermediaries, to report such information anonymously and in confidence' (Bloomfield, 1998: 38). In order to facilitate the disclosure of the places of burial of the disappeared, both governments agreed to grant immunity to those who would come forward with information regarding the location of the bodies. The Northern Ireland (Location of Victims' Remains) Bill, voted on by the House of Commons in June 1999, set up an independent commission to help find the disappeared. This legislation was quite controversial within some political circles, particularly unionist, who criticised what they saw as a blanket amnesty for those responsible for the disappearances. Arguing in favour of the Bill in the House of Commons, Adam Ingram, then Victims Minister, attempted to clarify the situation, explaining that immunity was granted only to those giving information, not to those ultimately responsible for those crimes: 'These were vicious and cowardly crimes and, if evidence is obtained from other sources, it will be used to seek to bring those responsible to justice' (BBC, 10 May 1999). Indeed, that distinction was fundamental for the legislation to be in accordance with a 1978 UN resolution on disappearances, as all states are required to bring those responsible to justice. The role of the commission which was led by Kenneth Bloomfield and former Tanaiste John Wilson was thus to collect information that it would then pass on to the Gardai and RUC.

In its March 1999 statement, the IRA, for the first time in the history of the Provisionals, had expressed a level of regret: 'in initiating this investigation, our intention has been to do all within our power to rectify any injustice, for which we accept full responsibility, and to alleviate the suffering of the families. We are sorry that this has taken so long to resolve and for the prolonged anguish caused to the families' (*AP*, 1 April 1999). This statement also revealed that an internal investigation had been under way within the IRA for the previous eighteen months, and that a special unit had been set up to collect information on the whereabouts of nine bodies. This was passed on to the Commission and then disclosed to the Gardai, which made it possible to locate three of the nine burial sites of the individuals identified as having been killed by the IRA. The searches began in June 1999 under the scrutiny of the international media, and led to some landscapes, particularly on the shores of Louth, being transformed into massive excavation sites. The work of the Gardai was made all the more difficult by the fact that the information on which they were relying was inaccurate. At the end of July, the searches were suspended, until such time as more reliable information would enable the excavations to resume.

The IRA disappeared all shared a common characteristic. All were branded traitors by the Republican Movement. Some were said to have betrayed the organisation from within, turning their backs on the Republican Movement and becoming informers in criminal court cases, some from outside, accused of giving information to the police or to the army. In its statement, the IRA thus explained that some of the disappeared were 'former members of Óglaigh na hÉireann who were executed for activities which put other Óglaigh na hÉireann personnel at risk or jeopardized the struggle' (*AP*, 1 April 1999). The crimes were denied by the relatives, and if there was ever any evidence against those who were disappeared, it was, obviously, never disclosed. Nevertheless, they were accused of the worst crimes that could be committed within republican circles, as they had, allegedly, turned informers and betrayed their own people. Within the IRA, this crime was quite unforgivable and has been punished severely down through the years, in some instances even by death. In IRA thinking, a turncoat was dangerous, not only for the risk to which he or she exposed the organisation, but also for the potential damage that might be caused to the morale and to the cohesion of the movement. Thus he or she had to be eliminated, a fate which befell a number of informers. One of the most notorious cases was that of Eamon Collins, former IRA Volunteer turned informer, who subsequently published a book, *Killing Rage*, and who was beaten to death in February 1999.

The profile of the nine disappeared as it was drawn by republicans themselves (*AP*, 6 April 1999) divided the nine disappeared into two categories: those who had been, allegedly, informers, and those who had stolen weapons from the IRA and used them in armed robberies. Of the former category, only three of the six people killed had been 'court-martialled'. The other three admitted that they were British agents. However, a number of questions were left unanswered by their fate, such as the reason for their bodies being hidden, when this was not the case with other informers. Whether or not those particular executions had been approved by the military council of the IRA, and whether these could have been operations that had gone badly wrong, was never quite clarified. Certainly, the rhetoric used against the victims probably contributed to the veil of silence that seemed to have sealed their fate. Few, other than their immediate relatives, would have felt comfortable starting a campaign in favour of those branded as traitors, the informers. Amnesty International never campaigned for the return of the bodies because it was a 'home country' issue and thus the Irish section of the organisation could not get involved.[15] The disappearances may also have been seen as a means of control insofar as the very community in which they happened could not show solidarity with the victims. This was particularly obvious in the case of Jean McConville who, in spite of her family situation (a young mother of ten whose husband had died of cancer some months previously), was abducted by a gang of twelve people (an operation that could not have gone unnoticed), and then disappeared.[16] Far from becoming a *cause célèbre*, her fate seemed silenced by the community at large until one of her daughters decided to seek justice for her. Her crime, according to her relatives, was to have given some comfort to a dying British soldier. To the IRA, she was an informer and thus deserved the fate that befell her.

The decision by the IRA to accede to the demand of the relatives and of the governments could also be seen as a pragmatic one. The organisation had nothing to gain by continuing to hide the location of bodies. On the contrary, this unresolved issue could be highly damaging to the strategy being pursued by Sinn Féin on the political front. After weeks of harrowing uncertainty for the relatives of the disappeared, only three bodies were found. The very first one was discovered in strange circumstances, having been apparently dug up by an IRA unit and left in a coffin for the Gardai to find. The fact that only three of the nine bodies were found in the first stages of the searches raised a certain number of criticisms over the sincerity of the IRA's gesture, some seeing it as a stunt meant to improve Sinn Féin's electoral prospects. Leaders such as Gerry Adams explained the difficulty that the commission was facing in locating the bodies by the fact that these events dated back more than twenty years, and information was consequently vague. Moreover, some of those responsible could not be tracked down, either because they were dead or because they had left the organisation. But these arguments probably rang hollow to those whose ordeal was continuing and was being witnessed by the cameras of the world.

The case of the disappeared was one that would come back to haunt the Republican Movement. Two years later, journalist Ed Moloney alleged, in his book on the IRA, that Gerry Adams must have known about the disappearances of the bodies, and insinuated that he might even have given the orders personally.[17] Adams strongly denied these allegations and further stressed that the IRA had made 'genuine efforts to try to bring closure to the families'. In the spring of 2003, the IRA resumed its internal investigation and revisited the possible locations where the bodies might have been buried. The body of Jean McConville was found in a shallow grave in early October 2003, by a man who was walking with his children. The fact that this grave was a mile away from the sites initially identified by the IRA again raised questions as to the accuracy of the information originally passed on to the commission. The IRA reiterated its apologies but confirmed that it had acted in good faith. However, the surviving relatives of the disappeared had mixed emotions.

Michael McConville, son of Jean McConville, said he forgave his mother's killers but denied the reason given for her abduction and wanted to know the truth about her killing and subsequent disappearance. Margaret McKinney, whose son Brian disappeared in 1978, was far more distressed, as she explained: 'What use are apologies to me? I want peace. I want to know why he was murdered' (*IT*, 5 October 2003).

In its statement, the IRA expressed regret for having disappeared a certain number of bodies, but not for having killed those people. While it admitted that disappearances were wrong, it did not leave its right to enforce justice within the community open to question. It was not so much the fact of killing these informants that the IRA was regretting as the absence of a proper burial. The IRA did, in some way, reaffirm its belief that retribution was part of its remit as a revolutionary army. The limit that was placed on such acts was a directive, issued subsequently to these disappearances, according to which 'anyone killed by Óglaigh na hÉireann should be left for burial by their relatives' (*AP*, 1 April 1999). Nevertheless, the IRA has begun a journey towards partial atonement, insofar as it has apologised for its actions on several occasions. Republican leaders have also stressed that they support all the efforts made by the IRA in finding the remains of the disappeared, and point to the fact that, in their view, the IRA has done everything in its power.

However, whether the IRA is ready to embark on a further process that would entail explaining why it acted in certain ways remains to be seen, and would surely raise far deeper questions about the organisation as a whole. The truth that some relatives are seeking also concerns the reasons why these people were disappeared and the circumstances in which this happened. Apologies and cooperation from the IRA to locate the remains are not sufficient, especially in the light of the republicans' regular calls for the truth to be established in many other instances. When asked whether the IRA would be willing to go further and explain why it acted in such a way, Martin McGuinness replied: 'Maybe they can't produce the evidence. The IRA is an organisation that doesn't have the structures of a regular army or of the police. It's a guerrilla army. Maybe they didn't retain the information' (McGuinness, interview). Nevertheless, no matter how far the IRA is prepared to go, it is doubtful whether this will correspond to the 'repentance' that the DUP was demanding in the aftermath of the November 2003 assembly elections.

The reading of history

Revisiting the past not only involves accepting responsibility for past actions and offering apologies; it also entails an analysis of the way in which history had been constructed as a tool of division and dual-identity formation. Within the republican camp, the manner in which history is presented can be contentious, as it is an issue where divisions between those who advocate tradition and those who preach openness can come to the fore. To put forward a vision of history that does not correspond to the accepted version of events may be seen as an attempt to blur the lines between the different identities, and perhaps even to undermine a substantial part of the traditions, events and principles from which the legitimacy of the struggle was derived.

In the summer of 2002, when the newly elected Sinn Féin Mayor of Belfast, Alex Maskey, announced his intention to lay a wreath for those fallen at the Battle of the Somme in 1916, quite a heated debate ensued. Maskey's decision stirred a controversy not only within unionism but also within the ranks of his own party. This gesture was seen as highly symbolic. As he put it himself, 'This is a major step for republicans and nationalists on this island. . . . I hope that this initiative will be seen at face value and as a positive gesture' (*IE*, 2 July 2002). But it was probably more than a gesture. Alex Maskey was commemorating the dead, which are at the core of the identity of a party that celebrates with great regularity those whom it sees as its forefathers. This is precisely where Sinn Féin draws a substantial part of its legitimacy as the representative of an oppressed people. Republicans gather to celebrate failures and deaths, which are turned into achievements in terms of the capacity for suffering and for resistance.

Commemorating the dead of the First World War was seen by some within the Republican Movement as an act of revisionism, as this war had always been strongly identified with the British. Nevertheless, some 210,000 Irishmen fought in the First World War, of whom the vast majority joined as volunteers, since there was no conscription at the time. Not all these men were from the northeast of the country. Some 170,000 men heeded John Redmond's call and joined the British troops.[18] But the memory of the First World War is also associated, in the republicans' and, to a large extent, in the Republic's collective memory, with the 1916 Easter Rising. The rising was orchestrated by those among the Irish Volunteers who had rejected the call to support the British war effort and had seen this war as not only alien to them but also as an opportunity to advance their own cause.[19] Because the Republic has been closely identified with this particular event, it took its leaders some time to officially acknowledge the role of Ireland in the First World War, in a process which historian Keith Jeffery has termed 'national amnesia', as 'their history [of the First World War dead] and their experiences did not fit in with either the republican legacy of southern Ireland or the unionist tradition of the North' (Jeffery, 2002, available online). Indeed, it was only in 1998 that a memorial to all the Irish people fallen in the First World War was inaugurated in Messines (Belgium) by the President of Ireland and Queen Elizabeth II. The divisions of history are all the more obvious in the case of the Battle of the Somme. Of all the killed and wounded on the 1 and 2 July 1916, some 5,500, over one-third, belonged to the 36th (Ulster) Division, which was predominantly, if not exclusively, Protestant and unionist, and whose members, for a large part, were also affiliated to the Ulster Volunteer Force. Because this date coincided with the original anniversary of the Battle of the Boyne, these two events were linked in collective memory and made the Battle of the Somme the biggest First World War event to be commemorated in Ireland, but it was seen as belonging solely to the Protestant, or unionist, heritage. The fact that Alex Maskey was commemorating such a heavily loaded event was unprecedented.

This gesture was not isolated. At least one other Sinn Féin elected representative, Francie Molloy, had taken a similar initiative. Having been elected Mayor of Dungannon in 2001, he hosted a reception for the British Legion on Remembrance Day of that year. His approach was similar to that of Maskey, insofar as he was seeking to represent all his constituents, but also to acknowledge those who died in the war. This, according to him, led to some 'nervousness' among his own supporters, who were not used to this type of initiative. But he stresses that it was important to reach out in this manner to the other side as it showed a willingness to take on board historical or cultural differences between the two sides and this was seen as an opportunity for people to 'understand each other' (Molloy, interview, 2003).

Those gestures might not have only been concerned with acknowledging the memory of those who fell during the First World War. They could also have been directed at the relatives of those who died in Enniskillen on Remembrance Day, in November 1987, when a bomb detonated under the memorial killed eleven people. This tragedy was highly damaging for the IRA, and was one that the leaders of Sinn Féin found difficult to justify. Hence laying a wreath for the Battle of the Somme could be seen as a manner of showing atonement for that particular incident. When asked about this interpretation, however, Molloy replies that 'maybe people saw me trying to compensate for what had happened in Enniskillen. I never thought of Enniskillen, what I was doing was to give recognition for those who died in the war and what was done on the ground, in terms of welfare' (Molloy, interview).

These types of initiatives, however, generate a level of controversy. Alex Maskey was criticised by unionist politicians for not attending the official ceremony of the Battle of the Somme and deciding instead to lay a wreath two hours beforehand. The former DUP Mayor of Belfast, Sammy Wilson, did see this gesture as a step forward, but he strongly criticised Maskey for making the ceremony into 'a political football for his own ends', as he saw his absence from the ceremony as an insult to the dead. Nevertheless, it could be argued that the presence of a Sinn Féin representative would have been at least as difficult, if not more so, to accept for the DUP. But Maskey's gesture was also controversial within the ranks of his movement because it raised fundamental questions about how far the leadership of the Republican Movement was prepared to go on the road to peace, and whether it was not going too much out of its way to accommodate unionism when it was felt that this gesture was not being reciprocated.

As history seems to be one of the main components of the movement's identity and references, the reading made of it is thus crucial. Historical legitimacy is paramount, and the movement is aware of its highly symbolic value. Legitimacy is not only driven by the manner in which the leadership conducts its business, but also by the manner in which it retains a certain code of conduct that is consistent with its past. Very few parties commemorate their history with such regularity and such ostentation. The columns of *An Phoblacht* are full every week of the different commemorations that are held by the party. Until the early 1980s, it could be said that this constituted a substantial part of Sinn Féin's activities. When entering into politics, the balance was gradually shifted to one where Sinn Féin also started to build up a track record in politics, with its involvement in electoral politics, the dropping of the abstentionist policy for the local councils and the opening of constituency or local clinics.

However, the historical figures that Sinn Féin decides to commemorate might seem, at times, like odd choices. One such instance was the commemoration organised in September 2003 for Seán Russell, chief-of-staff of the IRA in the late 1930s. This was a strange decision if only because Russell would be considered by historians as a militaristic leader, one who, as was reported by *An Phoblacht*, had led a 'disastrous campaign in England during the Second World War' (*AP*, 21 August 2003). But Russell was also the leader who established contacts with Nazi Germany during the Second World War, acting on the age-old adage that the enemies of Britain were not the enemies of Ireland and could even be seen as potential allies for a particular cause. The IRA's involvement with some agents of Nazi Germany has been a source of perplexity over the years, but also, to some extent, of embarrassment. In this light, it might seem puzzling that some sixty years later, several speakers, including Sinn Féin's Leinster candidate for the 2004 EU election Mary Lou McDonald, paid tribute to him. Gerry Adams does not have any particular issue with this incident. According to him, the decision to hold local commemorations is taken not by the party but by the local cumain. 'You have to judge people in their own time. You can commemorate aspects of people and dissent from aspects of what they are doing. The reality is that someone held a commemoration for someone who was involved as a leader for the IRA' (Adams, interview, 2004). However, *Irish Times* columnist Fintan O'Toole saw it in a different light, concluding that 'Sinn Féin itself has a weirdly dysfunctional relationship with the past' (*IT*, 2 September 2003), claiming on the one hand socialist credentials and rekindling, on the other, a past where there was overt cooperation with the Nazis. The fact that the commemoration's speaker was the EU candidate undoubtedly added an intriguing dimension to this decision.

Nevertheless, history is still paramount as a source of inspiration for republicans, if only to vindicate the choices made by the leadership. One of the most radical choices in recent years is undoubtedly that of the peace process in general, considering the significant implications it has had for the Republican Movement as a whole. For this reason, it was important to root it in history in order to strengthen its legitimacy. One of the ways in which this was done was by grounding this choice within the episode of the hunger strikes.

The year 2001 marked the twentieth anniversary of the hunger strikes, which Sinn Féin chose to commemorate on both sides of the border, in an effort, in its own words, to 'make sure that a lot of people, and particularly young people, learn from the hunger strike, and [to] remember the sacrifice as it is' (*AP*, 15 February 2001). Indeed, in the previous twenty years, the memory of Sands and his comrades had been regularly honoured. But what characterised 2001 was the diversity and the frequency of the events. Beyond the marches and public meetings that were regularly held all over the country, the organisers tried to capture the imagination of their contemporaries by playing on the visual aspect of the protest. The 1981 commemoration committee attempted to diversify the different events as much as possible.[20]

The celebrations organised throughout 2001 were a testimony to the importance given by republicans to the legacy of Sands and his comrades who died. To synthesise the republican message, the hunger strikers died in the name of a cause, political status, and the recognition of their struggle for a united Ireland. Obviously, the value of this memory is not universal, being, by definition, selective and reductive. The interpretation of the hunger strikes twenty years later could not be consensual. Some would contend that the deaths of the hunger strikers were the result of macabre and cynical manipulation by their leaders, or, at best, of a total miscalculation on the part of the British government. Within the republican family, the value of the legacy of Sands and his comrades differed. A number of organisations and groups that chose diverging political and strategic paths could claim, just as much as Sinn Féin, to be the heirs of the men who died in 1981. This phenomenon is all the more complicated given that the ten strikers who died were not all IRA volunteers, three of them being members of the rival republican group the INLA (Irish National Liberation Army). Consequently, members of smaller formations such as the Irish republican Socialist Party, the thirty-two-County Sovereignty Movement or republican Sinn Féin, who have been at odds with the direction chosen by Sinn Féin and the IRA throughout the peace process, did not identify with the manner in which the hunger strikes were remembered and commemorated. In contrast, at the time of the protest, all shades of republicanism were able to cast aside their differences to agree on the immediate demands of the strikers (mainly that of the status of political prisoner, and thus the recognition by the British of the political nature of the conflict).

Because they were, and still are, so emotionally and politically charged, the hunger strikes epitomise the fundamental contradictions that have riven the republican camp. For those who continue to oppose the direction that Sinn Féin has taken since the early 1990s, and, more particularly, since the 1994 IRA ceasefire, the values attributed to this episode are identical but the political conclusions that they draw from it are very different. Simply put, the position of dissident republicans could be summed up in the following axiom: 'the hunger strikers didn't die for this', *this* being, according to them, the renunciation of the armed struggle (this break with tradition, in their eyes, has been made all the more obvious by the acts of decommissioning of the IRA, the implicit acceptance of partition, the choice of parliamentarianism and consequently the betrayal of the revolutionary mandate inherited from the First Dáil of 1919). The list is much longer, but the debate over the hunger strikes contains, in essence, the main contentious points that divide the leaders of mainstream republicanism from others within their own camp. For Ruairí Ó Brádaigh, who was President of Provisional Sinn Féin from 1970 to 1983, Sands' ideals have been 'constantly perverted', the hunger strikers did not die 'for simple civil rights under British rule or for a spurious equality but for human dignity and for the POW status within the national liberation struggle' (*IT*, 7 May 2001). Ironically, these same criticisms have been voiced many times in the past against parties such as Fianna Fáil, Fine Gael or Official Sinn Féin, all originally descendants of Sinn Féin. But if the hunger strikers did not die for this, what exactly did they die for? There are different possible answers to this question. The prisoners were, as one mural put it, on hunger strike for justice; they were seeking an immediate goal (the five demands), but also the reunification of Ireland. Ultimately, they were also fighting for the respect of their physical and moral integrity. Tommy McKearney, an IRA Volunteer on hunger strike in 1980, believes that one can only speculate as to what the hunger strikers would have said about the Belfast Agreement, adding: 'What we can say is that at the time of his death, Sands was part of an ongoing campaign to break the link with Britain' (*IT* 7 May 2001). This question is thus unsolvable and no one, be they historians, politicians, relatives of the hunger strikers or even former protesting prisoners, can reply to it fully. Margaret McCauley, sister of dead hunger striker Michael Devine, commented on the death of her brother: 'I have been asked many times: was it worth it? and I always answer: I don't know, but ten young men were convinced it was. I made a promise and I kept it' (*AP*, 8 February 2001). The position of those who were close to the strikers, such as Adams or Brendan McFarlane, who was the prisoners' Officer in Command at the time of the hunger strikes, was as difficult, since they had little control over the events. Adams had hinted at his own impotence during a conversation with the father of a hunger striker, who had begged him to do something to save his son. Adams replied 'I can't, but you can' (Beresford, 1987: 347).[21]

Nevertheless, the memory of the hunger strikes and their commemorations enabled republican leaders to justify their strategic and political choices in the name of a sacrifice made by people other than them but closely associated with them. Sinn Féin needed this commemoration to project the image of a united movement, in the face of some decisions that were more than controversial, such as acts of decommissioning, which some republicans, not necessarily only those who have joined the ranks of the dissident groups, find a bitter pill to swallow. The memory of this event and the manner in which it has been promoted up to this day might then be ascribed to the necessity for republicans to revisit their own history in order to justify their political choices to their supporters and adversaries alike.

Within the republican camp, there are several organisations that claim to be the real heirs of the men of the 1916 Rising, of the war of independence or of the hunger strikes. One of them, Republican Sinn Féin (Sinn Féin Poblachtach), was formed in 1986, when the former leaders of Provisional Sinn Féin, Ruairí Ó Brádaigh and Daithí Ó Conaill, left the party in protest against the end of the abstentionist rule for the Dáil, although the party, since it sees itself as the true heir of Sinn Féin, claims to have been formed, 'in 1905 and to be 'the oldest political organisation in the country' (RSF, available online). Their party claims to be the true Sinn Féin, the one that has not sold out on its basic principle, abstentionism, the one that still upholds the sovereignty of the 1916 Republic. As such, it sees the Belfast Agreement as a flawed arrangement, guaranteeing the consolidation of the 'link with England' to the unionists while at the same time promising a weakening of that link to the nationalists. Republican Sinn Féin promotes a federal solution, much along the same lines as that advocated in the 1970s, and its policy programme has retained the name of that of the Provisionals, *Éire Nua*. Its criticism of the current leadership of Sinn Féin can be scathing, since it sees the acceptance of the new institutions as a collaborationist choice: 'all parties who broke from the republican Movement and accepted partitionist institutions, abandoned the 32-County Republic and ended up collaborating in the maintenance of English rule in Ireland' (RSF, 2003, available online). Therefore, for party leader Ó Brádaigh, 'Republican Sinn Féin labelled

2001 "the year of the hunger striker" . . . but for the Provisionals 2001
will always be "the year of the traitor".' Adding therefore that 'the
ultimate betrayal was made with the illegal surrendering of arms achieved
to defend and re-establish the All-Ireland Republic' (*Saoirse*, December
2002). However, although this party has retained the same structural
organisation as Sinn Féin, its operations are hardly likely to threaten
mainstream republicanism. Most of its activities seem to be centred
around commemorations, which attract, according to the figures cited in
the party's monthly publication *Saoirse* (Freedom), between 100 and 200
people. Since it observes a strict abstentionist policy at a national level,
it does not compete for the republican vote, and it further claims that
its representatives are prevented from standing in local council elections,
the only institution where successful candidates would take their seats,
as they refuse to take the oath introduced in Northern Ireland in 1989
by which candidates must accept not to express support for or approval
of any proscribed organisation. This, in RSF's view, means 'a repudiation
of the right of the Irish people to use force of arms to end British
occupation' (RSF, 2003).

The ideas put forward by this organisation have probably little
currency in twenty-first-century Ireland, and it is doubtful whether its
largely traditional, outdated rhetoric is viewed as a challenge to mainstream republicanism. Of much more concern is the armed expression
of dissenting republicanism. Open opposition to the manner in which
the Sinn Féin leadership was handling the peace process was originally
expressed with the formation of a political grouping, the Thirty-two-
County Sovereignty Movement, which subsequently led to the creation
of the Real IRA, presumably in early 1998. This organisation has been
responsible for most of the acts of violence in Northern Ireland since the
1997 ceasefire on the republican side, the worst one being the bomb in
Omagh in August 1998 that killed thirty people. The Real IRA is deemed
quite small (some reports put its total membership somewhere between
seventy and 170[22]) and vulnerable, probably heavily infiltrated on both
sides of the border and suffering from internal tensions and a lack of
organisation. But it has shown on various occasions its capacity to inflict
substantial damage. It fired an anti-tank rocket at MI6 headquarters in
London in September 2000, exploded a car bomb in London in August
2002, injuring seven people and causing extensive damage, and in that
same month it planted an explosive device in an army base in Derry,
killing a 51 year old civilian. The Real IRA suffered a serious setback
when its presumed leader, Michael McKevitt, was sentenced to thirty
years' imprisonment in July 2003 on charges of directing terrorism and
being the leader of the illegal organisation.

However, there is evidence that the organisation has the potential to
destabilise the situation, and, more particularly, of generating tensions

within republican ranks. In two instances, the IRA has been suspected of having killed members of the Real IRA. One, of them, Joe O'Connor, was shot dead in Belfast in October 2000, the other, Danny McGurk, in August 2003. Some newspaper reports talked of a possible internal feud. The Real IRA was also suspected of having conspired against Gerry Adams, although the organisation dismissed these reports as 'ludicrous'. However, in September 2003, it admitted being responsible for having sent an incendiary device to the home of a member of the District Policing Partnership, injuring her husband. The organisation subsequently claimed that all 541 members of those DPPs were deemed 'legitimate threats'. This led Martin McGuinness to state: 'I think the intimidation is absolutely deplorable. It is unjustifiable and the gang who are using these threats should withdraw these threats and should go further and disband' (*IT*, 18 September 2003). Calls for a republican organisation to disband emanating from a member of Sinn Féin might sound ironic, in the context of the numerous calls made on republicans for the IRA to disband. One such call came, precisely, from the leader of RSF: 'I would say that the Provisional IRA should disband because they no longer have any republican function. If they remain they will deteriorate to the level of a party militia, where they will be controlling certain areas for their own benefit' (*Saoirse*, December 2002).

Dissident republicans seem to found their legitimacy on a reading of history which vindicates armed struggle, political dogmatism and where compromise is equated with betrayal. It is on their analysis of historical precedents that they condemn the choices made by the present Sinn Féin leadership. They claim a lineage that goes back to Wolfe Tone and that, in their view, they are the only ones not to have broken. History is their credo, a feature which they share with many other actors in Northern Ireland. Indeed, history remains a conflictual issue, one that divides both communities in Northern Ireland, the bitterness of which finds its most obvious expression in the Twelfth of July parades tradition. These are upheld by the loyalist and Orange Order organisations as part of their cultural heritage, and are seen by republicans as a show of force. This is an area where a middle ground seems hard to find, since one side sees the other's interpretation of events as an attempt to undermine its identity and its right to express it, as the reading on a particular chapter of history is by definition exclusive of one community.

Parading

Parades are held annually in Northern Ireland and are viewed by both communities as an opportunity to perpetuate their cultural heritage, but also to show their respective levels of support. On the republican side, the high points of the year are the commemorations of the 1916 Easter

Rising, which are held all over the island. On this occasion, parades are organised throughout the island, and consist of colourful marches which generally culminate with the reading of the 1916 Proclamation. The days when Volunteers in balaclavas and military uniforms led the marches seem to be in the past. On the unionist side, the highlight of the year is the Twelfth of July, which commemorates the victory of William of Orange over the Catholic King James II at the Battle of the Boyne in 1690. This date, which is also a national holiday in Northern Ireland, is celebrated by the Orange Order, through its local lodges, which hold marches in virtually every town and city. On that occasion, Orangemen and women parade in traditional costumes and march to the beat of the drums, marking the victory of their tradition over that of Catholicism. To the Orange Order, this is a fundamental element of loyalism and it is a manner of emphasising their cultural difference. In their own words, 'parades therefore are very much part of the Orange tradition and heritage as two hundred years ago the founding fathers decided that parades were an appropriate medium to witness for their faith and to celebrate their cultural heritage' (Orange Order, available online).

Although both communities organise and participate in parades, it is undeniable that, for the most part, the unionist/loyalist tradition is the most visible. The statistics released by the Police Service of Northern Ireland and the Parades Commission (see below) clearly illustrate this phenomenon. Of a total of 3,390 parades notified for the year 1999, 2,661 were loyalist, 204 nationalist while the remaining 525 were labelled as 'others'.[23] Three years later, the figures were similar: 3,280 parades were notified to the Parades Commission, of which approximately 75 per cent were loyalist. Interestingly, the parades which tend to be most controversial and consequently get most media coverage represent only a small number: 6.8 per cent in 2001, and 5.8 per cent in 2002. Of these contentious parades, a quarter have no restrictions imposed on them, while the rest are either rerouted or some limitations are imposed regarding the music or the timing. Furthermore, the overwhelming majority of contentious parades are loyalist (93 per cent), but this figure is artificially inflated given that there is notification of a parade in Drumcree almost every Sunday. It is worth noting that the vast majority of parades pass off peacefully. The PSNI recorded a total of only twelve parades at which disorder occurred (nine loyalist and three republican respectively) in 1999, six in 2000 (five and one) and twenty-nine the following year (twenty-six and two, with an additional one in the 'other' category (PSNI)). Finally, most of the nationalist parades that are considered contentious tend to be notified as protest parades, inevitably being set against a loyalist parade.

Republicans tend to see the loyalist parades as inherently violent, as 'violence isn't an aberration to Orangeism, it's all part of the spectacle'

(*AP*, 20 July 2000). This analysis obviously needs to be qualified, as the figures show that, indeed, most parades pass off peacefully. Nevertheless, some routes are more prone to raising tensions than others, as is the case with Drumcree, which has been the highlight of disturbances in recent years. The Orange parade that takes place in Portadown every year is one of the oldest, dating back to 1807. It is in great part its longevity that makes it, in the eyes of the organisers, legitimate and justified. The march goes from the Orange Hall situated in the centre of the city to the Church of Ireland on the Drumcree Hill and back to the Hall through the Garvaghy Road. Although this route is considered traditional, and thus justified, by the Orange Lodge, it has become probably the most contentious parade in recent years. In 1995, the residents of the nationalist Garvaghy Road strongly objected to this parade being brought to their doorsteps. A compromise was reached whereby the marchers would still be allowed to take that particular route but would have to keep a low profile, which meant that the parade would be silent. This, according to the residents, was not respected by the marchers who clearly felt justified in their right and in their tradition. Among the marchers were unionist leaders such as David Trimble, MP for the area (he was to be elected leader of his party the following September) and Ian Paisley. This episode was seen by the nationalist residents, and to a large extent by that whole community, as a display of triumphalism on the part of unionists and loyalists alike.

The parade in Drumcree led to significant protests and stand-offs at the foot of the Drumcree Hill, when the march was banned from going down the Garvaghy Road by the RUC in 1996. This led the then Secretary of State for Northern Ireland, Patrick Mayhew, to announce in July 1996 the setting up of a commission to review parades and marches. Submissions were invited from all parties, individuals and organisations interested in the issue, and by the closing date in October 1996, some 300 had been received. Of the main political parties, the SDLP, the Alliance Party and Sinn Féin immediately contributed, whereas on the unionist side, the submissions (apart from the DUP which did not contribute) were not made public. The subsequent findings of the review, confined in the North report, recommended the establishment of an independent Parades Commission whose role would be, among others, one of mediation, review and monitoring of contentious parades. In March 1998, with the Public Processions (Northern Ireland) Act, the Parades Commission was established, with a view to 'grapple with the consequences of a legacy of bitterness and mistrust' and to 'promote greater public understanding, promote and facilitate mediation'. One of the first decisions of the newly appointed commission was to reroute the Drumcree parade and not to allow it to go down the Garvaghy Road, which was welcomed by the residents as the 'only possible correct decision that could be made'

(*IT*, 3 July 1998) and was condemned by the Orange Order as an act of repression.

The same scenario as that of the previous year was repeated, with tensions reaching a new height when, on the Twelfth of July, three Catholic brothers aged 10, 9 and 7 died when their house was the object of an arson attack. The sectarian nature of the crime and its tragic consequences led the leaders of the Church of Ireland, as well as David Trimble and the Reverend William Bringham, to ask for the protest to be called off. The marchers refused, and some, including Ian Paisley who came to show his support, stayed on to show their refusal to accept the outcome of the Parades Commission's decision.

Since 1998, all parades in Drumcree have been rerouted. Consequently, they must go back the way they came and avoid the Garvaghy Road. However, the marching season is still a period of tensions, one when, as columnist Mary Holland put it, 'the legacy of bitterness and grief from a quarter of a century of violence' comes to the fore (*IT*, 25 July 1996). For foreign journalists and observers, it is difficult to comprehend why there is so much grief, so much anger and violence over a march that takes, in total, ten minutes. To the local Orange Order, the residents' uncompromising refusal to allow them to take the traditional route was unfounded, given that, in their eyes, they had made significant concessions, such as the fact that the parade would pass off silently and that no triumphalism would be allowed to be shown.

Drumcree is not the only scene of contentious parades, although since it has been rerouted there are now over forty parades notified to the Commission every year, which would tend to show the resolve of the local Orange Lodge not to be deflected by the decision. Other potential flashpoints are generally locations which house a nationalist majority but are considered main routes for loyalist marches, either because of their so-called historical significance or their strategic location, being 'feeder routes' to bigger parades. Such is the case of the Lower Ormeau Road in Belfast, which is one of the main feeder routes towards main parades in the city. The march is seen as particularly contentious by the residents since February 1992 when the loyalist Ulster Freedom Fighters (UFF) shot dead five Catholic men in a betting shop. This prompted the residents to set up their own organisation, the Lower Ormeau Concerned Community. The following July marchers chanted and jeered as they passed the betting shop. Down the years, the parade along the Lower Ormeau Road has been seen as one of the most contentious ones. The decision of the Parades Commission reflects the difficulty of finding an acceptable middle ground over the issue: 'We cannot ignore the importance of perceptions in Northern Ireland and there is now a clear emerging sense of deep hurt amongst loyalists which arises from our decisions to reroute' (Annual Report, 1998). Republicans see some of these annual parades as confrontational and even provocative. In its 1996 submission, Sinn Féin laid out its views on this tradition, and described the Twelfth of July celebrations as 'expressions of unionist domination over nationalists [which] have always been a source of resentment and often of conflict' (Sinn Féin, Submission, 1996). Republicans see what they call a show of strength as inevitably sectarian, since it asserts one side's domination over the other. For the residents and their spokespersons, this issue is highly sensitive. Mitchell McLaughlin recognises the emotional implications of the situation: 'At various times over the past four years, I have heard republicans state a belief that intellectually Trimble is with the agreement but emotionally he is on Drumcree Hill with his Orange regalia, hectoring his neighbours and fellow Orangemen in the RUC who are blocking his way from marching down the Garvaghy Road' (*AP*, 25 July 2002). The parades issue could be seen as a test for both communities of how far they are prepared to go not only to coexist peacefully and accept each other's cultures and traditions, but also to accommodate the other side. Sinn Fein recognises that the right to march must be upheld, but it adds that this right 'cannot be absolute'. It contends that if the parade in question is seen as contentious to the local residents, then it must be rerouted. The Sinn Féin document adds that 'where a march had potential to cause offence to the loyalist community we have voluntarily re-routed' (Sinn Féin, Submission, 1996: 5). Whatever accommodation should be reached by dialogue and negotiation, Sinn Féin wants to be seen to be taking the lead on this issue, and points the way by adopting a compromising and conciliatory attitude towards the Apprentice Boys' march in Derry. 'We negotiated a deal in Derry City that sees the Apprentice Boys bringing their people by the thousands, into an area that is about 98 per cent nationalist or republican. It's not entirely trouble-free but it's mostly trouble free' (McLaughlin, interview).

Sinn Féin advocates the same method for local and national issues; that is, mediation and talks. Gerry Kelly therefore urged DUP representatives to discuss contentious parades with Sinn Féin and to encourage the Orange Order to dialogue with nationalist residents groups, as, according to him, the DUP 'are currently sitting on the North and West parades forums with three loyalist paramilitary groups. Let's show political leadership by meeting on the parades issue' (*IT*, 2 July 2004). It is interesting to note that the same approaches were suggested to resolve the parades issue as those prior to the signing of the Good Friday Agreement. Tony Blair proposed in 1998 that 'proximity talks' be held, along the same type of formula that was devised when the UP still refused to talk directly to Sinn Féin. Direct talks between the Garvaghy Road Residents' Association and the Orange Order were ruled out by the latter because the spokesperson of the association had served eighteen years in prison for a terrorist offence. The Orange Order thus perceived the Residents'

Association as a front for Sinn Féin. Whether or not this is the case, it is probable that both organisations entertain close links, and publicly, Sinn Féin leaders have supported the Residents' Association, although they are careful not to intervene directly, the associations being seen as the best intermediary to find a solution.

The Orange Order and some unionist politicians have accused the nationalist residents of being disingenuous about the issue of parades, especially at Drumcree. They point to the long-standing tradition of marching down a particular route that had never created any problem until the mid-1990s. They accuse Sinn Féin of exploiting the issue for its own ends. The Sinn Féin leaders retort that there are two reasons for this apparent change of heart. The first is that 'natural movements of population will cause changes in the demography of areas and therefore the tradition of marching a particular road or route cannot be used as the main criterion for the right to march' (Sinn Féin, Submission, 1996). But, and perhaps more importantly, the reaction to the march by the local residents is, according to Martin McGuinness, a sign that the political climate has changed and that the nationalist community is more capable of standing up for what it sees as its fundamental rights: 'The reality is that the people we represent are no longer going to be second-class citizens in their own country' (*IT*, 10 July 1998). But this newly found confidence among the nationalists is matched by a feeling of uncertainty on the part of unionists, a feeling of being, once again, bypassed by nationalists and by the peace process. According to a survey, only one-third of Protestant respondents agreed with the statement: 'I am confident that my own cultural tradition is protected in Northern Ireland these days', in contrast to 70 per cent of Catholics (Hughes, 2003: 3). Archbishop R. Eames encapsulated this dichotomy in attitudes, when he explained that Drumcree 'spoke of more than rights or duties. It enforced the raw nerve of traditional Protestant expression of a part of its historic ethos – and the growing confidence of nationalists to express its own perceived rights' (Eames, 2000: 11).

History and the future would then seem to be inextricably linked in Northern Ireland, as the visions that both communities have of each other are fuelled by their analysis of their respective pasts. The discourse on history, traditions and rights that republicans have developed in recent years, one that strives to be both conciliatory and firm, to uphold nationalist rights while not being seen to deny those of unionists, does not seem to have convinced those who feel threatened by the peace process and by the old-standard advances made by Sinn Féin. The rhetoric that is still used at times by party spokespersons, one that presents reunification as inevitable, that prophesies the victory of republicanism, is not helpful as it reinforces unionists' suspicions. As Martin McGuinness concedes, 'we all have to be sensitive about the language we use' (McGuinness, interview). But actions are probably more significant than words in contributing to reconciliation and dialogue, actions such as those of Alex Maskey while Mayor of Belfast. The Irish correspondent of the London *Observer*, Henry McDonald, who can be critical in his comments on republicans, talked of Maskey's meeting with UDA's Johnny Adair in prison in 2002 to discuss sectarian violence in North Belfast in the following terms:

> if future historians are looking for a pivotal point in the peace process when they could say the war was well and truly over, they could highlight this act of incredible generosity on Maskey's part. To be prepared to sit down face-to-face with a man once hell-bent on ensuring your annihilation sends out a signal that all can be forgiven, that the past can be put behind us.
>
> (*Observer*, 8 June 2003)

Maskey was able to show that 'despite his pugnacious exterior', he was 'the epitome of moderation, tolerance and understanding' (*Observer*). The day when this description can be used as a metaphor for the whole of Sinn Féin, then the hope and history that Gerry Adams wrote about[24] will indeed have been reconciled.

Conclusion

Beyond the IRA?

When Bairbre de Brún, then Sinn Féin Minister for Health in the Northern Ireland executive, was interviewed by an *Irish Times* journalist in May 2002, she seemed slightly irritated to be asked about decommissioning when she obviously wanted to talk about health. 'I knew I would not get to the end of an interview without somebody plucking the word out of nowhere' (*IT*, 2 May 2002), she said. Yet the word was not plucked out of nowhere. However tedious or difficult it might be for republican leaders to be constantly asked about when the IRA will disarm, and when it will eventually disband, this question is central to the understanding not only of the peace process but of the future role that Sinn Féin might play on both sides of the border.

Sinn Féin has many well-rehearsed answers to questions relating to decommissioning. It asserts that it possesses no weapons, that the process of putting arms beyond use has been effectively started, that time is needed to gain the confidence of the broad republican constituency in order to avoid splits. All these arguments undoubtedly have their merits. However, they have so far failed to convince the majority of political parties on both sides of the border. These parties still regard Sinn Féin as an organisation whose democratic credentials are not fully established, as its attitude towards paramilitary-style activities is seen as ambivalent. As long as this perceived contradiction within republicanism is not resolved, Sinn Féin will continue to be partly shunned by other parties who still regard republicans, at least publicly, as unacceptable potential government partners. Indeed, their policies and standpoints are at times dismissed as lacking credibility because the party still allegedly has links with the IRA. But Sinn Féin does have a political and social vision, no matter how strongly one agrees or disagrees with it.

Nevertheless, the lines between Sinn Féin and the IRA have been blurred for so many decades that it is difficult to extricate one or the other from their common historical, cultural and political roots. There is no doubt that Sinn Féin has become far more than the political wing of the IRA, in many different ways. Nevertheless, the IRA is an integral part of republican culture. The commemorations that are regularly held, the speeches made at the Ard Fheis, the mythology surrounding some of the past leaders or volunteers, all show how deeply rooted the IRA is within republican identity. Doing away with that component is not an easy task. Indeed, weapons can, and have been, put beyond use. And with sufficient political skill, Sinn Féin could potentially turn this difficulty into a strong negotiating card. They are very adept at cultivating a discourse in which the IRA is presented as having played a positive part in the peace process, contributing to carrying it forward and doing more on the decommissioning issue than other organisations. But this does not hold much sway with the main political formations of the island, which simply see the continued existence of the IRA as unacceptable.

The unionists are not the only ones to castigate Sinn Féin on its association with the IRA and to question its democratic credentials. The criticism of Sinn Féin's relationship to the IRA emanating from other political parties such as the SDLP or Fianna Fáil, which is also that of the British government, can be quite scathing. The position of the Republican Movement is seen as not wholly consistent, since it is considered impossible to reconcile a peace strategy with continued paramilitary activities. Republicans are seen as living in a culture that is complacent towards paramilitary operations. Despite the difficulties involved in disbanding an organisation that commands such respect within republican circles (a point on which most parties are ready to concede) both the SDLP and the UUP point to the fact that there is the need for some time scale on which to hinge the process of disarmament. 'You can't have a period of transition for 30 years. Wars end. Armies go home' (Farren, interview, 2004). In his view, if the IRA continues to operate, Sinn Féin should simply disown it and let the police deal with the criminal activities in which its members are allegedly involved. Fergus Finlay (Labour Party) mentions the vigilantism-type operations that take place in Dublin and in other parts of the country which, combined with a party structure which he sees as rigid and military-like, cast a shadow over Sinn Féin's democratic credentials. In fact, he goes further by denying republicans the title of socialist. 'You can't be a socialist if you're not democratic. Their relation to violence is too recent, they are too unwilling to repudiate it. You can mouth all the platitudes you want about equality, but these are not convincing if you're not prepared to condemn vigilantism' (Finlay, interview, 2004). In some respect, neither the SDLP nor the Labour Party see the quantity of arms that the IRA possesses as the issue, as much as the capacity of republicans to keep to their commitments on decommissioning. If republicans were to announce a time frame within which decommissioning would happen, and stick to it, then progress would be considered substantial, and arms would no longer be seen as being used as a bargaining tool.

What, indeed, are the options for the IRA? One, which is favoured by most political parties, is that the organisation disband, be legalised and become an old comrades association. However, there is little doubt that this is a difficult route to take for a number of republicans. Most seem to believe that the direction taken by their leadership is, globally speaking, the correct one. But some think that this same leadership has betrayed their movement and destroyed the struggle. Nevertheless, those disgruntled members concede that it is too late to turn back, and that there would be no point in taking up the struggle anew.

The other option for the IRA is to remain as it is at present. This implies that Sinn Féin maintains the perceived ambiguity that exists between the two organisations and obtains some political gains in return. This ambiguity is very much fuelled by the media, which speculate regularly on the identity of the men (or women) who sit on the commanding body of the IRA, the Army Council. Journalist Vincent Browne asked Adams whether he was P. O'Neill, the trademark signature of all IRA statements since the early 1970s. Indeed, a number of statements from the IRA contain striking similarities with the language used by the Sinn Féin press releases. Adams has constantly denied ever having been a member of the IRA, and continues to do so. But whether the identity of P. O'Neill is revealed or not, the more profound question is whether Sinn Féin is prepared to become totally free of the IRA, or indeed, if it is willing to do so. As long as it does not do so, speculations about the future intentions of the Republican Movement will continue to abound. Some observers have therefore talked of a strategy that borrows from the long war experience and translates it into a lengthy negotiation process. In such a scenario, republican intransigence is met by unionist intransigence, but it is the Ulster Unionist Party which gets the blame and ultimately stands to lose, as was shown by the November 2003 electoral results. Indeed, republicans have been quite adept at presenting their party as being the one that makes concessions and sacrifices, and unionism as rigid and unyielding in its stance. This rhetoric is, according to David Ervine, what explains Sinn Féin's successes in the November 2003 elections.

Other observers point to the repeated messages emanating from Sinn Féin that express their willingness to work within the institutions and to operate as a political party within a devolved assembly and government as a sign that the party is indeed prepared to put its own past, one where the party and the IRA were historically linked, behind. But Fergus Finlay remarks that there is no need for the IRA to disband for Sinn Féin to play a full political role, as it has sat in government without prior decommissioning. More importantly perhaps, the IRA is, in Finlay's words, 'an undefeated army', something which republicans are also keen to insist on. In Joe Cahill's words, they have 'won the war'. What they need to do to 'win the peace' is in great part predicated, however, on their capacity to retain the balance they have struck between their electoral successes and their radical edge.

One of Sinn Féin's greatest assets is undoubtedly the fact that it is, first and foremost, a party of activists. For this reason, it emphasises what it describes as the bottom-up organisation of its decision-making process and of its structures. However, it is also a party driven strongly by its leadership. It relies, principally, on a handful of personalities who seem to have the trust of the overwhelming majority of its members. But relying on charismatic figures such as Gerry Adams, Martin McGuinness or Alex Maskey could be one of the party's weaknesses in the longer term. The party has yet to find a voice that would speak for the southern part of the country. Although it has five elected representatives in the Dáil, none of these have succeeded in attaining the stature of their northern colleagues. Sinn Féin is an all-Ireland party; therefore the fact that its leadership seems to be based principally in the north is obviously problematic.

Furthermore, the difficulties experienced by the SDLP might carry a lesson for Sinn Féin. Although its current leaders see themselves as the victims of a governmental strategy that has focused strongly on the 'problem parties', leaving them on the margins of the decision-making process, the loss of John Hume or Seamus Mallon, whose names had been closely identified with moderate nationalism in the north, undoubtedly contributed to the party's crisis of identity. Sinn Féin is aware that relying on its present leadership could pose a problem if no alternative personalities come forward who could carry the party into the future, when Adams or McGuinness step down. This is currently being addressed, according to Sinn Féin's Director of Publicity Dawn Doyle, not only by ensuring that more individual representatives are given greater prominence and a higher public profile, but also by making sure that there is a dedicated and solid base. 'The key thing that the ANC drilled into us is that when people come in, they have to be grounded in the policy, that they know the full extent of why they're coming in' (Doyle, interview, 2004).

Sinn Féin's highly efficient organisational machine has contributed to the party's recent electoral successes, particularly since the start of the millennium. Unlike other parties in the island, Sinn Féin fights elections on both sides of the border, a fact that implies a strain on its financial and human resources. Between 2001 and 2004, it will have fought two general elections (one in the south and one in the north), one local, one European, and one for the assembly of Northern Ireland. The danger of becoming too focused on electioneering cannot be ignored, as this would run contrary to what Sinn Féin professes to fundamentally believe in: street politics, activism and involvement in local politics and campaigns. As the party's national organiser, Pat Treanor, reminded the readers of *An Phoblacht* in January 2004, electoralism is a permanent site of struggle and we must maximise support for our party next June, but we also need to develop in a radical way all the other sites of struggle. There are other watersheds. As activists of a radical movement, we should ask ourselves regularly some questions that challenge us. Are each of the party's organisational structures as strong as we will need them to be, to achieve our objectives?

(*AP*, 8 January 2004)

Republicans still emphasise the importance of their work outside of the institutions. 'One of the crucial things is not to privilege electoral representatives', says North Belfast councillor Eoin Ó Broin. Being an electioneering party while not becoming institutionalised is therefore another challenge that the party will face in the years to come.

The very word 'institutionalisation' conjures up a series of negative precedents, since it is perceived as the root cause of major splits which have fragmented and, ultimately, weakened the movement. More fundamentally, institutionalisation also means a loss of identity. Yet is it possible, in the longer term, to keep wining elections and parliamentary seats and to retain its identity as an activist-led, radical organisation? The examples of Clann na Phoblachta or the Workers' Party as former abstentionist Sinn Féin parties entering the mainstream and losing their edge are frequently quoted. Their short-lived experiences have taught present-day republicans that 'when they went into government, they moved away from the organisation and ideological culture that got them to where they were. Their great mistake was to have actively broken that link' (Ó Broin, interview, 2004). Republicans therefore see it as fundamental that they succeed in remaining as true to their radical roots as possible while not confining themselves to the margins. How this is done is undoubtedly problematic, because if the party does increase its share of the vote, it may be necessary to start compromising on some issues. Striking a balance between being a successful electoral party while retaining its identity and not becoming 'neutralised by the state', as Ó Broin puts it, is one of the main tasks that will face republicans in the years to come.

For the time being, Sinn Féin has to manage the strains that the recent growth in activity has implied. The structures of the party have been slightly amended to adapt them to the 'equality agenda' with which the party wants to be identified, with the appointment of regional equality officers, the organisation of in house training, internal conferences and so on. The policies of the party on some issues remain outdated and therefore unconvincing in some respects. This could impact on whether the electorate is willing to trust Sinn Féin with its social and economic vision of Ireland. Gerry Adams claims that one way of measuring Sinn Féin's successes is not only in electoral terms, but also in terms of the impact that it will have made, in a few years time, on society (Adams, interview, 2004). On some issues at least, republicans still have some way to go before they can demonstrate convincingly that they are the bearers of a social vision that can translate into the governing of a country. However, a lot of work needs to be carried out on issues that have been identified as key areas, such as education, the fight against racism, or gender. The concrete measures and the rethinking of policies in the latter area seem to indicate that the party is genuinely committed to the aim of being a gender-balanced party. In the shorter term, Sinn Féin has set more pragmatic objectives, such as building on its electoral strength. In some way, the next general election in the Republic will be seen as a critical indicator for its future prospects, in the sense that it will reveal whether the 2002 results represented a breakthrough or simply the result of good local policies. It will also reveal whether the support for Sinn Féin has reached a ceiling. Avoiding such a ceiling will require that Sinn Féin overcome some of its existing difficulties, such as its poor performance when it comes to transfer of votes and its weak incursion into the middle classes.

Sinn Féin's progress is highly dependent on the manner in which the situation unfolds in Northern Ireland and on the outcome of the review procedure initiated in February 2004. Ultimately, however, Adams' ambition is to look beyond the peace process and to develop a network of relations with other parties and organisations that will eventually lead to 'a realignment of Irish politics along right and left lines', as was the case, in his view, during the Nice referendum campaign (Adams, interview). However, the question of the IRA will probably keep coming back to haunt republicans, and will make alliances or coalitions difficult. For the time being, most politicians in the Republic of Ireland still profess not to intend to enter into any coalitions with republicans. But public opinion is more pragmatic, and increasingly willing to trust Sinn Féin with their votes, according to the findings of surveys. Consequently, political parties may have to alter their stance if Sinn Féin continues to increase its share of the vote. Ultimately, however, how Sinn Féin fares in the years to come may not have so much to do with the policies that it is capable of putting forward as with its ability to manage its internal contradictions.

Notes

Introduction

1 The party of that name first emerged in 1905, when Arthur Griffith, in front of a gathering of nationalist groups, presented his proposals for an autonomous Ireland under the name *Sinn Féin Policy*. The present organisation called Sinn Féin has little in common with the one founded in the early years of the last century, and on its website it takes some distance from that particular party, stating somewhat elliptically that 'the name Sinn Féin ("We Ourselves") first emerged in the early 1890s as a federation of nationalist clubs'

2 This phrase is borrowed from Theobald Wolfe Tone, the eighteenth-century leader who is considered the father of Irish republicanism and whose fight and eventual fall in 1798 are seen as the first modern manifestation of Irish national liberation.

3 'Republican' in the Irish political context refers, generally speaking, to political parties or groups that aspire to a united Ireland. Those include Fianna Fáil or smaller groups such as the Continuity IRA or the thirty-two-county Sovereignty movement. However, for practical reasons and in order to avoid any confusion, republican or Republican Movement will be used here to designate Sinn Féin and the IRA.

4 This phrase referred to the strategy adopted in the early 1980s, in which armed struggle and electoral policies were conducted in parallel. See Chapter 1.

1 Historical overview

1 At the time, Ireland was represented in Westminster by twenty-eight Lords and a hundred Members of Parliament.

2 Charles Stewart Parnell, leader of the Home Rule Party, suggested in a speech in May 1878 that if the Irish Members were expelled from Westminster for their obstructionist tactics, they should be prepared to formally secede and assemble in Ireland (Lyons, 1983: 162).

3 This secret organisation was founded in 1848 with the aim of overthrowing British rule in Ireland and creating an Irish Republic. According to its 1873 constitution, its members swore allegiance to the Supreme Council, or governing body, of the organisation, and its soldiers were called the Irish Republican Army.

4 This was in fact the third Home Rule Bill; the first one had been defeated by the House of Commons in 1886, the second by the House of Lords in 1893. This bill provided limited autonomy for Ireland, which retained representatives in the Imperial Parliament. The third bill met with fierce opposition

from the Conservatives and the Unionists, and was defeated by the House of Lords in 1913, which would delay it for two years. It was eventually signed into law by King George V in September 1914, but an agreement reached between the Unionists and the Irish Parliamentary Party suspended its implementation for the duration of the war.

5 This association, created in 1893, sought to promote the Irish language, and the study and publication of Irish literature.

6 Sinn Féin made it very clear in its electoral literature that its candidates would not take their seats in Westminster if elected. In an electoral tract, *Parliamentarism in a Nutshell*, the party asked: 'Are you going to continue the farce of sending Irishmen to this treacherous Assembly?' (Sinn Féin, Electoral tract, 1918).

7 The Black and Tans were responsible, among others, for the killings in Croke Park on Bloody Sunday, on 21 November 1921, when they fired into a crowd attending a match as a reprisal against the killing of eleven British agents by the IRA the previous day, killing twelve people and wounding many more.

8 The IRA had suffered severe losses during the Second World War, when its members had been interned on both sides of the border and some of them had been executed. Its reorganisation was slow and it only became operational again three years after the war.

9 The 'Republic of Ireland Act' was introduced in 1948 and declared that 'The description of the State shall be a Republic'. The Republic of Ireland formally came into existence on Easter Monday, 1949.

10 Two years previously, in 1955, two republican prisoners had been elected to Westminster.

11 The 'Northern Ireland Civil Rights Association' (NICRA), formed in 1967, put forward fundamental demands: the end of discrimination in the attribution of public housing and employment by local authorities; the removal of gerrymandered electoral boundaries and the reform of the 1946 Electoral law which led to some reforms such as universal franchise, the repeal of the Special Powers Act which gave the Minister of Home Affairs extensive powers such as arresting without warrant, introducing internment without trial, banning organisations and prohibiting meetings, and even flogging and executing.

12 The term *Provisional* has two explanations. It was chosen in the name of the Provisional Republic declared in 1916. It was also a reflection of the fact that the organisation created in January 1970 as a result of a walkout of some delegates of the Ard Fheis in Dublin was provisional, and did not at that time have firmly established structures. The Provisionals, or Provos, soon became a household name, and the adjective took on a life of its own. It was also a necessary linguistic device in the early 1970s to distinguish them from the other Sinn Féin and IRA, the Officials, who became known, derogatorily, as the 'Stickies', because of the Easter Lily that they wore every year which was a sticker instead of a pin.

13 This report was published at the time in its entirety in the pages of *An Phoblacht-Republican News* under its original title: *Northern Ireland, Future Terrorist Trends*.

14 A Tribunal of Enquiry was set up by the British government in 1999. See Chapter 6, 'The legacy of the conflict'.

15 Figures for casualties during the conflict vary slightly according to the sources. *The Cost of the Troubles* survey put the total number of deaths at 3,601, of which 1,573 had died before 1975 (Fay *et al.*, 1999: 137).

16 According to the 1975 report by Lord Gardiner, whose recommendations eventually led to the withdrawal of special category status, the total male prison population at the end of 1974 was 2,648, of which the vast majority, 1,881 (71%), benefited from special category status and thus, presumably, had been convicted of offences related to the conflict (Gardiner, 1975: 33).

17 There were also protesting prisoners among the loyalist ranks. Although they did not observe the dirty protest, they opposed the withdrawal of special category status. No coordination was put in place between the two sides of the prison, which meant that the protests were held separately. Some loyalist prisoners embarked on a hunger strike in early December 1980, which lasted a few days. On the other hand, IRA prisoners in the all-female Maghebery Prison also joined the protest, some as early as 1978, and three of them observed a fast for a few days before deciding to abandon that type of action.

18 Hunger strikes have been undertaken at many different times by republican prisoners throughout the twentieth century, either by individuals (Terence McSwiney, Mayor of Cork, died in 1919 after having fasted for seventy-four days; Frank Stagg, who was seeking his transfer from a British to an Irish gaol, died in 1976) or collectively (several thousand prisoners embarked on a hunger strike in several prisons throughout the Free State in 1923); in 1939, six men fasted and two died before the Free State government granted them political status. More recently, in 1972, over thirty men embarked on a hunger strike in Crumlin Road Prison in Belfast, demanding political status. They obtained what was then termed 'special category status' which was at the heart of the dispute in 1980 and 1981.

19 At the time of the prison protest, there were two main republican organisations. The Provisional IRA (Provos) had been formed in 1970 as a result of a split with the Official IRA. The latter operated in Northern Ireland until they declared an unlimited and unconditional ceasefire in 1972. Some of their members resented this decision, and either joined the Provisionals or subsequently formed a new organisation, the Irish National Liberation Army, whose political arm was the Irish Republican Socialist Party.

20 This change of tone was already perceptible from the late 1970s onward, when a new leadership, composed mainly of Northern leaders, emerged. Yet it was fully endorsed by the movement as a whole thanks to the hunger strikes.

21 See Chapter 4.

22 Some years previously, a movement had attempted to break away from the sectarian divide between Catholics and Protestants by rallying opinion around one theme: peace. However, the Peace People was a relatively short-lived phenomenon, which did not succeed in building on its initial success and gradually faded, though not before its leaders were awarded the Nobel Peace Prize in 1977.

23 In 1955, two prisoners were elected in the Westminster general election.

24 The 'rolling devolution' principle meant that devolution could be delivered in stages once agreement had been reached; if this did not arise, the Secretary of State would retain responsibility for governing Northern Ireland.

25 The political parties had to affirm their commitment to six principles: democratic and peaceful means of resolving political issues, disarmament of paramilitary organisations, the verification of such disarmament by an independent commission, the renunciation of violence and the opposition to the use of violence by others, adherence to any agreement reached as a result of all-party negotiation, and the prevention of punishment killings and beatings.

26 This is the time of the year when most marches are held, especially in the unionist/loyalist community. See Chapter 6.
27 The two prisoners who were elected in 1981 to the Dáil were, technically, not Sinn Féin candidates, as they stood for the H-Blocks-Armagh Committee.
28 The DUP did not participate in the negotiations leading up to the Agreement and is therefore not a signatory to the document.
29 This Act effectively partitioned the country by creating two different jurisdictions and giving them limited autonomy.
30 Article 2 of the 1937 Constitution stipulated that 'the national territory consist of the whole island of Ireland, its islands and the territorial seas', although Article 3 qualified this statement, adding that 'pending the reintegration of the national territory', the laws enacted by Dáil Éireann would only apply to the twenty-six counties. These two articles were frequently flagged by unionists as evidence of the hostility of the Irish Republic towards Northern Ireland and used to justify their refusal to engage in any mechanism that gave their southern neighbours a say in the affairs of Northern Ireland.
31 Frente Armado Revolucionario de Colombia (Colombian Revolutionary Armed Front). See Chapter 5.

2 The peace process

1 Secretary of State Patrick Mayhew spelled out three conditions for Sinn Féin to be included in the talks: the IRA had to be prepared to disarm progressively, it had to agree on the way to proceed, and it had to decommission part of its weapons prior to the talks.
2 Illegal weapons should not be handed to the security forces, since this would have been perceived as an act of surrender; instead, they were to be destroyed, or 'put beyond use' in order to ensure that they would not be used by anyone but also that they would not be submitted to forensic testing and subsequently used as evidence in judicial proceedings.
3 Jeffrey Donaldson remained David Trimble's strongest critic within the Ulster Unionist Party in the following years. He eventually left the party for the DUP in December 2003, following the results of the assembly election.
4 The DUP, as well as some UUP politicians, refers to Sinn Féin as 'IRA-Sinn Féin', and seems to be profoundly convinced that the links between the two are not simply organic, but that they are the same organisation.
5 The Police Service of Northern Ireland raided the Sinn Féin Stormont offices on 6 October 2002 on the basis that an employee had been suspected of copying documents in September 2001. The documents retrieved allegedly included information on a PSNI officer and British soldiers, details on known loyalists and confidential documents from the NIO. A laptop with information on the Northern Ireland prison services was also seized. According to a journalist, this amounted to 'hundreds of documents, which, stacked, were more than one foot high' (IT, 7 October 2002). This episode put the IRA ceasefire into question, since, if the organisation was effectively collecting information which targeted specific individuals, it was in breach of its ceasefire. Two Sinn Féin officials were brought to the Magistrates Court. Sinn Féin, however, pointed out that the timing of this raid, one-and-a half years after the alleged infiltrator had left Stormont, could not have been a coincidence, and concluded that the operation was politically motivated, giving Trimble the opportunity to take the heat off himself and to switch the blame to Sinn Féin.

6 The IRA subsequently decided to publish its statement which, in the first weeks of the controversy, had remained confidential, as had the Joint Declaration. The statement contained some indications on the future intentions of the IRA: it committed the organisation to 'put arms beyond use at the earliest opportunity', although it did not set a date or a time scale; it affirmed that republicans were 'resolved to see the complete and final closure of this conflict. The IRA leadership is determined to ensure that our activities, disciplines and strategies will be consistent with this.' However, the following sentence could have been of some concern to the authorities and political parties alike: 'furthermore, the full and irreversible implementation of the Agreement and other commitments will provide a context in which the IRA can proceed to definitively set aside arms to further our political objectives. When there is such a context this decision can be taken only by a General Army Convention representing all our volunteers' (IRA statement, 13 April 2003, available online).

7 This is the police station that was broken into in March 2002. Several republicans were arrested, suspected of having stolen highly sensitive files. However, all were subsequently released without charge.

8 In his essay on war, military strategist Von Clauzewitz wrote: 'War is, therefore, the continuation of policies.'

9 This view was echoed by a study commissioned by the Sinn Féin minister's Department of Health, the report of the Acute Hospitals Review Group, chaired by the north's former ombudsman, Dr Maurice Hayes, which stated that: 'There are things we can't do for a population of 1.5 million, there are things that can't be done in the South with a population of 3.5 million but you could do them for five million' (IT, 21 June 2001). It could be argued, nevertheless, that the views of the report were not entirely partial, as it was commissioned by a Sinn Féin minister. However, there is nothing to suggest that this particular agenda was part of the brief of the survey.

10 The areas of cooperation were the following: Agriculture (animal and plant health), Education (teacher qualifications and training), Transport (strategic transport planning), Environment (environmental protection, pollution, water quality and waste management), Waterways (inland), Social Security/Social Welfare (entitlements of cross-border workers and fraud control), Tourism (promotion, marketing, research and product development), Relevant EU programmes, Inland fisheries, Aquaculture and marine matters, Health (accident and emergency services and other related cross-border issues), Urban and rural development.

11 The portfolios were distributed along the d'Hondt lines of proportional representation, according to which the number of ministries for each party depended on the number of seats obtained in the Assembly. Moreover, parties take turns choosing the ministries, starting from the strongest down to the weakest. Once all parties have chosen their first ministry, the procedure is started again. The Northern Ireland Executive was thus composed of the following ministries, chosen in the following order: G. Empey (UUP), Enterprise, Trade and Investment; M. Durkan (SDLP), Finance and Personnel; P. Robinson (DUP), Regional Development; M. McGuinness (Sinn Féin), Education; I. Foster (UUP), Environment; S. Farren (SDLP), Higher and Further Education, Training and Development; N. Dodds (DUP), Social Development; M. McGimpsey (UUP), Culture, Art and Leisure; B. De Brun (Sinn Féin), Health, Social Services and Public Safety, and B. Rodgers (SDLP), Agriculture.

12 The Bogside is a predominantly nationalist area of Derry. In 1969, its inhabitants raised barricades and renamed the area 'Free Derry'. It was in the Bogside that the shootings on Bloody Sunday took place.

13 The survey does not measure the work of other ministries held by different parties. The fact that only Health and Education were chosen is not justified in the study, but could be explained by the attention that these two ministers attracted, not only because of their political affiliation, but also because of the very departments they held. However, it would have been interesting to measure their performance compared to that of their colleagues.

14 This undated pamphlet, probably dating from the mid-1980s, was part of a series of documents designed for internal training for future members of Sinn Féin.

15 To each department was attached a committee, whose chairperson had to be from a party which was different from the one of the minister. Therefore, for every nationalist minister, the corresponding committee chair was held by a unionist, and vice versa. The Minister for Finance was DUP's Peter Robinson.

16 The electoral results for the SDLP and Sinn Féin at Westminster general elections show a relatively stable share of the vote for both parties. In 1983, Sinn Féin obtained 13.4 per cent of the vote, to 17. 9 per cent for the SDLP. The 1987 general elections showed a decline in the Sinn Féin vote (11.4 per cent to 21.1 per cent). Sinn Féin regained the lost ground in 1992, with 13.1 per cent to 23.5 per cent, and increased its share of the vote to 16.1 per cent, with the SDLP still ahead (24.1 per cent).

3 From political wing to political party

1 Unless stated otherwise, the opinion polls quoted in this section are all taken from the following website: http://www.tcd.ie/Political_Science/cgi/File.html

2 Shooting the kneecap, known as 'kneecapping', was considered to be a typical IRA punishment.

4 The equality agenda

1 The GNP rose from 2.3 per cent in 1991 to 10.4 per cent in 2000. Similarly, employment in the services and industry rose from 1,133,000 to 1,671,000 in 2000, amounting to a net creation of over 500,000 jobs. Unemployment, on the other hand, dropped dramatically to reach less than 4 per cent in 2000 (O'Hearn, 2003: 42).

2 The point made here about foreign investment is quite fundamental, as figures show how much the economic recovery of the Irish Republic relies on the fixed industrial investment: the US share of the total was 32.5 per cent in 1990 and rose to 65.7 per cent, whereas the Irish total fell from 42.7 per cent in 1990 to 16 per cent in 2000 (O'Hearn, 39).

3 This campaign was started as a result of a decision by Dublin County Council to impose a tax on bin collections. Several political parties and trade unions, along with individual citizens, organised protests against what they perceived as a double taxation. Several people were gaoled for obstructing the bin collection, among them Socialist Party TD Joe Higgins and local councillor Clare Daly.

4 When Seamus Twomey, presumed chief-of-staff of the IRA, was arrested in 1977, a document outlining the proposed reorganisation of the paramilitary organisation was seized. This document stated, among other things, that

cumman na mBan would be dissolved, its best elements would be incorporated into IRA cells and the rest would be going towards the civil and military administration (Coogan, 1980: 580).

5 In total, for the years 1919 to 1969, there were twenty-two women in Dáil Eireann.

6 Terence McSwiney, Mayor of Cork, died in 1917 after a seventy-four-day hunger strike, in search of political status. He set a sort of record within republican mythology, as the length of his fast was never equalled down the years.

7 Mary McSwiney had taken part in the 1916 Rising, and then became elected TD when her brother died. However, throughout the late 1920s and early 1930s, she became known for her intransigence and her visceral opposition to anything that deviated from the republican dogma. She resigned from Sinn Féin in 1934 when the party admitted into its ranks those who were state pensioners, a move which she viewed as a betrayal of the revolutionary mandate inherited from the 1918 elections.

8 Maire Drumm was assassinated in 1976 while in hospital in Belfast. This was the first political assassination to deliberately target a woman since the start of the Troubles.

9 Article 40.3.3 was amended as follows: 'The State acknowledges the right to life of the unborn and with due regard to the equal right to life of the mother, guarantees in its laws to respect and, as far as practicable, by its laws to defend and vindicate that right.'

10 At the 1986 Ard Fheis, one infuriated member talked of abortion in the following terms: 'Abortion is counter-republican and counter-revolutionary. It is disgraceful that as Republicans we should be talking of the destruction of future Irish people' (Ard Fheis, 1986).

11 About 4,000 women were said to travel overseas in the early 1990s to have an abortion.

12 Sinn Féin was not the only political party to successfully apply for funding under the general heading 'Promoting gender balance in decision making'. Fianna Fáil and Fine Gael both obtained finance to encourage and promote full participation of women at all levels.

13 The women candidates were put forward in six constituencies, and obtained the following results: Dublin West (8.02 per cent), Dublin North Central (5.74 per cent), Dublin South (3.93 per cent), Wicklow (2.80 per cent), Cork East (5.73 per cent) and Cork South West (5.85 per cent).

14 Ireland has experienced a notable growth in applications for asylum since the early 1990s. The number of asylum seekers grew from thirty-nine in 1992 to more than 10,000 in 2001. To this must be added the increase in the work permits and work visas being granted to non-EU citizens: 1,103 in 1993, a figure which rose to 18,017 by the end of 2000 and to 36,431 by the end of 2001 (Loyal, 2003: 80).

15 Travellers suffer from well-documented social problems, such as poor health or standards of education (see e.g. the websites of travellers' organisations such as Pavee Point or Exchange House). As far as discrimination is concerned, an article in the *Sunday Business Post* stated that 'The Office of the Director of Equality Investigations, which was set up in October 1999 as the main forum for investigating discrimination claims, has dealt with 1,111 cases, of which 918 came from Travellers' (SBP, 21 April 2002).

16 The Macpherson report, published in February 1999, followed an inquiry into the Metropolitan Police's investigation of the murder of a black teenager,

Stephen Lawrence. It surveyed the instances of 'institutional racism' within the Metropolitan Police and policing generally, and gave seventy recommendations as to how to tackle this problem. Among others, it advocated the strengthening of the 1976 Race Relations Act, by extending its provisions to public authorities and bodies, obliging them to ensure that their workforce reflects their communities, and that policies and practices do not discriminate indirectly.

17 Manifestations of racism on both sides of the island have become more obvious since the mid-1990s. The National Consultative Committee on Racism and Interculturalism started establishing biannual reports on racist incidents in 2001, including racist abuse, assault and harassment, provision of services and circulation of offensive material. The figures for May to October 2003 were forty-eight, of which 75 per cent had occurred in the Greater Dublin area (NCCRI, available online). A survey carried out by the Irish section of Amnesty International in 2001 showed that 80 per cent of the ethnic minorities surveyed had experienced racism or discrimination in Ireland (AI, 2001, available online).

18 Under this system, asylum seekers are housed in accommodation provided by the state and are given a weekly allowance of 19 euros per week and 9.50 euros per child, in addition to the provision of meals.

19 In order to avoid a concentration of asylum seekers in the capital, the government introduced their dispersal to towns and villages across the country. They do not have an option, and organisations working on their behalf have called for more flexibility on this issue as dispersal generally entails isolation of ethnic minorities and more difficult access to services such as health and counselling.

20 This is also the figure quoted by the government as part of the National Development Plan.

5 The international dimension

1 The IRA did maintain some contacts abroad. In 1936, volunteers joined the Connolly Column of the International Brigade to fight alongside the republican government in the Spanish Civil War. Some 161 republicans fought in that war, of whom sixty-one were killed. Some contacts were established at the outset of the Second World War between Seán Russell, former chief-of-staff, and the German Abwehr.

2 Republicans tend to draw a parallel between their struggle and that of the Basque Country. Examples of this abound. In one instance, Alex Maskey, who was then local councillor for South Belfast, referred to the French Basque Country as a region 'under French occupation', a phrase reminiscent of the 'British occupation' phrase used by Sinn Féin when referring to the north in the 1970s and 1980s. Similarly, an article in *An Phoblacht* on ETA prisoners on hunger strike in late 1999 made reference to ETA's 'five demands', which automatically evoked the 'five demands' made by IRA and INLA prisoners on protest from 1976 to 1981, even for those having only a cursory knowledge of recent republican history.

3 In its opening statement, the document explained that the 'British and the IRA were aware that neither was going to win the war militarily and they consequently accepted that the conflict could last for a long time'.

4 In June 2002, the Spanish House of Representatives (Cortes) voted by a 90 per cent majority in favour of a law on political parties, the main objective of

which was to allow for the dissolution of parties that support terrorism, overtly or tacitly.

5 Indeed, in an article posted on the Spanish Interior Ministry's website entitled 'IRA–ETA, peace process – War Process' (which was a synthesis of different articles written on the subject and was not, as such, to be seen as the official line), the republicans' courage was praised, and the Adams factor cited as one of the keys to the Irish peace process.

6 This fund was established by the British and Irish governments in 1986 as an independent, international organisation. The main donors are the USA, the EU, Canada, Australia and New Zealand. According to its 2002 report, it had received £383 million. The share of the US contribution in 2002 represented more than half of the total donations (IFI, *Annual Report*, 2002: 46).

7 Richard Haass was replaced by Mitchell Reiss in December 2003.

8 The Real IRA was re-designated as a 'Foreign Terrorist Organisation' in May 2003.

9 At the moment, the five larger member states nominate two commissioners each, and this number will be reduced to one commissioner per state in 2005. Ireland has currently three votes out of eighty-seven in the Council of Ministers, representing 3.45 per cent of the total vote. This will be extended to seven votes with enlargement, but as the number of votes will be 345, its share decreases to 2.02 per cent. The Irish population will represent 0.8 per cent of the total enlarged EU.

10 Some 70.9 per cent of the Irish electorate voted massively (83.1 per cent) for accession in 1972. Both figures declined in subsequent referenda: 69.1 per cent voted in favour of the 1992 Treaty of Maastricht (with a turnout of 57.3 per cent) and 61.7 per cent for the 1998 Amsterdam Treaty (56.2 per cent).

6 The legacy of the conflict

1 According to the 2001 census figures, the population of Northern Ireland stands at 1,685,267 (*IT*, 29 April 2001).

2 These figures are taken from the Cost of the Conflict Study, a limited company working in partnership between victims of the Troubles and researchers, which analysed in detail the human cost of the conflict from 1969 to the first IRA ceasefire in 1994. Thus these figures do not take into account the casualties that have occurred since, such as the thirty victims of the Omagh bombing in August 1998 and the victims of interface conflicts.

   Those figures, however, differ slightly from those of the RUC, which give a total of 3,322 deaths for the period between 1969 and 2001. Furthermore, those statistics, entitled 'Deaths as a result of the security situation', do not include a category for paramilitary deaths, which are, presumably, included in the overall civilian column, which totals 2,365 deaths (statistics available online).

3 The RUC total figure for the number of persons injured is 44,881, of whom 28,683 are civilians.

4 Michael Ancram was replaced by Des Browne in 2001, and in August 2003, following a reshuffle in the NIO, Angela Smith was appointed to that post.

5 A Victims Unit was also established under the devolved institutions, which was responsible for supporting the minister's work and the implementation of programmes within the devolved administration.

6 This measure was one of the reasons why some members of the Ulster Unionist Party, including Jeffrey Donaldson, strongly disagreed with the

Agreement when it was signed. When the issue of the 'On the Run' prisoners, those men and women who had been convicted *in absentia* for a crime related to the conflict but had managed to escape, was discussed with the British and Irish governments from 2002, some unionists, including the DUP, voiced their concern that these people would never have served any time for the crimes that they had committed.

7 Some of the most successful campaigns that were associated with the issue of prisoners were those of the Birmingham Six, the Guildford Four and the Maguire Seven. However, all three were cases of miscarriages of justice, as it was clearly demonstrated that they were not guilty of the crimes for which they had been sentenced to serve lengthy times. However, the case of the Castlereagh Five is far less straightforward, as there was public outcry at the time of the incident.

8 Coiste itself puts this figure into perspective: 7,525 people have been identified as having been imprisoned between 1973 and 1990, which, according to the organisation, does not take into account the people imprisoned before and after those dates, but also those interned and those imprisoned abroad. In light of these recalculations, the figure may need to be viewed with some caution.

9 This IRA unit was responsible for a number of attacks in the UK in the mid-1970s, until their arrest in 1975. The four men were imprisoned in the UK, but transferred to the Republic shortly before the signing of the GFA.

10 According to figures quoted in John McGuffin's study on internment, there were, after six months, '2,357 arrested under the Special Powers Act, 598 interned, 159 detained, and 1,600 completely innocent men (by even the government's standards) released after "interrogation" – nearly 67 per cent' (McGuffin, 1973: 87).

11 The inquiry began in Derry in March 2000, hearing from over 1,000 witnesses (among whom were civilians, journalists, government officials, and also soldiers) before reporting in 2004, with a total cost estimated at £50m (*Guardian*, 25 April 2002).

12 Foundeer and leader of the Loyalist Volunteer Force (LVF), Billy Wright was murdered while in prison by three members of the INLA in December 1997.

13 Among these are the bombs in Dublin in Monaghan in May 1974, which killed thirty-four people. These were later claimed by the UVF, but strong suspicions as to possible collusion between the loyalist paramilitary organisation and the security forces have been repeatedly voiced. The victims and relatives of the bombings are demanding a full public inquiry, as the Garda investigation was closed after six weeks. No one was prosecuted for the bombings.

14 On 5 January 1976, an IRA unit, operating under the name of 'South Armagh Republican Action Force', stopped a minibus of workers, eleven Protestants and one Catholic, in Kingsmill, South Armagh. The Catholic was let go, the other eleven men were shot and only one survived. On 11 November 1987, a bomb exploded during the Remembrance Day ceremony in Enniskillen, Co. Tyrone. Eleven Protestants were killed. On 23 October 1993, a bomb apparently intended for what was thought to be a UDA meeting on the Shankill Road in Belfast exploded in a fish shop, killing nine Protestants and the bomber, and injuring more than sixty people.

15 According to Amnesty International, 'A disappearance occurs whenever there are reasonable grounds to believe that a person has been deprived of freedom by the authorities or their agents, with the authorization, support or acquiescence of the state, and the authorities deny that the victim is held in their custody, thus concealing the victim's whereabouts and fate, thereby

placing the person outside the protection of the law.' This definition is obviously problematic as it does not include non-government agents, and is not workable in the case of the IRA. Yet it might serve to explain why the phenomenon of IRA disappearances has attracted so little attention from human rights groups until recently, and why the fight to discover the truth was left solely to the relatives of the disappeared.

16 Jean McConville's abduction was narrated by her daughter's husband Séamus McKentrick in his book *Disappeared*, who started the Families of the Disappeared organisation in 1994.

17 Ed Moloney wrote that 'Whether, as alleged by one well-informed source, or not the order was given by Adams himself, it is inconceivable that such an order would have been issued without his knowledge' (Moloney, 2002: 124).

18 John Redmond was the leader of the Nationalist Party. He called for the Irish Volunteers to join in the war effort in the hope that this would be later compensated by the implementation of the Home Rule bill by Westminster.

19 Nationalists such as Griffith considered that this war was not theirs. 'Germany is nothing to us in herself, but she is not our enemy', he said in 1915 (Colum, 1959: 131). James Connolly opposed the war for the same reasons, although, in line with socialist thinking at the time, he also condemned it as an imperial war. He just wrote that the working class would be entitled to join a German army 'if by doing so we could rid this country once and for all from its connection with the Brigand Empire that drags us unwillingly into this war' (Lyons, 1983: 343).

20 This ranged from the commissioning of sculptures from Irish artists to travelling exhibitions including photos and memorabilia of the hunger strikes, such as the very small letters know as 'comms' which the prisoners smuggled out of the prison throughout the protest; from visual manifestations like the building of a makeshift H-Block cell on the Falls Road to more symbolic ceremonies such as the planting of ten trees in Derry. The narrative of the hunger strike was mainly explored through a play, *Diary of a Hunger Strike*, which toured Ireland in the spring of 2001 and in which the role of Bobby Sands was played by Gerry Adams' cousin, and through the film *H3*, co-written by Lawrence McKeown, himself on hunger strike for seventy days during the summer of 1981. Although Sinn Féin had not directly commissioned these two events, they were an integral element of the reconstitution of this episode. The objective was that the hunger strike would become part not just of the Irish political identity, but of the cultural identity as well.

21 Adams was certainly talking about the fact that the only people who could ask for a medical intervention on a hunger striker once he had fallen into a coma were the relatives. This is how the 1981 hunger strikes ended, when some relatives asked for their sons/husbands to be taken off their fast.

22 The US State Department, in April 2003, talked of '100 to 200 activists plus possible limited support from IRA hardliners dissatisfied with the IRA cease-fire and other republican sympathisers. Approximately 40 RIRA members are in Irish jails.'

23 The category of 'others' includes, according to the Parades Commission, 'civic parades and galas, ex-service organisations of and uniformed youth organisation' (Report, 2003: 12)

24 *Hope and History* is the title of Gerry Adams' book published in 2003. It is also a line of a poem by Seamus Heaney, 'Doubletake', which reads: 'History says, Don't hope/on this side of the grave. /But then, once in a lifetime/the longed for tidal wave/of justice can rise up,/and hope and history rhyme.'

Bibliography

Books and articles

Adams, G. (1988) *A Pathway to Peace*, Dublin: Mercier Press.

—— (1996) *Before the Dawn: An Autobiography*, London: Heinemann.

—— (1997) *An Irish Voice: The Quest for Peace*, Dingle: Mount Eagle.

—— (1999) *Cage Eleven*, Dingle: Brandon.

—— (2003) *Hope and History: Making Peace in Ireland*, Dingle: Brandon.

Allport, G.W. (1966) *The Nature of Prejudice*, London: Addison-Wesley.

Amnesty International (2001) *Racism in Ireland: The Views of the Black and Ethnic Minorities*, available online (www.amnesty.ie/act/racism/ire13.shtml).

Anderson, B. (2001) *Joe Cahill: A Life in the IRA*, Dublin: O'Brien Press.

Arthur, P. (2000) *Special Relationships: Britain, Ireland and the Northern Ireland Problem*, Belfast: Blackstaff Press, available online (http://cain.ulst.ac.uk/events/peace/murray/murray00.htm).

Beresford, D. (1987) *Ten Men Dead: The Story of the 1981 Irish Hunger Strikes*, London: Grafton Books.

Bew, P. (1997) *Northern Ireland: Between War and Peace*, London: Lawrence & Wishart.

Bew, P. and Gillespie, G. (1996) *The Northern Ireland Peace Process 1993–1996: A Chronology*, London: Serif.

Bew, P., Gibbon, P. and Patterson, H. (2002) *Northern Ireland 1921/2001: Political Forces and Social Classes*, London: Serif.

Bishop, P. and Mallie, E. (1987) *The Provisional IRA*, London: Heinemann.

Bloomfield, K. (1998) *We Will Remember Them: Report of the Northern Ireland Victims Commissioner*, Belfast: NIO.

Bourke, R. (2003) *Peace in Ireland: The War of Ideas*, London: Pimlico.

Bowyer Bell, J. (1983) *The Secret Army: the IRA 1916–1979*, Dublin: Academy Press.

—— (1993) *The Irish Troubles*, Dublin: Gill and Macmillan

—— (2000) *The IRA 1968–2000: Analysis of a Secret Army*, London: Frank Cass.

Boyce, G. (1992) *Nationalism in Ireland*, Dublin: Gill and Macmillan.

Briand, R.J. (2002) 'Bush, Clinton, Irish America and the Irish Peace Process', *Political Quarterly*, 73 (2).

Byrne, A. and Leonard, M. (eds) (1997) *Women in Irish Society: A Sociological Reader*, Belfast: Beyond the Pale.

Campbell, G. (2000) 'The Peace Process and the Protestants', in D. Murray (ed.) *Protestant Perceptions of the Peace Process*, Limerick: UL.

Cash, J.D. (1996) *Identity, Ideology and Conflict: The Structuration of Politics in Northern Ireland*, Cambridge: Cambridge University Press.

Clancy, P. (1995) *Irish Society: Sociological Perspectives*, Dublin: Institute of Public Administration.

Clinch, P., Convery, F. and Walsh, B. (eds) (2002) *After the Celtic Tiger: Challenges Ahead*, Dublin: O'Brien Press.

Coakley, J. (ed.) (2002) *Changing Shades of Orange and Green: Redefining the Union and the Nation in Contemporary Ireland*, Dublin: UCD Press.

Coakley, J. and Gallagher, M. (1999) *Politics in the Republic of Ireland* (3rd edn), London: Routledge.

Cochrane, F. (1997) *Unionist Politics and the Politics of Unionism since the Anglo-Irish Agreement*, Cork: Cork University Press.

Collins, E. (1997) *Killing Rage*, London: Granta Books.

Colum, P. (1959) *Arthur Griffith*, Dublin: Browne and Nolan.

Connolly, P. (2002) *Race and Racism in Northern Ireland: A Review of the Research Evidence*, Belfast: Office of the First Minister and Deputy First Minister.

Constitution of Ireland, available online (http://www.taoiseach.gov.ie/upload/publications/297.htm).

Coogan, T.P. (1980) *On the Blanket: The H-Block Story*, Dublin: Ward River Press.

—— (1987) *The IRA*, London: Fontana.

Cory (2003a) *Cory Collusion Inquiry Report, Lord Justice Gibson and Lady Gibson.*

—— (2003b) *Cory Collusion Inquiry Report, Chief Superintendent Breen and Superintendent Buchanan.*

—— (2004a) *Cory Collusion Inquiry Report, Patrick Finucane.*

—— (2004b) *Cory Collusion Inquiry Report, Rosemary Nelson.*

—— (2004c) *Cory Collusion Inquiry Report, Billy Wright.*

—— (2004d) *Cory Collusion Inquiry Report, Robert Hamill.*

All available online on Northern Ireland Office website (http://www.nio.gov.uk).

Coulter, C. and Coleman, S. (2003) *The End of Irish History? Critical Reflections on the Celtic Tiger*, Manchester: Manchester University Press.

Cox, M., Guelke, A. and Stephen, F. (2000) *A Farewell to Arms? From 'Long War' to Long Peace in Northern Ireland*, Manchester: Manchester University Press.

Cunningham, M. (2001) *British Government Policy in Northern Ireland 1969–2000*, Manchester: Manchester University Press.

Curtis, L. (1984) *Ireland: The Propaganda War*, London: Pluto.

Darby, J. and McGinty, R. (eds) (2002) *Contemporary Peace Making: Conflict, Violence and Peace Processes*, Basingstoke: Palgrave Macmillan.

Department of the Taoiseach (2002) *Treaty of Nice and Seville Declaration – Information Guide*, Dublin: Department of Foreign Affairs.

Dixon, P. (2002) 'Political Skills or Lying and Manipulation? The Choreography of the Northern Ireland Peace Process', *Political Studies*, 50.

Doyle, J. and Connolly, E. (2002) 'Foreign Policy and Domestic Politics: A Study of the 2002 Election in the Republic of Ireland', *Irish Studies in International Affairs*, 13.

Eames, R. (2000) 'The Religious Factor', in D. Murray (ed.) *Protestant Perceptions of the Peace Process*, Limerick: UL.

EMCDDA (European Monitoring Centre for Drugs and Drug Addiction) (2002) *National Report, Ireland*, available online (http://www.emcdda.eu.int)

English, R. (2003) *Armed Struggle: A History of the IRA*, London: Macmillan.

Equality for Women Measure (2001) *Annual Report*, Dublin: Department of Justice, Equality and Law Reform.

Fanning, B. (2003) *Positive Politics: Participation of Immigrants and Ethnic Minorities in the Electoral Process*, Dublin: Africa Solidarity Centre.

Farrell, M. (1976) *Northern Ireland: The Orange State*, London: Pluto Press.

Fawcett, L. (2001) 'Journalists Vote Sinn Féin and DUP Best at Media Relations', available online (http://www.ulster.ac.uk/news/releases/2001/340.html).

Fay, M.T., Morrissey, M. and Smyth, M. (1999) *Northern Ireland's Troubles: The Human Costs*, London: Pluto Press.

Feeney, B. (2002) *Sinn Féin: A Hundred Turbulent Years*, Dublin: O'Brien Press.

Finlay, F. (1997) *Snakes and Ladders*, Dublin: New Ireland Books.

Gallagher, M., Marsh, M. and Mitchell, P. (eds) (2003) *How Ireland Voted 2002*, Basingstoke: Palgrave Macmillan.

Galligan, Y. (1998) *Women and Politics In Contemporary Ireland: From the Margins to the Mainstream*, London: Pinter.

Gardiner (1975) *Report of a Committee to Consider, in the Context of Civil Liberties and Human Rights, Measures to Deal with Terrorism in Northern Ireland*, London: HMSO.

Gilland, K. (2003) 'Ireland at the Polls: Thirty Years of Europe Related Referendums', available online (http://www.iri-europe.org/reports/York-KarinGilland.ppt).

Griffith, A. (1904) *The Resurrection of Hungary*, Dublin: James Duffy.

Haass, R. (2002), 'Address to Business and Community Leaders of Northern Ireland', US State Department, Press Release, available online (http://www.state.gov/s/p/rem/15318.htm).

Hackett, C. (1995) 'Self-determination: The Republican Feminist Agenda', *Feminist Review*, 50.

Hainsworth, P. (ed.) (1998) *Divided Societies: Ethnic Minorities and Racism In Northern Ireland*, London: Pluto Press.

Hamber, B. (1998) 'A Truth Commission for Northern Ireland?', in B. Hamber (ed.), *Past Imperfect: Dealing with the Past in Northern Ireland and Societies in Transition*, University of Ulster, Incore.

Hamber, B., Kulle, D. and Wilson, R. (eds) (2001) *Future Policies for the Past*, Belfast: Democratic Dialogue.

Hanley, B. (2002) *The IRA, 1926–1936*, Dublin: Four Courts Press.

Hughes, J. (2003) 'Attitudes to Community Relations in Northern Ireland: Grounds for Optimism?', *Social and Political Archive*, November.

Hughes, J., Donnelly, C., Robinson, G. and Dowds, L. (2003) 'Community Relations in Northern Ireland: The Long View', *Social and Political Archive*, March.

Irish Council for Civil Liberties (ICCL) (1993) 'A Free Media is the Lifeblood of

Democracy', Submission on Section 31, available online (http://www.iccl.ie/constitution/fos/93_s311.htm).

Jarman, N. (2002) *Managing Disorder: Responding to Interface Violence in North Belfast*, Belfast: Office of the First Minister and Deputy Prime Minister.

Jeffery, K (2002), 'Ireland and World War One', available online (http://www.bbc.co.uk/history/war/wwone/ireland_wwone_06.shtml).

Kee, R. (1976) *The Green Flag: A History of Irish Nationalism*, London: Quartet Books.

Knox, C. and Quirk, P. (2000) *Peace Building in Northern Ireland, Israel and Palestine: Transition, Transformation and Reconciliation*, Basingstoke: Macmillan.

Lee, J.J. (1989) *Ireland 1912–1985: Politics and Society*, Cambridge: Cambridge University Press.

Lentin, R. and McVeigh, R. (eds) (2002) *Racism and Anti-Racism in Ireland*, Belfast: Beyond the Pale.

Lovenduski, J. and Norris, P. (eds) (1993) *Gender and Party Politics*, London: Sage.

Loyal, S. (2003) 'Welcome to the Celtic Tiger: Racism Immigration and the State', in C. Coulter and S. Coleman, *The End of Irish History? Critical Reflections on the Celtic Tiger*, Manchester: Manchester University Press.

Lyons, F.S.L. (1983) *Ireland Since the Famine*, London: Fontana.

McCann, E. (1980) *War and an Irish Town*, London: Pluto.

Macardle, D. (1951) *The Irish Republic*, Dublin: Irish Press.

McGarry, J. (ed.) (2001) *Northern Ireland and the Divided World*, Oxford: Oxford University Press.

McGinty, R. (1999) '"Biting the Bullet": Decommissioning in the Transition from War to Peace in Northern Ireland', *Irish Studies in International Affairs*, 10.

—— (2002) 'Better, Worse or Just the Same? Public Attitudes Towards the Northern Ireland Assembly', *Social and Political Archive*, May.

—— (2003) 'What our Politicians Should Know', *Social and Political Archive*, April.

McGinty, R. and Darby, J. (1999) 'Government not Politics', *Social and Political Archive*, June.

McGinty, R. and Darby, J. (2002) *Guns and Government: The Management of the Northern Ireland Peace Process*, Basingstoke: Palgrave.

McGinty, R. and Wilford, R. (2003a) 'Now What: Attitudes to Devolution in Northern Ireland', *Social and Political Archive*, February.

McGinty, R. and Wilford, R. (2003b) 'Police and the Youth Vote', *Social and Political Archive*, June.

McGough, S. (2002) 'Sinn Féin: The Political Marketing of a Party in Conflict Resolution', *Political Association*, available online (http://www.psa.ac.uk/cps/2002M-Z.htm).

McGuffin, J. (1973) *Internment*, Tralee: Anvil Books.

McKeown, L. (1999) 'Gender and the Social Construction of an Irish Republican Prisoner Community', Annual Convention of the International Studies Association Washington, available online (http://www.coiste.ie/articles/laurence/gender.htm).

—— (2001) *Out of Time: Irish Republican Prisoners Long Kesh, 1972–2000*, Belfast: Beyond the Pale.

McKittrik, D. (1997) *The Nervous Peace*, Belfast: Blackstaff Press.

McKittrick, D. and McVea, D. (2000) *Making Sense of the Troubles*, London: Penguin.

MacStiofáin, S. (1975) *Memoirs of a Revolutionary*, Edinburgh: Gordon Cremonesi.

McVeigh, R. (1996) *The Racialization of Irishness: Racism and Anti-racism in Ireland*, Belfast: Centre for Research and Documentation.

Maginnis, K. (1999) *Disarmament, Pathway to Peace*, available online (http://cain.ulst.ac.uk/events/peace/docs/disarmament.htm).

Meaney, G. (1991) *Sex and Nation: Women in Irish Culture*, Dublin: Attic Press.

Mitchell, G. (1999) *Making Peace: The Inside Story of the Making of the Good Friday Agreement*, London: Heinemann.

Moloney, E. (1991) 'Closing Down the Airwaves: The Story of the Broadcasting Ban', in B. Rolston, *The Media in Northern Ireland*, Basingstoke: Macmillan, available online (http://cain.ulst.ac.uk/othelem/media/moloney.htm).

—— (2002) *A Secret History of the IRA*, London: Penguin.

Morrison, D. (1999) *Then The Walls Came Down: A Prison Journal*, Dublin: Mercier Press.

Morrissey, M. and Smyth, M. (2002) *Northern Ireland after the Good Friday Agreement*, London: Pluto Press.

Morrow, D. (2000) 'Nothing to Fear But . . .? Unionists and the Northern Ireland Peace Process', in D. Murray (ed.) *Protestant Perceptions of the Peace Process*, Limerick: UL, available online (http://cain.ulst.ac.uk/events/peace/murray/morrow.htm#one).

Mulholland, M. (2002) *The Longest War: Northern Ireland's Troubled History*, Oxford: Oxford University Press.

Murray, D. (ed) (2000.) *Protestant Perceptions of the Peace Process*, Limerick: UL, available online (cain.ulst.ac.uk/events/peace/murray/white.htm).

National Women's Council of Ireland (NWCI) (2002) *Irish Politics: Jobs for the Boys!*, Dublin: NWCI.

Northern Ireland Council of Ethnic Minorities (NICEM) (2000) *Position Paper on Core Funding for Black and Ethnic Minority Organisations in Northern Ireland*, Belfast: NICEM.

Northern Ireland Human Rights Commission (NIHRC) (2003) *Human Rights and Victims of Violence*, Belfast: NIHRC.

O'Clery, C. (1996) *The Greening of the White House*, Dublin: Gill and Macmillan.

O'Connell, J. (1999) *Policy Issues in Ireland*, Dublin: Higher Education Equality Unit.

O'Dwyer, E. (2003) *Ann Devlin Remembered*, Dublin, Sinn Féin National Conference, 1 November.

O'Hearn, D. (2003) 'Macroecomic Policy in the Celtic Tiger: A Critical Reassessment', in C. Coulter and S. Coleman, *The End of Irish History? Critical Reflections on the Celtic Tiger*, Manchester: Manchester University Press.

O'Leary, B. (2002) 'The Belfast Agreement and the British-Irish Agreement', in A. Reynolds (ed.), *The Architecture of Democracy: Constitutional Design, Conflict Management, and Democracy*, Oxford: Oxford University Press.

O'Leary, B. and McGarry, J. (1997) *The Politics of Antagonism: Understanding Northern Ireland*, London: Athlone Press.

O'Malley, D. (2000) 'Redefining Southern Nationalism', Progressive Democrats Press Release, available online (http://www.iol.ie/pd/pressreleases/200001/omalley001.html).

O'Toole, F. (1998) *The Lie of the Land: Irish Identities*, Dublin: New Island Books.

Pettit, L. (1997) 'Ireland's Alternative Press: Writing from the Margins', *Irish Communications Review*, 7.

Porter, C. (2002) 'US, Colombia Investigate Expansion of Terrorist Alliances', US State Department, available online (http://usinfo.state.gov/topical/pol/terror/02042500.htm).

Public Office Commission (2002) *Annual Report*, available online (http://www.sipo.gov.ie/281e_246.htm).

Rees, M. (1985) *Northern Ireland: A Personal Perspective*, London: Methuen.

Roulston, C. and Davies, C. (2000) *Gender, Democracy and Inclusion in Northern Ireland*, Basingstoke: Palgrave.

Ruane, J. (1996) *The Dynamics of the Conflict in Northern Ireland*, Cambridge: Cambridge University Press.

Ruane, J. and Todd, J. (1999) *After the Good Friday Agreement: Analysing Political Change in Northern Ireland*, Dublin: UCD Press.

Ruane, J. and Todd, J. (2001) 'The Politics of Transition: Political Crises in the Implementation of the Belfast Good Friday Agreement', *Political Studies*, 49.

Ryder, C. and Kearney, V. (2002) *Drumcree: The Orange Order's Last Stand*, London: Methuen.

Sales, R. (1997) *Women Divided: Gender, Religion and Politics in Northern Ireland*, London: Routledge.

Sands, R. (1983) *One Day in My Life*, London, Pluto Press.

Smyth, M. (1998) 'Remembering in Northern Ireland: Victims, Perpetrators and Hierarchies of Pain and Responsibility', in B. Hamber, *Past Imperfect: Dealing with the Past in Northern Ireland and Societies in Transition*, University of Ulster: Incore, available online (http://www.incore.ulst.ac.uk/home/publication/research/dwtp/index.html).

Stevens, J. (2003) *Stevens Inquiry: Summary and Recommendations*, London: HMSO.

Taylor, P. (1997) *Provos: The IRA and Sinn Féin*, London: Bloomsbury Press.

—— (2002) *Brits: The War Against the IRA*, London: Bloomsbury Press.

Toolis, K. (2000) *Rebel Hearts: Journey Within the IRA's Soul*, London: Picador.

Trumbore, P.F. (2001) 'Electoral Politics as Domestic Ratification in International Negotiations: Insights from the Anglo-Irish Peace Process', *Irish Studies in International Affairs*, 12.

Ulster Unionist Party (1999) *Disarmament: Pathway to Peace*, Belfast: UUP.

US State Department (1996) *Patterns of Global Terrorism 1995*, available online (http://usinfo.state.gov/journals/itgic/0297/ijge/gj-10.htm).

Wilford, R. and Wilson, R. (2003) *A Route to Stability: The Review of the Belfast Agreement*, Belfast: Democratic Dialogue.

Wilkinson, P. (ed.) (1981) *British Perspectives on Terrorism*, London: Allen & Unwin.

Wilson, R. (ed.) (2001) *Agreeing to Disagree? A Guide to the Northern Ireland Assembly*, Norwich: Stationery Office.
Wong, M. (2002) *The IRA in Colombia – The Global Links of International Terrorism*, available online (http://wwwc.house.gov/International_Relations/107/wong0424.htm).
Yuval-Davis, N. (1997) *Gender and Nation*, London: Sage.

Official reports (www.nio.gov.uk)

Among those most frequently quoted are:
Agreement between the British and Irish governments, April 2003.
Agreement Reached in the Multi-Party Negotiations (Good Friday Agreement), Belfast, April 1998.
The Community and the Police Service, Patten Report, 2001.
Joint Declaration by the British and Irish Governments, April 2003.
A New Beginning: Policing in Northern Ireland, Report of the Independent Commission on Policing for Northern Ireland, September 1999.
Parades Commission, *Annual Report*, 2001 to 2002, 2002 to 2003.
Parades Organisers Guide, September 2003.
Proposals in relation to *On the Runs* (OTRs), April 2003.
Responding to a Changing Security Situation, updated October 2003.
Stevens Enquiry: Overview and Recommendations, John Stevens, 17 April 2003.

Newspapers

An Phoblacht, available online (http://www.anphoblacht.com/).
Fortnight (Belfast).
Guardian/Observer available online (http://www.guardian.co.uk/) (free access to archives).
Irish Times, available online (www.ireland.com) (subscription-only access to archives).
Magill (Dublin).
Sunrise, available online (http://www.ireland.ie/ quarter/)
Sunday Business Post, *Irish Examiner* and other Irish publications, available online: (http://archives.tcm.ie/index.asp).

Websites most frequently used

www.sinnfein.ie
www.paveepoint.ie
http://www.taoiseach.gov.ie
www.paradescommission.org
www.psni.police.uk/ines/statistics_branch.htm
http://www.grandorange.org.uk/parades/tradition_parades.html
http://www.nisra.gov.uk/Census/Start.html
http://www.knowracism.ie/
www.internationalfundforireland.com

www.medialive.ie
http://www.state.gov
http://www.sipo.gov.ie/about.htm
www.bringthemhome.ie
http://www.ni-forum.gov.uk/debates.htm
www.rsf.ie
(All websites were accessed in February 2004.)

Interviews carried out between February 2003 and January 2004

Sinn Féin representatives

Adams, Gerry – President of Sinn Féin and MP for West Belfast
Anderson, Martina – All Ireland Coordinator
Bhreatnach, Lucilita – Head of the party's Equality Department, former Secretary General
Coleman, Caroline – Policy adviser on multiculturalism
de Brún, Bairbre – EU candidate for the Six Counties, former Health Minister
Doyle, Dawn – Publicity Officer
Ferris, Martin – TD for Kerry North
Gibney, Jim – Sinn Féin Ard Chomhairle member
Kelly, Gerry – MLA for North Belfast
McDonald, Mary Lou – Dublin EU Candidate
McGuinness, Martin – Sinn Féin Chief Negotiator and MP for Mid Ulster
McLaughlin, Mitchel – Chairperson, MLA for Foyle
Maskey, Alex – MLA for South Belfast, former Mayor of Belfast
Molloy, Francie – MLA for Mid Ulster
Moran, Justin – Parliamentary assistant to Sean Crowe TD
Murphy, Conor – MLA for Newry Armagh, head of party group in the assembly
Ó Broin, Eoin – Councillor in the north
O'Connor, Joan – Head of the International Department
O'Hare, Rita – party representative in the United States
Ó Snodaigh, Aengus – TD for Dublin South Central and Party Whip in Leinster House
O'Toole, Larry – Dublin City Councillor
Pierse, Michael – In charge of membership and education department
Smyth, Robbie – General Secretary
Spain, Martin – Editor of *An Phoblacht*

Other representatives

Campbell, Gregory – DUP MP for East Derry, former Minister for Rural Development
Collins, Martin – Pavee Point, Dublin
Ervine, David – Progressive Unionist Party leader
Farren, Séan – SDLP, former Minister for Further Edutation
Finlay, Fergus – Chef de Cabinet of Labour Party leader Pat Rabitte

Finnegan, Brian – Editor of *Gay Community News* and *GI*
Garland, Roy – Member of the Ulster Unionist Party
Lenihan, Brian – Fianna Fáil TD for Dublin South West
National Women's Council of Ireland
Noonan, Paul – Travellers' Resource Centre, Belfast

Interviews carried out for former research used in this book

Hartley, Tom – former Sinn Féin Secretary General (1987)
McKeown, Lawrence – former hunger striker (1988)
Montague, Pat – Media consultant (1998)
Morrison, Danny – former Sinn Féin Director of Publicity (1987)
Ó Bradáigh, Ruarí – former President of Provisional Sinn Féin (1986)

Selected Sinn Féin documents (in chronological order)

Eire Nua, (1972), Dublin
Eire Nua, the Social, Economic and Political Dimensions (1979)
The Road to Peace in Ireland (1979)
Loyalism, Parts 1 and 2 (not dated, probably mid-1980s)
A Scenario For Peace – Discussion Paper (1987)
Submission to the Review of the Parades Commission (1996)
Empowering Communities – Sinn Féin's Response to the Drugs Epidemic (1996)
Sinn Féin Submission to Multi-Party Talks (1998)
Putting People First (1998)
Sinn Féin Programme for Government – Governing Equally for All (1999)
Health for All – A Health Strategy Discussion Paper (2001)
Housing for All – A Basic Right 2001 (2001)
Many Voices, One Country (2001)
Moving On – A Policy for Gay, Lesbian and Bi-Sexual Equality (n.d.)
Arts, Culture and Leisure – A Policy Review Paper (2001)
Women in an Ireland of Equals (2002)
Educate that You Might Be Free (2003)
Who Sanctioned Britain's Dumb Squads (2003)
Sinn Féin and the European Union (2003)
No Right Turn: Sinn Féin's Call to Action Against the Thatcherisation of Ireland (2003)
Eliminating Poverty: A Twenty-First Century Goal (2004)
Transfer of Policing and Justice Powers (2003)
Rights for All – A Sinn Féin Discussion Document (2004)
Template for Interface Violence (2004)
Campaigning for Full Equality – An Election Manifesto (2004)
Local Government Manifesto, Delivering Real Change (2004)

All electoral manifestos, IRA statements and main speeches from 1996 onward, as well as most of the policy documents, may be found on the website

Index

eBooks

eBooks – at www.eBookstore.tandf.co.uk

A library at your fingertips!

eBooks are electronic versions of printed books. You can store them on your PC/laptop or browse them online.

They have advantages for anyone needing rapid access to a wide variety of published, copyright information.

eBooks can help your research by enabling you to bookmark chapters, annotate text and use instant searches to find specific words or phrases. Several eBook files would fit on even a small laptop or PDA.

NEW: Save money by eSubscribing: cheap, online access to any eBook for as long as you need it.

Annual subscription packages

We now offer special low cost bulk subscriptions to packages of eBooks in certain subject areas. These are available to libraries or to individuals.

For more information please contact webmaster.ebooks@tandf.co.uk

We're continually developing the eBook concept, so keep up to date by visiting the website.

www.eBookstore.tandf.co.uk